T0300223

Routledge Revivals

Economic Developments in Victorian Scotland

Marwick argues that economic development in Scotland was severely delayed until the 18th Century unlike neighbouring countries. Originally published in 1936, this study aims to explore key features of economic development in Victorian Scotland to promote more understanding of this issue. Issues discussed include ownership of land and capital, administration and finances of industry, organisation of trade and marketing, labour and recruitment, trade unions, housing and other aspects which impact on the standard of life. This title will be of interest to students of Economics and Industrial History.

Economic Developments in Victorian Scotland

W.H. Marwick

Routledge
Taylor & Francis Group

First published in 1936
By George Allen & Unwin Ltd

This edition first published in 2016 by Routledge
2 Park Square, Milton Park, Abingdon, Oxon, OX14 4RN
and by Routledge
711 Third Avenue, New York, NY 10017

Routledge is an imprint of the Taylor & Francis Group, an informa business

© 1936 W.H. Marwick

All rights reserved. No part of this book may be reprinted or reproduced or
utilised in any form or by any electronic, mechanical, or other means, now
known or hereafter invented, including photocopying and recording, or in any
information storage or retrieval system, without permission in writing from the
publishers.

Publisher's Note
The publisher has gone to great lengths to ensure the quality of this reprint but
points out that some imperfections in the original copies may be apparent.

Disclaimer
The publisher has made every effort to trace copyright holders and welcomes
correspondence from those they have been unable to contact.

A Library of Congress record exists under LC control number: 37038318

ISBN 13: 978-1-138-64847-0 (hbk)
ISBN 13: 978-1-315-62636-9 (ebk)

W. H. MARWICK, M.A.

Carnegie Teaching Fellow and Extra-Mural Lecturer, University of Edinburgh

Economic Developments
in
Victorian Scotland

With a Foreword by

F. W. OGILVIE, M.A.

President of the Queen's University of Belfast

LONDON

George Allen & Unwin Ltd

MUSEUM STREET

FIRST PUBLISHED IN 1936

All rights reserved

PRINTED IN GREAT BRITAIN BY
UNWIN BROTHERS LTD., WOKING

PREFACE

THANKS are especially due to Mr. F. W. Ogilvie, President of Queen's University, Belfast, and late Professor of Political Economy, University of Edinburgh, for constant help and advice in the preparation of this work, and for his Foreword Among others to whom acknowledgment is due are the Librarians and staff of the University Library, Edinburgh; National Library of Scotland; Edinburgh Public Library; Mitchell Library, Glasgow, and University Library, Glasgow, for facilities afforded in the prosecution of research. Access to information on special points has been kindly given by Dr. Marguerite Wood, Keeper of Records, Corporation of Edinburgh; Mr. J. MacKenna, of Messrs. W. Collins & Sons; the manager of Edinburgh Co-operative Building Co. Ltd., and the officials of Edinburgh Trades Council. I am indebted to Dr. Mary Rankin, Lecturer in Political Economy, University of Edinburgh, for helpful criticism of my manuscript, and to Dr. W. S. Cormack, Stow College, Glasgow, for permission to utilize his unpublished thesis. Dr. A. Morgan, Hon. Sec., Edinburgh University Extra-Mural Committee; Mr. A. Birnie, Lecturer in Economic History, University of Edinburgh; Dr. H. Hamilton, Lecturer in Economic History, University of Aberdeen; Dr. A. McPhee, University of Sheffield, and Dr. G. P. Insh, Training College, Jordanhill, Glasgow, have assisted throughout by their advice and encouragement. Finally, tribute must be paid to Mr. J. F. Rees, Principal of University College, Cardiff, and sometime Lecturer in Economic History in the University of Edinburgh, whose teaching first inspired me with an interest in the subject.

The substance of certain sections of this work has already appeared in the following periodicals, to whose editors acknowledgment is made for permission to reproduce:

Juridical Review ("Paternalism in Victorian Scotland," March 1935).

Economic History Review ("Early Trade Unionism in Scotland," April 1935).

Scottish Bankers' Magazine ("Scottish Overseas Investment in the Nineteenth Century," July 1935).

Scotland ("The Scottish Mineral Oil Industry," Autumn 1935; "Housing in Scotland," Spring 1936).

The Scottish Educational Journal (series of biographical sketches, intermittently since 1930).

The Carnegie Trust for the Universities of Scotland has by the award of a Teaching Fellowship at the University of Edinburgh during sessions 1932–36 rendered it possible for half my working time to be devoted to the necessary research; their munificence is gratefully acknowledged.

W. H. MARWICK

EDINBURGH
August 1936

FOREWORD

by F. W. OGILVIE, M.A.

President of the Queen's University of Belfast; lately Professor of Political Economy in the University of Edinburgh

IT is curious that the story of the economic development of Scotland should have remained so long unwritten; that the country which produced *The Wealth of Nations* and *The Statistical Account*, two path-breakers of economic history, should have had to wait well into the twentieth century before her own economic fortunes were described and analysed. Excellent monographs, of course, there had been in plenty, on guilds, or banks, or the staple, or particular industries; but no attempt had been made to survey the field as a whole, or to apply to the rich and varied material which lay there the ordered principles of economic reasoning.

Whatever may have been the causes of this strange neglect —and every inquirer will probably advance his own explanation—the charge against Scotland no longer holds. In the last few years Scottish economic history has come into being, in Professor James Mackinnon's outline sketch and particularly in the work of Miss I. F. Grant on *The Social and Economic Development of Scotland before 1603*, and of Dr. Henry Hamilton on *The Industrial Revolution in Scotland*. And now there appears the book before us, *Economic Developments in Victorian Scotland*. The author, Mr. W. H. Marwick, Carnegie Teaching Fellow and Extra-Mural Lecturer in the University of Edinburgh, is singularly well fitted for this task. He has brought to it not only a well-trained and a well-stored mind, but qualities of historical sympathy and insight without which work of this kind can easily slip into antiquarianism.

Mr. Marwick's work is based upon original research, and there is a great deal of new material in it; especially perhaps in the sections of Part II which deal with the intricacies of industrial organization, and in those of Part IV which deal with trade unionism, a subject which in Scotland, as Mr. Marwick says, is still without its Webbs. But while the book is likely to remain important for many years on account of the facts which it presents, its purpose is not so much to array information as to analyse it; to portray the main trends of Scottish economic development, and to lay bare the causes which made the economic scene in Scotland at the Diamond Jubilee so different from what it had been at the Queen's Accession.

It is this element in the book which should make it of lively interest and value, not only to professed students of history, but to a wide circle of readers. Business men, for example, will see there, writ plain, the lessons of the generation from which their own is sprung—lessons often of foresight and enterprise, sometimes of somnolence or of stubborn resistance to change. And members of the general public who have watched the growth of national sentiment, in Scotland as elsewhere, in recent years, and are anxious to reconcile the apparent advantages of small areas for certain purposes of political life with the obvious economic necessity of large units for purposes of industry and trade, will find themselves richly rewarded by the account which is given in these pages of a small country forced, as the nineteenth century wore on, into closer and closer contact with the large world. Mr. Marwick concludes his careful study of the period by remarking that the industrial development of Scotland during the Victorian age "suggests the successful elaboration of means toward an end unknown and unconsidered." How long will things continue so?

QUEEN'S UNIVERSITY, BELFAST
September 1936

CONTENTS

PART THREE

Life and Labour

PART FOUR

Social Organizations and Movements

Scotland at the End of the Nineteenth Century

INTRODUCTION

IT is coming to be realized that economically Scotland remained in the Middle Ages until the eighteenth century. The Reformation, however important in religion and politics, made no such breach in the social life of Scotland as has been assumed. To the ordinary man the transition from Catholicism to Protestantism made little difference in the regular course of life. The Union of the Crowns and even the Union of Parliaments made less direct difference for good and ill than ardent partisans have asserted.

A complex of causes, for which the two Unions have a certain responsibility, stimulated changes in the eighteenth century. Internal peace and order encouraged a secularization of interests and enabled Scottish energies to be devoted at last to material progress. Scotland thus shared in those vast transformations which historians still term "the Industrial Revolution," a process now realized to have been more varied and protracted than was at first supposed.

Dr. Hamilton has recently surveyed "the Industrial Revolution in Scotland." To his work the present study in some respects aims at being a sequel, but it is designed upon a rather different plan. It seeks to analyse some of the main features of economic development rather than to describe the growth of the several industries. It endeavours to deal with such matters as the ownership of land and capital, the administration and finance of industrial enterprise, the organization of trade and marketing, the recruitment and remuneration of labour and its conditions of employment, Trade Unions and other economic associations, housing and other elements in the standard of life.

The subject is too vast and detailed, and ascertainable knowledge of it as yet too imperfect, to permit of a complete and ordered presentation. Some aspects, particularly those relating to the technique of industry, have been almost entirely omitted, the more readily because nearly all previous publications are predominantly of that character. The topics elaborated have been largely ignored in previous work, and are therefore emphasized, at the expense of a disproportionate treatment. A whole generation of co-operative effort, especially in the form of regional and industrial studies, will be necessary before anything like an adequate or definitive economic history of the period can be written; it is hoped that some suggestions for further research may have been indicated.

It is becoming clearer that the problems of the present day cannot be understood, far less solved, without some understanding of their historic origin. The economic society of modern Scotland is in essentials a product of the Victorian Age, and it is the possibility of throwing a little light on its development that offers the most valid excuse for such research as is incorporated in this volume.

SCOTLAND AT THE COMMENCEMENT
OF THE VICTORIAN AGE

SCOTLAND in the eighteen-thirties was in the midst of economic as well as of political change. The fabric of government was transformed by the Reform Bill of 1832, and the immediately consequent Municipal Reform of 1833, which together gave a measure of national and local self-control. While the spirit of *laissez-faire* was in the ascendant, it was still restrained by survivals of the older paternalism, and the extension of political democracy almost inevitably entailed a renewed intervention of the State in economic matters.

The population of Scotland at this date (1831) was some two and one-third million, of whom 84,000 are returned as "manufacturing" and 76,000 as "other labourers," together constituting already a larger group than those engaged in agriculture (*c.* 140,000).(1)

The Industrial Revolution meant for Scotland, unlike England, no change in the hub of economic activity. The Midland Belt, or Forth and Clyde Valley, retained its pre-eminence, in manufacture as in agriculture. The tendency was for industry and commerce to become more concentrated in the West, and Glasgow was assuming the position of economic capital. The second Statistical Account (1838–45) affords much data for this period. Twenty-six thousand, six hundred and seventy-seven of the "manufacturing labourers" (almost one-third) were domiciled in Lanarkshire, and of these 19,313 were within the limited bounds of Glasgow.(1)

This industrial ascendancy was at first based chiefly on the textiles, especially cotton, that typical if exotic product of the machine age. Glasgow had found in it employment for much of the capital and labour left derelict through the blow given to colonial trade by the American Revolt. The major branches of the industry, the spinning and weaving of cotton fabrics, had passed their brief heyday by the dawn of the Victorian Age, as the superiority of Lancashire was demonstrated. The

B

introduction of steam power had involved considerable concentration of the industry, at first dispersed throughout Scotland by the attraction of water supplies; apart from the famous
mills at Deanston (Perthshire) and Catrine (Ayrshire) practically all the factories of importance were now in Lanarkshire.
In 1834 there were 134 cotton mills in Scotland.(2)

Two important subsidiaries flourished. Calico printing,
illustrated by the notable firm of Crum of Thornliebank,
developed in the southern suburbs of Glasgow, on the slopes
of the Campsies and in the Vale of Leven. In the latter area
dyeing was also rising to importance, in the hands of the
prolific clans of Ewings and Stirlings. Another offshoot was
the thread industry, concentrated in Paisley, where the Coats
and the Clarks were already conspicuous among the numerous
small concerns.

The textile industry also contributed to the rise of that
which in part supplanted it—viz. engineering, of which an
early branch was the construction of spinning and weaving
machinery. This was frequently carried on as an adjunct to
the textile business, e.g. by Smith of Deanston and at first by
Houldsworth of Anderston. Glasgow soon became noted for
its "millwright engineers," from whom the various branches
of the modern industry descend. The demand for coal to
supply motive power, and for shipping to transport the raw
material and the finished article, are obvious instances of the
lasting stimulus given by cotton to other enterprises.

The two other great textile trades were of more ancient
origin and more enduring existence, though changed in form.
Wool and linen were both domestic industries, and their
relative merits were a subject of chronic controversy in the
early industrial period, as witness the writings of Loch, Anderson, and Naismith. Out of the sheep-rearing of the Southern
Uplands sprang the tweed and hosiery factories of the Border
Burghs; the carpets of Kilmarnock and elsewhere were also an
offshoot.

The chief home of flax was in the eastern lowland strip,
especially the county of Angus, consecrated in literature in
the classic example of Thrums. Native flax-growing, despite

recurrent propaganda (e.g. by Robert Brown of Hamilton),(3) was inadequate, and supplies from the Baltic were a feature of foreign trade. Over 400,000 tons were imported in 1845.(4) With the development of linen as a factory product is peculiarly associated the Baxter dynasty of Dundee. The damasks of Dunfermline are the aristocrats of linen wares. The history of the linen industry was the theme of a peculiarly exhaustive work by Alexander J. Warden, a Dundee merchant who with elaborate statistics traced its growth from the Garden of Eden to his own days. In 1822 there were seventeen spinning-mills in Dundee, and thirty-two in the neighbourhood, with a total of nearly 15,000 spindles.(5) A concession to the rising "Manchesterism" was afforded by the abolition of the long-standing bounty on linen in 1832.(6)

A kindred but exotic manufacture, that of jute, was just being introduced into Dundee by the import of a few hundred tons from India by James Aytoun, a linen manufacturer, noted also for his hostility to the Factory Act agitation.(7)

The heavy industries as yet played but a secondary part in Scotland's industrial structure.

Coal had been worked for many centuries, especially in the Lothians and in Fife; its exploitation was normally carried on with rather primitive methods and on patriarchal lines, incidentally to landownership. The coal measures of the Clyde were now being developed, mainly by small contractors.

Local supplies of iron ore, aided by native inventions, such as J. B. Neilson's hot blast and Nasmyth's steam hammer, gave opportunity for the rise of the iron industry; blast furnaces were erected "actually at the pit's mouth, directly upon carboniferous strata."(8) In 1825 there were twenty-five blast furnaces, and 36,500 tons of pig iron were produced in 1828; in 1830 twenty-seven furnaces had an output of 39,400 tons; by 1839 they had risen to fifty-four, with an output of about 200,000 tons.(9) Bairds of Gartsherrie had just laid the foundation of what was to become their gigantic enterprise (1829). Thus a Scottish Black Country, centring in Motherwell and Coatbridge, devastated a landscape of æsthetic and historic interest.

With the introduction of the steamship, pioneered by the Scots Symington and Bell, marine engineering came into being. The Napier cousins were already initiating what was to be Glasgow's most typical industry. Other branches of engineering as yet hardly constituted an industry apart.

Anticipations of that modern type of industry based on applied science were to be found in the various chemical works sprung from the numerous inventions of the Mackintoshes, father and son; and in the originally allied firm of Tennants of St. Rollox, one of the largest of the time, with its 1,200 employees, and annual consumption of 80,000 tons of raw material.(10)

The "domestic system" persisted, if on the down-grade. Apart from a few paper mills, only the textile industry seems to have been regarded as within the scope of Factory legislation. Building, while doubtless much expanded by the increased industrial and residential demand, continued almost unchanged in technique and organization; and other manufactures were small and localized, with little influence on general economic development.

Hand-loom weavers, some 37,000 in number,(11) were engaged in a "customer" trade, producing directly for consumers, or (probably to a growing degree) were virtually employees of manufacturers and merchants, especially in Glasgow; the latter supplied materials and paid for workmanship to tradesmen throughout the countryside, notably Paisley and the townships at the foot of the Ochils and Campsies. Once the aristocracy of labour, the hand-loom weavers had fallen to conditions of destitution. Their cause, agitated by the Maxwells of Pollok, was investigated by successive Parliamentary Committees, which reported that the decay was irretrievable. The hapless burgh of Paisley also suffered from the decline of its shawls with a change in fickle and luxurious feminine fashion. Aberdeenshire hand-made stockings survived the century. In the coal mines there was much sub-contracting, and the persistence of the "family unit" of labour, here as in textiles, was partially responsible for the exploitation of women and children.

To turn to commerce—the Clyde was making tentative essays in shipping, under the guidance of men like the brothers Burns, soon to be among the founders of the Cunard Line (1839). Glasgow firms like Pollok, Gilmour & Co., James Finlay & Co., and Wm. Connal & Co., were developing a world-wide wholesale trade; the "nabob" tradition, fostered by "King Harry" Dundas, was maintained in a novel form by the enterprise of Scottish merchants like Jardine, Matheson & Co.

Telford, the Rennies, and Macadam had played their part in that improvement of communications which some have deemed the key of the Industrial Revolution. Telford as Commissioner had been responsible for a great advance in the quantity and quality of Scottish roads. The stage-coach was in the ascendant; the beginning of opposition was to be seen in the light railway or "tram" lines, chiefly associated with coal mines and other industrial establishments. Horse traction was at first utilized, but Stephenson's locomotive was introduced into Scotland about 1830, and during the decade a number of small lines were built in the industrial area, usually conveying passengers and relying on steam power.(12)

The Forth and Clyde and the Monkland Canals meantime flourished on the conveyance of the output of the growing heavy industries; many of the railways were virtually their subsidiaries, connecting them with a works; it was in the 'forties that the "railway mania" spread, and unplanned small-scale undertakings established the confused and overlapping network of communications from which Scottish industry has since suffered.

The Scottish banks, not yet legally regulated, continued their traditional policy of note issue and cash credits. They already displayed a tendency to concentration; by 1837 there survived only five chartered, twelve joint stock, and seven private banks.(13) Fire insurance was already a century old; life assurance had just come into vogue, and several important and lasting companies were formed in Scotland in the years around 1830.

Some minor improvements in communications are credited

to Scots. Robert Wallace of Kelly, M.P. for Greenock, a stalwart of Parliamentary Reform, was also an early advocate of the penny post;(14) James Chalmers, bookseller, Dundee (1782–1853), it is claimed, first suggested the adhesive stamp.(15)

The sharpness of the breach between feudalism and industrialism, like that between Catholicism and Protestantism, has often been exaggerated. Landowners were often "sleeping partners" in industrial concerns, sometimes even their promoters; e.g. the foundation of the village of Castle Douglas (Stewartry), the partnership with Dale of Alexander of Ballochmyle, the ill-fated schemes of the inventive Earl of Dundonald. Some, like the Alexanders of Airdrie House and the Buchanans of Drumpellier, derived large incomes from mining royalties. Other industrial magnates were of humble origin, and uncultured, starting in a small way and prospering on Smilesian principles; this was the case with most of the ironworks of Coatbridge and many of the textile factories of Glasgow.

The mental attitude expressed in patriarchalism survived in many of the new industrial concerns; New Lanark is but the earliest and best-known example. Schools were provided at nominal fees by many ironworks and collieries and some cotton-mills, and some form of medical service was not infrequent; the linen factories of the East, however, were rarely equipped with either service. The provision of "tied houses" as an incident of employment spread from agriculture by an easy transition to mining, and the precedent was commonly followed by iron and textile works established in unpopulated areas; few came up to the standard of the model village attached to Deanston Cotton Mills (Doune). Remoteness from settled centres likewise accounts for and partly justifies the establishment in mines and ironworks of company stores, which by a variety of expedients circumvented or defied the legal prohibition of Truck (1831).

The merchant and craft guilds, though still existing, mainly as charitable trusts, had become economically obsolescent, and the last vestiges of their trading privileges were abolished in 1846. Henceforth *laissez-faire* was the accepted principle in determining working conditions, though soon modified piecemeal by collectivist legislation. The abuses attaching to the employment of women and children in the mines and factories led to the first public investigation and subsequent legal restriction of the modern type (Factory Inquiry 1833), resulting in the appointment of permanent inspectors, including Leonard Horner, brother of the "Edinburgh Reviewer" and founder of the Edinburgh School of Arts. Similar action was taken in the coal industry nine years later. The unavailing attempts, sponsored by the Maxwells of Pollok, to establish wages boards for the hand-loom weavers, perhaps belong rather to the paternalist tradition.

While the Midland Belt had been and continued to be the most populated area, the balance was further weighed in its favour by Highland depopulation. The "Clearances" combined with the greater attractiveness of industry and of urban life to aggregate masses on the Clyde. The population of Lanarkshire increased well over 100 per cent between 1801 and 1831.(16) Many Highland emigrants went overseas, and the "Celtic" element in Scotland was recruited by Irish immigration, to some degree from Ulster, but mainly from farther south. There seems some warrant for the popular view that a number were deliberately introduced by employers to depress wages and break strikes. Emigration to the Colonies had been recommended as a panacea after the Napoleonic Wars by such writers as the Glasgow magnate and statistician Patrick Colquhoun,(17) and was spasmodically fostered in times of acute depression by Government and by private agencies, including some Trade Unions, as a means of relieving the labour market.

Early Scottish Trade Unionism shared in the ambitious flights of revolutionary Owenism and in their debacle; it flourished chiefly among the cotton operatives and the building trades, the two industries most advanced in size and importance. Both suffered in the late 'thirties from legal restriction and penalization of their activities as well as from trade depression.

The prophet of Co-operation, Robert Owen, achieved his business success and pioneered his welfare schemes and social experiments in Scotland, which had already dabbled in small consumers' societies. The most active propagandist of the

Co-operative ideal, resembling his master in temperament as in doctrine, was the long-lived and versatile Alexander Campbell, a Glasgow Scot.(18) The early experiments in co-operative production and distribution, notably the Orbiston Colony (1828) and the Glasgow Bazaar (1831), had a brief existence. Owen had lost the superficial patronage of high society, and the vision of a voluntarist community was cherished only by a few idealists. The rapid growth of co-operative retail societies commences a generation later.

Friendly Societies and Building Societies exemplify other attempts at collective self-help among the masses. Those then existent were usually of a small-scale temporary type, and many were in a chronic state of actuarial unsoundness. The Trustee Savings Bank, pioneered early in the century by Dr. Henry Duncan of Ruthwell,(19) had taken root in many places, and received legislative sanction.

Proposals to establish a public system of poor relief provided a famous controversy, which culminated in a verbal duel between two Edinburgh professors—William Pulteney Alison(20) and Thomas Chalmers.(21) The former, son of the literary critic and brother of the Tory historian, found ample evidence in support of statutory provision in his long and intimate medical experience in Edinburgh slums and hospitals, and a theoretical basis in his interpretation of Christian teaching. The distinguished divine and leader of the Free Church sought in prolific and prolix expositions to harmonize his theocratic prepossessions with his acceptance of the classical economics, while generalizing from his own limited and ephemeral experiment in a Glasgow parish. He was waging a losing battle; the aggregation of population in industrial areas rendered the old parochial economy obsolescent; though it was only after he had himself dealt it the final blow by heading the Disruption of 1843 that a qualified endorsement of obligatory public finance and control was given in the Poor Law Act of 1845.

Dr. Alison merits recognition also as a pioneer of public health services. He showed that the average mortality of Edinburgh and Glasgow was almost twice that of England, one-third higher than London (*c.* 1840), particularly among young children.(22) Recurrent epidemics of cholera and typhus, the information supplied by Poor Law Reports(23) and the advances of medical knowledge with regard to infectious diseases prepared the way for the painfully slow municipal and State action undertaken later in the century.

Scotland had a bad tradition of overcrowding, due partly to chronic English and civil wars, and Edinburgh had long been a by-word. The Industrial Revolution encouraged the multiplication of jerry-built slums; subdivision of existing structures and building over of intervening spaces (backlands) were frequent; these substantial erections were a hindrance to improvement. The supply of houses for the growing population was left to the small speculative builder and to the works owner; it was only gradually that a social conscience, sharpened by a realization of the social danger of the slums, awakened to its first inadequate efforts at betterment.

Scotland was just passing through the last days of its penultimate literary Renaissance; an influence more hostile to culture than Calvinistic Puritanism or English domination was gathering force as industrialization proceeded. The lust of wealth was only temporarily and superficially countered by the revived ecclesiastical controversies anent "non-Intrusion" and the other issues of the "Ten Years' Conflict." The Church, with few and late exceptions, failed even to suggest an adequate social ethic for the new society or to maintain its traditional rôle as a vehicle of popular culture. The parochial system of education, like that of poor relief, was fast becoming insufficient; recent research has discounted some of the traditional eulogy.(24) The Mechanics' Institutes and kindred bodies were spreading in industrial centres, but soon tended to evolve into technical schools or degenerate into social clubs, if they outlived the initial enthusiasm.(25) Political organizations, chiefly associated with Parliamentary Reform, were the resort of most of those with intellectual interests. Thus Scotland entered the Victorian era materially well equipped, but rather deficient in the intellectual and moral qualities requisite to utilize these resources to the highest communal good.

PART I

LANDOWNERSHIP

CHAPTER I

MINERAL VALUES

LAND is obviously a primary necessity for industrial production, of which it is traditionally reckoned as one of the three "agents." Here we are concerned with it in respect not of its agricultural uses but of its site values, whether arising from the presence of minerals in the subsoil, or because of the erection of factories and other industrial structures or of dwelling-houses upon its surface. The concern of the ground landlord may be active, if he controls or participates in the exploitation of mineral resources or other revenue-producing enterprises carried on upon his estate; or passive, as the recipient of royalties from minerals and of rent of land let for industrial and kindred purposes (e.g. housing, transport). We deal first with the extraction of minerals; in a subsequent section the use of land for manufacturing and housing purposes will be considered.

Where the landlord was also entrepreneur, there is at least a partial survival of the paternalist regime; the oldtime agricultural relations were then not sensibly modified. Coal, by reason of its isolated location and peculiar methods of working, lent itself particularly to such arrangements. The early working of coal by monastic and other landlords (e.g. Newbattle, Culross) is a familiar story. Professor J. U. Nef, in his erudite work on *The Rise of the British Coal Industry*, corroborates the continuance of the practice during the seventeenth century, when the "estate of many Scottish noblemen gentlemen and others," according to the then Earl of Wemyss (1658), "doth consist very much in coalworks." "In Adam Smith's time many Scottish coal mines were still exploited by the landlords," probably because "the great landlords were almost alone in having money to invest."(1)

In the Eastern Lowlands in particular, the great landlords themselves retained the working of the pits. The ubiquitous Dukes of Buccleugh, the Marquesses of Lothian, descendants of a Commendator of Newbattle Abbey, the Dundases of Arniston, foremost of senatorial dynasties, the Cockburns of Ormiston, the Hopes of Pinkie, the Clerks of Penicuik, were all in this position early in the nineteenth century.(2) Similarly in Fife the Earls of Elgin and of Dundonald worked coal at Dunfermline, Cardross, and Culross, the Hendersons at Fordel (Inverkeithing), the Wemysses at Methil, in each case for many generations.(3)

In the West of Scotland the leasing of mineral rights seems to have been more prevalent from an early date, as in the cases of the Bairds, the Dixons, and the Dunlops. The Grays at Carntyne (c. 1600–1875) (4) and the Faries at Farme (Ruther-glen),(5) afford small-scale exceptions. Less successful ventures in developing minerals on their estates were made by the second Marquis of Breadalbane in Perthshire,(6) the Duke of Gordon in Glenlivet,(7) and the Whig politician T. F. Kennedy of Dunure, in Ayrshire.(8)

In the course of the century, control commonly passes into the hands of joint-stock companies; the landlords either sell out, retaining only the right to royalties, or become shareholders and perhaps directors, in name or in actuality. Instances of the latter are supplied by the Lothian Coal Co., formed in 1890, of which the eighth and ninth Marquises were successive Chairmen,(9) and the Wemyss Coal Co. (1894), of which Randolph Erskine Wemyss remained Chairman till his premature death (1908).(10) Members of the prolific Dundas clan also figured on the Directorate of the Arniston Coal Co.(11)

By the end of the century, minerals were generally worked by lessees on a tenure normally of nineteen to thirty-one years, a result of the original prohibition of longer leases under the law of entail.(12) A preference for the patriarchal system was expressed by Robert Brown, a former Newbattle employee, as spokesman of the miners at the Royalties Commission.(13)

The separation of the ownership of land and of minerals was not uncommon, e.g. the Earl of Elgin held certain minerals on a 999 years' lease from the ground landlords, the Halketts; for some time they were worked directly, but latterly contracted to Thomas Spowart & Co. The Burgh of Sanquhar leased

Commonty lands to Archibald McNab in 1809 for 999 years; right to work underlying minerals remained a perennial matter of doubt.(14) A County Assessor explained to the Royalties Commission that under the Scottish Land Valuation Act (17–18 Vict. C. 91) in the case of mining leases under thirty-one years' duration, the rent was the criterion; over that limit the lessee was considered as proprietor, and assessed on the rateable values of the minerals.(15) This divided ownership was a source of friction and litigation, and was regarded as an obstruction to mining development, especially in view of a legal decision (White v. Dixon, 1883) which debarred the creation of a subsidence by underground workings.(16) The charges for transmission over the land of another, whether above or below the surface, known as "wayleaves," were another obstacle to economical working. Improvements, in default of special provision to the contrary, were appropriated by the landlord on the termination of the lease.(17) Profits of lessees in the Lothians about 1840 were estimated at not more than about one shilling per ton, because of heavy "oncost" charges.(18)

The tribulations of the small-scale lessee are graphically depicted by the novelist, Henrietta Keddie ("Sarah Tytler"); her father, a solicitor (d. 1852), for many years leased Grange colliery near Elie (Fife) and injured health and fortune in the struggle to keep it going.(19)

Happier results were achieved by such Western adventurers as Alexander Baird, farmer at Kirkwood in the Old Monkland, who early in the century took leases of neighbouring coalfields, and thus laid the foundation of the gigantic enterprises developed by his sons.(20) The agricultural connection and tradition are further illustrated by the fact that his mining operations were carried on as a subsidiary to farming, a practice paralleled elsewhere in the locality; e.g. William Black of Whiterigg and Robert Addie of Langloan.(21) The Dunfermline area affords instances of "tacksmen" holding leases from the proprietors; e.g. Messrs. Henderson and Maclaren thus operated Cuttlehill Pits in the 'forties.(22)

In Dunfermline also there is an interesting survival of the

Burghal Common Good in the civic ownership of Townhill Colliery; it was worked by "direct labour" until 1838, then rented on a nineteen years' lease for about £1,000 a year; the lease appears to have been renewed at a higher figure, for in 1874 its annual value was assessed at £3,600, and in 1890 it yielded over £4,300 in royalties.(23) Glasgow preferred to preserve the amenities of its "Green" rather than exploit its subterranean coal measures.(24) The burgh of Hamilton still owns some untapped coal resources.(25) Dumbarton sold its burgh Common Muir to Sir John Maxwell of Pollok for £9,000 in 1845; it became part of the Strathleven estate.(26)

In cases where the landlord was a mere recipient of rent and royalties, his reward of course depended on "natural and social" causes outwith his control. The Buchanans of Drumpellier (Lanarkshire), descendants of a great Virginia House, who after vicissitudes of fortune had re-established their position through inheritance from "Robin" Carrick, the notorious manager of the Ship Bank,(27) were singularly lucky in the subsoil of the estates which they had acquired. Much of their land was feued or leased for coal and iron mines, iron-works, etc. Their gross rental from minerals was recorded as being over £15,000 in 1874, in addition to £8,700 from land.(28) Neighbouring absentee landlords, the Alexanders of Airdrie and Rochsilloch, latterly resident in America, were similarly favoured.(29) Land with a rental for agricultural purposes estimated at £650, produced at one period £12,500 per annum from minerals. Four ironworks and an iron mine were leased from them. The much sought blackband seams yielded them a royalty of 7s. 6d. per ton, but were soon exhausted, and the gross rental of the estate fell by 1874 to little over £2,000. Ironstone from Kirkintilloch and Cumbernauld yielded a small lordship of £4 per 100 tons to the proprietors.

The Callendar estates (Falkirk) owned by the descendants of William Forbes, an eighteenth-century Government con-tractor and alleged "war profiteer," included a colliery and an ironstone mine; the assessed rental in the 'seventies was £12,800, plus £3,400 for minerals.(30) On the Kerse estate of the Earl of Zetland (Grangemouth) coal was extensively wrought; he had here a rental of £4,250, along with one of £2,600 in Clackmannanshire.(31) The initial enterprise of the Bairds—the Gartsherrie coal pit—was leased in 1826 from the proprietor Hamilton Colt; in 1874 their rental was £8,400 from land and about half as much from minerals; while the share held by Colt's trustees amounted to £2,400 from land and £4,000 from minerals.(32) The Bairds subsequently leased Cairnhill ironstone (Airdrie) from George Muir Nisbet, a colliery at Kilsyth, and mineral fields in Ayrshire from the Earl of Eglinton.(33) This early champion of Scottish nationalism held respectable rank among royalty owners with a rental of £9,500, but was far transcended by the Duke of Hamilton with a total of £56,920 14s.

Among others of "our noble families" thus enriched may be cited the Duke of Portland (£16,200), Lord Belhaven (£19,500), the Earl of Glasgow (£8,700), the Marquis of Lothian (£6,300), and the Countess of Home (£4,700). Other names of interest are those of James Boswell's descendants at Auchlinleck (where coal was "wrought from time immemorial") (£3,600), the Trustees of William Dixon, founder of the iron industry at Govan (£9,100), the Rev. Sholto Douglas, a scion of the Blythswoods, in the Monklands (£6,400), and Hamilton of Dalzell, son of the Owenite (£11,000); while one Emily Muirhead, otherwise unknown, had a rental of £5,471 5s. at Motherwell.(34)

The usual system of leasing was described by an Inspector of Mines to the Commission on Coal (1871). The landlord generally defined the method of working, but did not specify particular seams, protecting himself by a fixed rent redeemable out of royalties payable on coal. There was usually a clause in the lease providing that the tenant could be quit if he proved to an arbiter that the mine could not be worked at a profit. The tenants were at that period insisting on a "break of term period," i.e. an option to terminate or review the lease after a fixed date; alternatively, a lease might be granted, allowing the tenant to quit at any time on payment of one year's rent in advance.(35)

A sliding scale of royalties was frequently in force at an

early date, but was abandoned owing to complexity of calculation during the "Railway Age"; it was being revived in some quarters about 1890, and was calculated in relation to the selling price. An authoritative estimate of royalties at that period gave the following averages: ironstone, sixpence to two and sixpence per ton; coal, fourpence to one and three; shale, fourpence to tenpence.(36)

How far expansion was checked and enterprises were abandoned owing to the burden of royalties was much debated. The "excessive lordship dues on minerals" were asserted to be a main cause of trade depression in the 'eighties, on the ground that they entered into the cost of production of the principal industries; e.g. they were estimated to represent three shillings per ton in the price of pig iron.(37) The allegation by miners' representatives that his extortionate demands had caused several stoppages on his estate were repelled by the Duke of Hamilton's agents; their assertion that royalty per ton was sometimes double wage per ton was apparently not contradicted.(38) Economic theory was also adduced to demonstrate that "rent does not enter into the cost of production."

As early as the date when Robert Forsyth surveyed from his study "the Beauties of Scotland," the different proprietors have had serious lawsuits on account of "interferences of interests" in the exploitation of minerals.(39) His legal soul doubtless rejoiced in the extent to which "surplus value" thus continued to be diverted into professional pockets throughout the century. The "Great Scottish Coalworking Question" legally debated in 1850 was occasioned by the removal of "coal pillars" at a Hurlet mine.(40)

A novel bone of contention was introduced by the invention of James Young enabling oil to be extracted from cannel coal. His pioneer venture was responsible for a lengthy lawsuit (1853–59), notable because of the parties as well as the issues involved. William Honyman Gillespie, proprietor by right of his wife (a descendant of Lord Braxfield), of Torbanehill estate (Bathgate), who was "receiving only a small fee," sued his lessees, Messrs. Russell of Falkirk, who were "reaping vast and unexpected profits" from the new use of the much sought

mineral. The issue turned on the definition of the latter substance, sometimes termed "torbanite." The pursuer claimed
that "it was not coal, and therefore the working of it was not
included in the lease." Many experts, including Hugh Miller
in his capacity as amateur geologist, were cited, but after their
fashion differed hopelessly. The laird lost his case, the jury
deciding that "whatever it might be, it was one of the minerals
included in the lease." He appealed, and a compromise was
reached, on terms profitable to him; his mineral rental was
assessed at £13,125. This perhaps added fervour to the zeal
with which Gillespie penned the successive "*a priori* demonstrations" of the existence and beneficence of the Deity, for
which he is still remembered by theologians. The proceeds
helped to endow the Trust which his widow established to
disseminate his publications. Mr. Russell sealed his reconcilia-
tion by subsidizing a cheap edition for workers of Gillespie's
magnum opus; the metaphysician showed a more practical
interest in their well-being by suggesting to his tenant schemes
for their better housing.(41)

The threatened exhaustion of the "torbanite," "bituminite,"
or "Boghead coal" (to quote some of its aliases) led to the
utilization about 1860 of oil shale proper, which abounded in
certain parts of the Lothians, but had hitherto been of little
commercial value.

Robert Bell (1824–94), a Wishaw coal and ironmaster, leased
minerals on the Broxburn estate from the Earl of Buchan, and
initiated the distillation of oil from shale; he thus became the
second founder of the industry. A large number of companies
for mining, distilling, and refining were established in the
'sixties; among the other landowners on whose estates shale was
now advantageously worked were Peter McLagan of Pumpherston, M.P., S. B. Hare of Calderhall, and George F. Maitland
of Hermand.(42)

Land was sometimes bought by industrial magnates or
companies in order to utilize its mineral resources. The Bairds
purchased from William Dixon coal-bearing land at Palacecraig
(1841); it cost them £90,000, but produced a handsome
revenue from "lordship" of shale.(43) The Carron Co. held

property in nine Stirlingshire parishes, with an income of nearly £9,000.(44) The Ayr Coal Co., with which the forebears of Dr. John Taylor the Chartist were connected, owned the lands of Blackhouse early in the century.(45) The Houldsworths purchased from Sir James Denham, son of the pre-Smithian economist, the Coltness estate (Lanarkshire), which proved to be "full of minerals."(46)

CHAPTER II

SITE VALUES:
THE USE OF LAND FOR BUILDING PURPOSES

The expansion of the cities was also a source of revenue to ground landlords. "Buildings in Scotland are erected either on land held for perpetuity from the Crown, or on land held for perpetuity on payment to an immediate feudal superior of a certain annual feu duty."(1) The essence of this feu-holding system, peculiar to Scotland, is "that it is a heritable tenure, granted in return for a fixed and single rent and for certain casualties";(2) it had a somewhat obscure origin during the fifteeenth and sixteenth centuries. "In 1746, practically the whole of the land of Scotland came to be held in feu-farm."(3) Before the days of the joint-stock company, land was of necessity the principal outlet for investment; all sorts and conditions of men became involved in the profits of land through feus, wadsets, and the other devices of the singularly complex and abstruse land law of Scotland. Feu duties have been purchased largely as an investment by religious and educational trusts.(4)

A now outstanding business quarter of Glasgow bears the name of the Lords Blythswood, on whose estate its erection was commenced about a century ago; it was the first of many areas to be absorbed within the city as it outgrew its ancient limits.(5) Its development commenced with the feus undertaken about 1800 by William Harley, the pioneer of Glasgow's water supply (afterwards relinquished on his failure to the Blythswoods and thus a source of immense revenue), and a little later by Lawrence Phillips, Dugald Bannatyne (of an eminent legal firm), Dr. James Cleland, the statistician, and others.(6) Once part of Glasgow's Common Good, its acquisition by the Campbells in the seventeenth century and its later history are alike obscure; as Mr. Johnston remarks, it is "unaccountably omitted" from the Landowners' Return of 1874.(7) Covering some 470 "Scotch acres," it had in 1799 a rental of

£223 1s. 3d.; about 1870 it was estimated to yield an annual income of about £25,000.(8)

Stobcross estate, bought in 1783 for £3,750, by John Phillips (d. 1829), was sold by his trustees in 1844 to a syndicate for £50,000, and was valued thirty years later at three and a half millions, having been laid out in streets and tenements.(9) Lands at Pointhouse, Partick, worth £400 in 1782, were sold in 1847 for £14,000 to A. and J. Inglis's shipyard.(10)

Cranstonhill, the estate of John Houldsworth, a founder of the engineering industry, was all feued by the 'seventies.(11) North Woodside estate was sold (1867) by John Bain of Morriston to the City of Glasgow Bank, and laid out about 1869 for feuing.(12) Allan Fullarton (d. 1865) developed the lands of South Woodside (c. 1830–50).(13) Improved tenements were erected at Garscube by John Duncanson.(14)

Thomas Binnie (1792–1867), a builder, feued lands south of the Clyde from David Laurie, a timber merchant and land speculator, and built the suburb of Laurieston.(15) James Scott, a versatile entrepreneur, erected Bothwell Buildings on his land in central Glasgow, and sold Holm Lands to the Caledonian Railway as a site for its Central Station.(16) Alexander Dennistoun of Golfhill, M.P. (1790–1864), who lost heavily through the failure of the Liverpool Borough Bank in 1857, recouped himself by purchasing land contiguous to his paternal estate on the east of Glasgow, and laid out the suburb now known by his name. He continued the operation commenced at Bellgrove by John Reid, merchant (c. 1838–43), and curtailed by his death in 1852, purchasing from his representatives Whitehill, Meadowpark, etc. (c. 1853). His acquisitions also included the estate of Craigpark (1850), formerly owned by James Mackenzie, a merchant who had worked whinstone quarries there; in the year of his death, Dennistoun was returned as the owner of 142 acres with a gross rental of £4,500.(17)

Glasgow Corporation sold an acre to Robert Smith for £645 in 1787, and less than a century later bought it back for £173,000 as the site of their new municipal buildings.(18) John Park Fleming (1790–1869), a procurator, acting in concert with his partner Montgomerie and with J. B. Neilson the inventor, bought and developed about 560 acres of land in Kelvinside (1839–45); 100 acres for which he paid an average of £111 were feued by 1884 at from £700 to £3,600 per acre.(19) The Glasgow Western Cemetery Co. (1845), which as the Gilmorehill Co. extended its care to the living, bought Gilmorehill and Hillhead lands, and sold them twenty years later to the University on its "flitting" from High Street, where it disposed of its old home for a railway goods yard.(20)

George Martin, St. Vincent Street, with one acre rented at £3,928 10s., James Scott, Woodside Place, five acres, rental £5,782, and J. and G. Roy, Buchanan Street, two acres, rental £5,057, are noteworthy in the Landowners' Return for Glasgow in 1874.(21)

These instances, drawn largely from the two monumental records of nineteenth-century Glasgow, the *Old Country Houses of the Glasgow Gentry* (1870) and the *Memoirs and Portraits of One Hundred Glasgow Men* (1886), illustrate what was obviously a uniquely large and rapid expansion.

In some cases inherited land rose in value merely through the chance of its situation; in others, the deliberate purchase of land to hold for a rise or to feu for speculative building is clearly indicated, and the demarcation of pure economic rent in the increment becomes complicated with the problem of the "reward of enterprise."

For other areas less concrete evidence is available. In Dundee a "remarkable increase of ground values" is noted, especially in the middle decades, while feuing increased threefold.(22)

James Steel, afterwards a Baronet and Lord Provost, built most of the industrial suburb of Dalry (Edinburgh) in the 'seventies, and acquired land from the Heriot Trust (*c.* 1877) and from the feuars of Colonel Learmouth of Comely Bank to construct middle-class residences; he became the largest feuar, builder, and ratepayer of Edinburgh.(23) Feu duty in Edinburgh (1855) ranged usually from 4s. 6d. to 10s. per foot of frontage.(24)

As Edinburgh and Leith drew nearer, the estates of the

Balfours of Pilrig, kinsmen of R.L.S., were reluctantly feued
(c. 1860). Sir George Warrender, sixth Baronet of Bruntsfield
(1835–1901), a keen financier prominent in American estate
companies, feued some sixty acres in the early 'seventies, and
thus created the tenements of Edinburgh's student quarter.
The family rights in part of the estate were much disputed;
but Mr. Moir Bryce after elaborate investigation claims to
have established them.(25) Other noted families who profited
by suburban expansion include the Gilmours of Craigmillar,
the Hopes of Pinkie, the Dick Lauders of Grange, and the
Fettes of Comely Bank, together with the collaterals of William
Miller of Craigentinny, the Quaker seed merchant, and his
son, the eccentric collector, self-commemorated in the "Roman"
mausoleum on his estate.(26)

In the industrial west were the Colquhouns of Killermont,
with a gross rental of £4,500 (1874), the Smolletts of Bonhill
(£3,300), Hinshelwood of Ibrox (£2,300), Paterson of Dowan-
hill (£7,200), and the Stirling Maxwells of Pollok (£8,700).(27)
The "Great Depression" involved a setback to building and a
check to the growth of "unearned increment" coincident with
Henry George's onslaught upon it.(28)

The endowments of ancient and charitable corporations,
trusts, and "mortifications," continually added to by the pious
benefactor, and occasionally redirected from obsolete use or
waste, have a distinguished place in Scottish social history.
As landowners some of these were favourably affected by
industrial progress, notably in Edinburgh the Heriot Trust
and the Merchant Company. The former by judicious purchases in the seventeenth century augmented the bequest of
its founder, and so acquired the Broughton and other estates,
enormously enhanced in value by the building of the New
Town. The latter owned over 7,000 acres in Edinburgh and
elsewhere, to the value of about £300,000. Much of its land,
especially in Merchiston, was feued for building after 1870.(29)

In Glasgow, some 200 acres owned by Hutcheson's Hospital
in the Gorbals had a rental in 1800 of £600, which by 1880
rose to over £17,000.(30) Glasgow Trades House in 1788
acquired sole rights in certain lands in Gorbals, held since

1640 in joint ownership with the Town Council and other bodies. These seventy-eight acres were feued by 1856, the rate rising from 1s. 6d. to £1 5s. per square yard, yielding about 1880 nearly £5,000.(31) The Trades House also bought in 1846 the lands of Kelvinbank and Sandyford for about £30,000 —land valued at £1,000 in 1792. They thus relieved from obligations rashly undertaken on their own account two of their members, Archibald McLellan (eponym of the Art Galleries) and James Smith, at whose expense the chronicler is somewhat sarcastic; but the charitable attitude of the House was financially justified, since by 1875 it had through sale or feu made gains reckoned at from £13,000 to £80,000.(32)

The Tailors' Incorporation, having profited by the feuing of Parson's Croft within the city, bought in 1876 the lands of Middlemuir (Lenzie); while the Bakers derived revenue from Dunhouse Lands and Mills on the Kelvin.(33) In Falkirk, a "feuars' corporation" managed an estate of long standing, and devoted its yearly income to general civic purposes.(34)

Complaints of high prices for land and of restriction of building by feuing regulations were frequent, especially in Edinburgh, where the Heriot Trust was censured on this account by Drs. Begg and Blaikie, in their zeal for working-class housing.(35) Considerably later, the protest was reiterated by the Chairman of the Trades Council and the manager of the Co-operative Building Company, in their evidence before the Royal Commission on Housing (1884–85).(36)

It was a long-standing practice for the successful in business to set up as landed proprietors, and the new industrialists were quick to follow suit; thus large tracts of rural land changed ownership. This "migration to the land" was commented on by Sheriff Alison as a characteristic of Glasgow social life,(37) and is amply illustrated in the two local volumes already mentioned. The prolific clan of Finlay was soon distributed throughout Great Britain;(38) the eight brothers Baird of Gartsherrie purchased estates all over Scotland to a total value of about two million pounds,(39) the majority preferring to crown a youth of toil with a middle age of ease as country gentlemen and sportsmen. Sir James Matheson, Bart., bought the Island of Lewis from the Seaforths in 1844 for £190,000, and thus became the second landowner in the kingdom, with an acreage of over 400,000; he expended on the crofters of his native isles, especially during the famine years, a further half-million of his spoils from the Chinese opium and tea trade; his efforts to render them self-supporting were vain, and his only rewards were a baronetcy and many compliments on his tribal philanthropy.(40)

Such purchases of land had a social and political value, owing to the voting power and prestige attaching to land-ownership. Thus Duncan McLaren, the Radical M.P., by acquiring Newington House, whose lands overlapped the Edinburgh city boundary (1852), became a Midlothian elector and a butt for the satire of the Tory *Courant*.(41) In the same year his colleague, Charles Cowan, M.P., the paper manufacturer of Penicuik, bought Logan House with three farms for £31,000.(42) Allan Gilmour, the timber merchant, had an estate of £12,000 a year in his ancestral parish of Eaglesham; his partners, Arthur and John Pollok, early began to invest their savings in land, partly owing to land hunger, partly because they were keen politicians. Besides acquiring an estate in Renfrewshire with a rental of £4,000, the former invested much of his gains in land at Lismany in Northern Ireland, where he ultimately lost much of his fortune in cattle rearing.(43) George Hope, the unique tenant farmer, Free Trader, and Unitarian, purchased sheep farms in Berwickshire and Peeblesshire in the 'sixties, and thus secured greater freedom in the exercise of the religious and political nonconformity which ultimately occasioned his eviction from Fenton Barns (East Lothian) on the expiry of his lease (1872).(44)

Another prestige factor was the "conspicuous waste" of sport; its relation to industrial development as cause and effect is indirect and twofold. The scions of business families devoted some of their enhanced wealth and leisure to the pursuit of game; the seclusion of considerable tracts for non-productive purposes encouraged migration of labour to the towns. A new era began in the late eighteenth century, with the introduction of sheep farming and prohibition of trespass; the letting of estates for shooting and consequent "English invasion" of the Highlands had definitely commenced by 1830.(45) The setting apart of ground in residential areas for golf courses and playing-fields appears to belong to the end of the century.

The spread to all classes of the "summer holiday" habit, illustrated by the transformation in character of the "Glasgow Fair,"(46) also provided opportunities for speculative building in popular resorts. A pioneer in this sphere as well as in naval engineering was David Napier, who in 1828 purchased Kilmun estate on the Holy Loch and developed its attractions by constructing a pier, hotel, and villas.(47) To James Ewing, sometime Lord Provost and M.P. for Glasgow, is attributed credit for similar enhancement of the attractions of Dunoon (c. 1835–40).(48)

The introduction of railways affords cases of special interest as regards the attitude of the landowners to industrial progress, involving complex issues of amenity as well as of finance. The early "railways" were devised as subsidiaries to collieries and similar enterprises—e.g. the pioneer Scottish venture from Kilmarnock to Troon (1810) was established to convey the Duke of Portland's coal to his harbour; the Edinburgh and Dalkeith (1826) to transport coal from Newbattle Colliery to St. Leonard's Depot; the Ardrossan and Johnstone (1827) as a supplement to the uncompleted Eglinton Canal, to convey coal to Ardrossan.(49)

As with the invention of the locomotive the railway became a serious competitor to older forms of transport, and projects of expansion multiplied throughout the country, some land-owners became actively hostile, some were energetic promoters, some (like Disraeli's Lord Marney) were "violent against railroads . . . until the compensation was settled . . . but gave up all opposition when (the promoters) agreed to his terms." The thirteenth Earl of Eglinton (1812–61), despite the medieval proclivities displayed in his revival of the feudal tournament (1839), was an eager champion of railway enterprise. Besides fostering the establishment by the Bairds of ironworks on his Ayrshire estates, he resumed his grandfather's enterprises, the Ardrossan Harbour and the Eglinton Canal, and promoted a railway designed to link the two; he thus became Chairman of the Glasgow and Paisley, and of the Glasgow, Kilmarnock, and Ardrossan lines.(50) The Earl of Glasgow, another magnate interested in the exploitation of local minerals, was a Director of the latter. The Nithsdale line (1846) was supported by the Marquis of Bute, and opposed by the Duke of Buccleugh;(51) here the mining interests of the former, in the Cumnock district, were probably the determining factor. Local landowners are described as apathetic to the project of an Edinburgh to London "East Coast Route."(52) John Hay of Lethan and other proprietors opposed the construction of the Arbroath and Forfar Railway (1835-36), but Lord Panmure gave land at a nominal feu duty for the Dundee and Arbroath Railway, reaping a reward in the enhanced value of land near the line.(53) The Edinburgh and Northern Railway Company (1841) was controlled chiefly by Fife proprietors;(54) The Highland Railway was generally supported by landowners, but the Duke of Atholl and others demanded large sums for loss of amenity.(55) A much more liberal attitude was shown by Berwickshire lairds at the formation of the local line in 1861-62, by which time the advantages of the railway had become recognized. "All the proprietors gave the land for the railway through their property without compensation. The Chairman, Sir Hugh Hume Campbell, Bart., of Marchmont, indeed is reported to have said that if it were necessary he would allow the line to go through his dining-room." He did at any rate give practical aid by subscribing at the outset for £5,000 of the stock.(56) Landed and titled gentry throughout the century were on the Boards of the principal companies.(57)

Harbours likewise owed much to the landed interest. The promotion of Ardrossan Harbour for Irish Sea traffic by successive Earls of Eglinton has already been mentioned. The fifth Duke of Buccleugh initiated the construction of Granton Harbour (1835-44) in connection with the export of coal from his Dalkeith estates;(58) the Wemysses similarly furthered the creation of the port of Methil towards the end of the century;(59) the Earls of Zetland had set an earlier example in facilitating the development of Grangemouth.(60) Conversely, William Baird of Gartsherrie through his purchase of the estate and harbour of Elie (Fife) was able to thwart the attempt of Philip and Robert Keddie (father and brother of the novelist) to further the export of iron ore to the Tyne.(61)

Analogous questions arose with regard to the utilization of rivers for manufacturing purposes. Water for power purposes was at first withheld from woollen mills in Hawick by the Duke of Buccleugh and Douglas of Cavers; the latter was subsequently convinced of the mutual advantage to be derived from manufacture on his estate.(62) Pollution of the Water of Leith and of the Esk by mineral workings and paper mills was a perennial subject of controversy in Midlothian, ameliorated as regards the latter by improved methods of treating the paper (1867), remedied by the Water of Leith Purification Commission (1889–93). A similar dispute between riparian landowners and tweed millowners in Galashiels was at length amicably settled (1878–85).(63)

The renting of land for the erection of factories and other industrial purposes seems normally to have gone on as a matter of course. Forsyth indeed generalizes about the obstacles to industrial progress occasioned by the prevalence of absentee ownership of large estates;(64) probably experience of the financial advantages induced a change of attitude ere long. Such cases of friction over the terms of lease as in a notorious case led the Craigs to abandon their paper mills at Newbattle after seventy years' possession appear to be rare.(65) In general, the intimate connection of landowners with the beginnings of mining and other extractive enterprises ensured their favour to later developments of manufacture, and precluded a distinct cleavage between the landed and the capitalist classes.

PART II
ORGANIZATION OF INDUSTRY

ORGANIZATION OF INDUSTRY

"BUSINESS history," "the history of business enterprise, how business has been organized and controlled through administration and management" is, as Professor Gras has recently argued,(1) a novel and difficult but essential part of historical study. "The change of organization in man's financial behaviour seems often to be strangely missing from the chronicles of the historian. The very omnipresence of the corporate form in business dulls the curiosity as to its antecedents, and perplexes effort to distinguish its characteristics."(2) The brilliant investigator of the "Migration of Capital," Professor L. H. Jenks, here voices an impression heartily echoed by the student of modern Scottish industrial development. The "one-man business" is always with us, and a natural outcome is the family concern. This shades imperceptibly into the private partnership.

We seek to illustrate the transition from these more primitive forms to the joint-stock company, latterly with limited liability; the composition of the directorate and kindred topics will be discussed. Transference of a business (plant, goodwill, etc.) to other hands, owing to the death, retiral or failure of its owners is common; in some notable cases the enterprise was carried on for a period by trustees. Interlocking of partnerships in a variety of undertakings introduces complications, and culminates in vertical and horizontal combines.

The more specifically financial aspect will next be considered, and the provision of capital exemplified by reference to the flotation of railways, the activities of banks, and the formation of investment trusts, building societies, and insurance companies. Under the head of internal administration, some indication will be given of the variety of expedients by which firms carried on their normal duties of manufacturing, buying, and selling. In the next section the commercial development of Scotland is described, and the areas and subjects of trade depicted. The general tendency to aggregation is further displayed in associations of capital for special purposes, particularly in relation to organized labour. Finally, some factors in the fluctuation of trade during the period will be reviewed.

D

CHAPTER I

OWNERSHIP AND CONTROL

THE "self-made man" of the Smiles tradition is the conventional hero of the Industrial Revolution, and is not altogether a myth. In the Hand-loom Weavers' Report, it is affirmed that some forty or fifty hand-loom weavers, including two Lord Provosts of Glasgow, James Monteith of Anderston and Robert Dalglish of Campsie, had risen to prominence as "men of capital and character."(1) (This appears to be inaccurate, as it was the son of the former, Henry Monteith of Carstairs, who attained the Lord Provostship (1814).(2)

In the more developed phase with which we are concerned, the career was perhaps not quite so open to the talents, but such instances may be cited as those of James Young, founder of the shale oil industry, Alexander Morton of Darvel, pioneer of the Ayrshire lace manufacture, and Sir William Arrol, the bridge builder. In the distributive trades, John Anderson of the Glasgow Polytechnic is an early example of the "universal provider," and a generation later Thomas Lipton of the multiple store; both had originally one-man shops in Glasgow.

Where the "representative business unit" continued to be small, as in the East Coast herring fishery,(3) in the building trades and in retail shopkeeping the family concern survived; but the larger scale enterprise almost necessarily involved transition to a more complex organization.

There are, however, certain well-known instances of large industrial enterprises which have for generations remained in the same family. The precondition of this is, of course, an "Act of God," in the sense of fecundity in the stock—one commonly satisfied in these pre-Stopesian days of reliance on "moral restraint." The dynastic potentiality afforded by nature was, however, frequently thwarted in practice by the preference which the inheritors displayed for leisured enjoyment over active accumulation.

Among family concerns of long standing, the shipbuilding

Scotts of Greenock, now entered on their third century, are pre-eminent, followed in the same sphere by the Dennys of Dumbarton and the Stephens of Linthouse. The shipowning Burnses (Lords Inverclyde) of the Cunard Line, the calico-printing Crums of Thornliebank, the thread-spinning Clarks and Coatses of Paisley, the Pullars of Perth Dyeworks, the Baxters and the Coxes, supreme in Dundee textiles, the Tennants of St. Rollox Chemical Works and the Tennents of Wellpark Brewery, afford other examples. Paper-making seems to have been peculiarly a hereditary trade, as witness the Cowans of Penicuik, the Annandales of Polton, the Craigs of Caldercruix, and the Tullises of Auchmuty.(4) The wholesale drapery firm of J. and W. Campbell (the family of Campbell-Bannerman) spanned the century in three generations. The successive heads of J. and J. White's chemical works, Shaw-field, Rutherglen, were equally noted as Free Churchmen, and the Collins have for a century been prominent in public life as well as in publishing; the descendants of the Temperance pioneer who founded the business have included a Lord Provost of Glasgow and a Secretary of State for Scotland. Among families of local note are the Websters of Arbroath, associated for many generations with the linen trade, who celebrated in 1896 their centenary as a manufacturing firm.(5) Two noted old Glasgow families terminated in the 'seventies a connection of several generations with the firms which they had founded; the Monteiths of Blantyre in 1873 and the Stirlings of Cordale printworks (Vale of Leven) in 1875.(6)

Private partnerships may be regarded as almost the typical form of early industrial organization, and were usually entered upon for a fixed and relatively short period of years, after which they were dissolved and probably reconstituted upon a somewhat different basis. The history of private banking supplies familiar illustrations. Falkirk Ironworks was founded in 1819 and carried on for thirty years by a co-partnery consisting chiefly of operatives from the Carron Works;(7) Strachan & Petrie, a shipbuilding firm in Montrose, was also founded by journeymen.(8) Several of the coal-pits and ironworks of the Monklands were opened by groups of petty operators, among whom Robert Addie of Langloan Ironworks and William Black of Whiterigg Coalfield dominated; both were, like the father of the Bairds, originally farmers, dabbling in coal extraction as a side-line.(9)

Such private partnerships from an early date occasionally took the style of company, but there were few genuine specimens of the joint-stock enterprise until the ratification, after preliminary legislation (1844, 1856), of the Limited Liability principle by the Companies Act of 1862 (amended 1867). (10) Now began "the modern era of investment."

Mr. Roberton Christie, writing from a legal standpoint, maintains that "the genius of the Scots law of Society was much more congenial to the development of the idea of a company as an entity independent of its constituent members and trading upon the credit of its own resources than was the common law of England";(11) and Mr. H. A. Shannon remarks that while "before the legal changes of 1844 and 1855 English law virtually prohibited joint-stock enterprise for ordinary trading and manufacturing purposes, Scots law was better." "By Scots Common Law," said Professor Rankine, "every company was a distinct persona."(12) It was held that a legal decision of 1860 (Cox v. Hickman), by repudiating "participation in profits as a test" and affirming "mutual agency and principalship, approximated to the Scots view of joint ownership."(13) However, as Mr. Christie continues, "economic backwardness counteracted this, and the Act of 1856, the first to apply to Scotland, substituted Statute for Common Law." Between 1825 and 1855 about a hundred cases relating to joint-stock companies came before the Scottish Courts; of these forty referred to railways.

In 1824 a speculative mania arose in Edinburgh, which displayed itself in attempts to form a great variety of joint-stock companies, most of which were short-lived.(14) In 1839 there were quoted on the London Exchange four classes of Scottish Companies—banks, insurance, railway, and miscellaneous, the latter comprising Edinburgh and Glasgow Water, Edinburgh Gas Cos., and Shotts Iron Co.(15)

The Scottish joint-stock companies existing in 1842 included

24 banks, 14 insurance companies, 18 gas companies, 10 marine insurance companies, and 26 miscellaneous—chiefly shipping, canal, and investment companies; that is, the system was almost unknown in manufacture. *Fenn's Compendium* for 1869 includes Railways, Banking, Finance, and Insurance Companies, Gas and Water Companies, and a few miscellaneous, such as Shotts Iron Co., Assam Tea Co., Scottish Wagon Co., Aberdeen, Leith, and Clyde Steamship Co., Glasgow Jute Co. Ltd., and two Cemetery Companies.(16) Companies whose shares were quoted on the Edinburgh Exchange in 1872 were similar, Railways much predominating.(17)

Of these, the Shotts Iron Co. is the most notable. It was formed in 1801 as a private company, with John Baird as managing partner till about 1840; it was converted into a public joint-stock company in 1825, and was one of the first industrial concerns to have its shares quoted on the Exchange. It was refused recognition under the Letters Patent Act of 1837, but was incorporated by Special Act in 1871, and on reconstruction in 1897 was registered under the Companies Act. In addition to blast furnaces at Shotts, the Company developed collieries and brickworks there; later, it acquired coal mines in Lanarkshire and leases of minerals (iron, coal, and lime) in the Lothians. It sustained considerable and continuous losses during the Great Depression, but recovered by the end of the century. It was latterly presided over by Robert Bell (1824–94), the shale oil magnate, and Charles Carlow (1849–1923), a Fife colliery owner.(18)

The doyen of survivors from the eighteenth century was the world-famed Carron Company. Successive related managers carried it on as a "strict family preserve, with an ultra-conservative policy" (1786–1870), but it was reorganized and its equipment modernized under the management of David Cowan in the 'seventies.(19)

The growing need of large capital involved collective provision, and the Act of 1862 stimulated the flotation of many and varied companies, either new creations to undertake some fresh enterprise or reincarnations of some private partnership or family business. The banks pursued a somewhat exceptional course, and underwent a slow and complicated process of legal reconstitution.(20) Clapham's generalization, that "the transformation of old businesses, though steady, was certainly slow," seems to hold good of Scotland.(21)

Among important industrial concerns which took a company form, private rather than public, the following may be noted.

The Hurlet & Campsie Alum Co. originated in Macintosh, Knox & Co., a private firm working alum at Hurlet (1797); it apparently assumed the title of the Hurlet Company in 1805; additional works at Campsie were acquired about 1835, and the name modified accordingly. It subsequently became a joint-stock company.(22)

The Coltness Iron Co. was formed about 1837 as one of the undertakings of the Houldsworths, who divagated, as regards the branch naturalized in Scotland, from textiles to heavy industry. It remained largely a family property, though taking joint-stock form (1881).(23)

The Cunard Company (at first officially the "British and North American Royal Mail Steam Packet Co.") was formed under distinguished auspices in 1839, with a capital of £270,000, to provide a regular steamship service to America. The original partners, thirty-two in number, included Samuel Cunard, an American, George Burns, the Glasgow shipowner, his former competitor, David McIver of Liverpool, and Robert Napier, the marine engineer. The co-partnery was drafted by J. P. Fleming, procurator and land speculator. The original shareholders were bought out by the families of Cunard, Burns, and McIver, who each retained one-third. Limited liability was adopted in 1878; shares were first offered to the public in 1880; but three-fifths of the nominal capital remained in the three families and the Burnses continued to dominate the directorate.(24)

Summerlee Ironworks, near Coatbridge, was established by Wilson & Co. in 1837. It soon passed into the hands of the brothers Walter and William Neilson, nephews of the inventor, who had founded Mossend Ironworks in 1839. They are said to have expanded the enterprise largely by aid of the gains of their uncle in his lawsuit with the Bairds. The former was converted into the Summerlee Iron Co. in 1870. They were united under the same family control as the Summerlee & Mossend Iron & Steel Co. in 1896; the Company also owned seven collieries, workmen's houses, etc. Colonel James Neilson, son of the founder, and a well-known Volunteer, was managing director until his death in 1903.(25)

The Glasgow Iron Co. was established in 1845 at Glasgow and Motherwell; in 1879 it undertook the making of steel at Wishaw.(26) The Lochgelly Iron Co. started in 1850; having undertaken considerable working of coal, it extended its title accordingly in 1872.(27) The Tharsis Sulphur & Copper Co. (1863), with mines in Spain and works in Glasgow and elsewhere, was closely connected with Tennants of St. Rollox, whose heads were successively its chairmen.(28) The Fife Coal Co. was formed in 1872 with Charles Carlow as general manager, and afterwards managing director and chairman; it leased Leven Colliery from the Wemysses (1878),(29) and extended its operations widely, absorbing the Lochore, Cowden-beath, and other concerns.

The Steel Company of Scotland was commenced in 1871 to work the Siemens process at Hallside (Lanarkshire); it purchased Blochairn Works in 1880.(30) The Lanarkshire Steel Co. established itself at Flemington (Motherwell) in 1890.(31)

Young's Paraffin Light & Mineral Oil Co. was formed in 1866 to carry on the extraction and manufacture of mineral oil at Bathgate and Addiewell commenced by James Young, and successfully developed through his inventive skill and the pugnacity with which he defended his patent. He retained about one-fourth of the capital of nearly half a million, and for some time acted as manager, while John Orr-Ewing, a Vale of Leven dyer, became chairman.(32)

The Guard Bridge Paper Co. was formed in 1874 to purchase the pulp works started on the Eden (Fife) some ten years earlier by Chalmers, an ex-schoolmaster of Tayport, to prepare pulp from wood for paper mills.(33) Perhaps the first newspaper company was that formed by the Conservative Party to carry on the old-established *Edinburgh Courant* as its official Scottish organ (1871); it was styled "the Scottish Newspaper Co. Ltd."(34)

The marine engineering business founded by John Elder and afterwards controlled by Sir William Pearce was converted by the latter into the Fairfield Engineering Company in 1885.(35) The old family firm of Crums became the Thornliebank Company in 1886.(36) Sir Thomas Lipton's grocery, which began as a small retail shop at Finnieston, Glasgow, about 1870, was converted into a public company in 1898; shares issued to the value of two million pounds were twenty-five times over-subscribed.(37)

As already indicated, many concerns, while retaining their identity and sometimes their name, soon became dissociated from the families of their founders; the frequent change of name along with change of partnership, or for some other reason, makes the process difficult to trace. Change of personnel, and in some degree of activities, might come about through failure of the owners, whether due to their own mismanagement or to circumstances outwith their control, such as one of the periodic crises.

Two of the greatest Glasgow houses, the Buchanans and the Dunlops, underwent such reverses, but recovered;(38) indeed, the "resilience" of many of the early capitalists is remarkable, and suggests less attachment to "safety first" and more genuine risk-taking than is always evident later. The failures of the Western (1857) and of the City of Glasgow Bank (1878) were responsible for many upheavals. In the early history of joint-stock enterprise there were not a few cases of fraudulent devices.(39)

Among businesses which survived many vicissitudes was Henderson, Semple & Co., calico printers, Campsie. Established in 1785, it came into the hands of Inglis, a clerk in the firm, who owing to inadequate capital thrice had to compound with his creditors; it was taken over by Messrs. Duncan, who were ruined by the stoppage of the Western Bank (1857), and was reopened three years later by Caldwell & Ritchie, Kelvinhaugh, Glasgow.(40) One of the oldest Scottish paper mills, that at Springfield, Polton (Midlothian), dating from 1742, also changed hands frequently, and was more than once sold up, until after sequestration in 1856 for behoof of the Union Bank as bondholders it was bought in 1866 by William Todd, and carried on thereafter successfully by him and his successors.(41) Print-works at Milton (Dumbartonshire), founded about 1800 by McDowall & Co., was bought in 1817 by Patrick Mitchell, former manager of Cordale Works, who concentrated other branches of the trade there. It survived a protracted and violent strike in 1833–34, and after his death in 1848 was carried on by his nephews Andrew Muter and James Millar till 1864; after some years' idleness it was converted into a paper mill by R. Biggart & Co. They soon failed, and from 1879 the paper works were conducted successfully by John Collins of Denny, but later discontinued permanently.(42)

The Ayrshire Iron Co., as a result of speculative over-expansion and mismanagement, failed for a quarter of a million in 1848. The managing partner was Alexander Alison, jun., who had lost £21,000 on the *North British Daily Mail*, the first Glasgow daily, of which he was chief proprietor. The Company's properties included the Blair ironworks, Dalry, with mineral fields on lease. After a reconstruction of its affairs, conducted by James Watson, stockbroker (afterwards Lord Provost of Glasgow), the works at Dalry were sold to Messrs. Baird for £20,000.(43)

The Benhar Coal Co. was formed in 1872 and bought part of the Duke of Abercorn's estate at Duddingston, where it wrought coal and manufactured oil and bricks; it soon absorbed the Niddrie Coal Co., formed in 1874. Partly owing to the City of Glasgow Bank failure, it went into liquidation in 1880. The properties were subsequently bought by a new company headed by Robert Bell, and the enterprise was resumed under the style of the Niddrie & Benhar Coal Co. (August 1882). It survived difficulties due to fire and flooding, and later came under the control of the distinguished mining family of Moore.(44)

The Monkland Iron & Steel Co. was originally a co-part-nery established by Francis Murray and John Buttery, who acquired works at Calderbank (1805) and Chapelhall (1826), and later at Moffat and Gartness. In 1839 they abandoned steel manufacture, and extended that of malleable iron. A private company owned by their families suspended payment in July 1861. In 1872 the Monkland Iron & Coal Co. was promoted with limited liability by Alexander McEwan, a Glasgow financier, with a capital of nearly half a million. This incurred persistent losses, and went into liquidation in 1881. The Company was reconstructed under the headship of Thomas Reid, a Glasgow merchant, but was short-lived. The properties were sold in 1888 for £50,000; Calderbank works were demolished. A new Calderbank Steel Co. was formed in February 1889, and was absorbed in 1900 by James Dunlop & Co., Tollcross.(45)

Such extreme cases of "resilience" are perhaps exceptional. They may, however, serve to illustrate both the continued vitality of enterprise and the difficulties of adapting it to the joint-stock system. Transference of ownership under happier financial circumstances affected the personnel of several notable firms.

William Baird & Co. was formed as a co-partnery in 1830 by the sons of Alexander Baird, a New Monkland farmer, who had leased collieries in the locality. Blast furnaces were established at Gartsherrie, and coal and iron mining carried on. In the 'forties operations were extended to Ayrshire, under the style of the Eglinton Iron Co., leases being obtained from the Earl of that name. Five of the famous brotherhood left no male offspring, and the sons of the other three took no active part in the business. A nephew, Alexander Whitelaw of Gartshore (1823–79), succeeded to the headship; subsequently it passed under quite unrelated control. It became a private company in 1894, with Andrew K. McCosh as managing director.(46)

Of the enterprises initiated by Robert Napier, pioneer of marine engineering, Parkhead Forge, opened in 1842, was acquired from him about 1860 by its manager, his son-in-law William Rigby, in partnership with William Beardmore. On Rigby's death (1863) it was carried on by Beardmore and his brother Isaac, and from 1886 by his son (afterwards Lord Invernairn), who in 1900 reunited the concern by obtaining control of Robert Napier & Sons. The parent firm had been constituted in 1853, when the original Napier assumed his sons as partners; the elder son soon retired, the younger, John, controlled the business during his father's last years; on his death (1876) it was taken over by Dr. Alexander C. Kirk, a former apprentice of Napier in his Vulcan Foundry, in partnership with the brothers John and James Hamilton, formerly of Barclay, Curle & Co.(47)

John Elder, the other great naval engineer, was in partnership with Charles Randolph from 1852 to 1868; on his premature death a year later a new firm was constituted by his brother-in-law J. F. Ure, along with William Pearce; the latter became sole partner in 1878, and transformed the firm into the Fairfield Shipbuilding & Engineering Co. in 1885.(48)

The Clyde heavy industries afford many such examples. Barclay, Curle & Co. began with a yard at Stobcross established by John Barclay (1818), his son Robert gave the firm its name by taking Robert Curle as partner in 1845; the business was transferred to Whiteinch in 1855, and engine works added two years later. The greatness of the firm dates from the 'sixties, when it was under the control of John Ferguson, Sir Andrew MacLean, and Archibald Gilchrist.(49) Tod & Macgregor, Shipbuilders, Partick, founded by managers in the service of David Napier and pioneers of iron vessels (1834), gave over their business in 1872 to D. & W. Henderson & Co., a firm closely associated with the Anchor Line; it was eventually absorbed by Harland and Wolff.(50) J. & G. Thomson, Engineers (1846) and Shipbuilders (1851) of Finnieston, transferred their yards farther down the river, and became (1890) a limited company, afterwards the Clydebank Co., virtual founders of the burgh of that name; the firm finally passed under the control of John Brown & Co. (1899).(51)

Walter Montgomerie Neilson (1819–1889) was son of the inventor of the hot blast. At first a partner in the Hyde Park Foundry, Finnieston, he in 1860 established the Hyde Park Locomotive Works, Springburn. On his retiral (1874) the former was carried on separately, the latter by James Reid his manager as sole partner until he assumed his four sons in

1893; the firm now styled Neilson, Reid & Co. became part of the North British Locomotive Co. in 1902.(52)

Among instances in other industries may be quoted the famous cotton mill at Ballindalloch (Stirlingshire); built by the local laird, Robert Dunmore, it passed through the notable hands of the Buchanans and the Finlays before being sold about 1845 to Robert Jeffrey & Son; in 1883 it was bought by J. M. Dawson of Balfron.(53) Portobello Paperworks, established in 1836 in a mill erected about 1780, passed through the hands of seven firms within sixty years; three of these, however, were controlled by members of the noted paper-making family, the Craigs of Newbattle.(54) The chief calico-printing firm in the Campsies was founded at Lennoxmill by Robert Dalglish (later Lord Provost of Glasgow) in 1805; it was long controlled by his son Robert (1808-80), sometime M.P., and after the latter's death was converted into a limited company as Dalglish, Falconer & Co., and later absorbed with Crums in the Calico Printers' Association (1899).(55)

After the death or failure of an owner, enterprises were sometimes carried on for a considerable period by his trustees —e.g. those of Neale Thomson of Adelphi Cotton Works (d. 1857);(56) of William Dixon of Govan (d. 1862);(57) John Wilson of Dundyvan Ironworks (d. 1851),(58) and Hugh Tennent of Wellpark Brewery—in this case from 1864 to 1884.(59)

While competition was conventionally regarded as the life of trade and even as the law of life, such theoretical prepossessions did not preclude a considerable degree of combination where it seemed advantageous. Illustrations may easily be found throughout the century of both forms of combination which economists call horizontal and vertical, and also of some which seem to involve both principles.

Particularly noteworthy is the interconnection of firms by partnerships, sometimes ephemeral, sometimes virtually constituting interlocking directorates. In some cases the relationship seems purely personal and almost accidental, in others it verges on an industrial combine, by reason of the intrinsic affinity of the businesses in question. "The system under which people were partners in other businesses besides their own was common. A man whose business outgrew his capital had not the financial facilities of our days, and a man whose capital outgrew his business had not our choice of investment."(60) David Dale and Kirkman Finlay, the outstanding figures of the first and second generations of industrialism, were early exemplars of such arrangements.

Robert Napier the marine engineer acquired interests in several concerns useful towards the expansion of his proper business. He was a shareholder in the Dundee, Perth & London Shipping Co., for which he built two of his first steamboats. He was connected with an unsuccessful coal mine at Barrowfield and an unspecified work at Port Glasgow. For ten years he held one-fourth of the shares in Muirkirk Ironworks (1834–44) besides acting as its engineer; not finding it lucrative he withdrew at the expiry of the co-partnery; James Ewing of Strathleven, a noted Glasgow merchant and politician, was then Chairman, and the Protectionist leader Lord George Bentinck "lord of the manor."(61) John Orr-Ewing (1809–78), at first a yarn dealer, afterwards a Turkey-red dyer in two distinct firms (1835–45, 1860–78), became a Director of the Edinburgh & Glasgow Railway Co., and Chairman of Young's Paraffin Oil Co.(62) Charles Randolph (1809–78) of Randolph Elder & Co., marine engineers, was first Chairman of the British Dynamite Co. (Nobels), and a Director of the British and African Steam Navigation Co.(63) Sir Matthew Arthur, Bart. (first Lord Glenarthur, 1852–1928), was Chairman of Arthur & Co., Merchants, Glasgow, and of the Lochgelly Iron & Coal Co., a Director of Young's Paraffin Oil Co., and of the Glasgow and South-Western Railway.(64) The bond in most such cases appears to have been personal, and snapped by the death, retiral, or dispossession of the individual partner.

Participation by industrial and commercial magnates in the control of railways is noticeable. Such pillars of local enterprise as Sir Alexander Anderson of Aberdeen (Lord Provost, 1859–66), founder of the North of Scotland Bank and of the North of Scotland Assurance Co. (1836),(65), and George Roberts (1806–77), founder of the Selkirk woollen manufacture,(66) were also conspicuous as promoters of railway development. The importance of transport to their industries doubtless accounts for the presence on rail directorates of such men as William Baird of Gartsherrie (Chairman, Caledonian Railway); Henry Dunlop of Craigton, cotton manufacturer (Deputy-Chairman, Edinburgh and Glasgow Railway); John Orr-Ewing, dyer, Vale of Leven (Director, Caledonian and Edinburgh and Glasgow Railways); John King of Campsie Alum Co. (Director, Glasgow and South-Western); John Leadbetter, linen merchant (Chairman, Edinburgh and Glasgow, etc.); Sir James Lumsden and Sir Andrew Orr, both wholesale stationers and successive chairmen of the Glasgow and South-Western; and Charles Cowan, paper manufacturer (Director, Edinburgh and Glasgow Railway).(67)

Commerce and industry were likewise represented in the sanctums of banking, which can hardly be regarded as constituting a divergent financial interest. Henry Dunlop was a Director of the ill-fated City of Glasgow, and perhaps fortunate in predeceasing it. The equally ubiquitous John King of Campsie sat on the board of the Clydesdale, along with Sir James Lumsden. Sir William Johnstone, the Edinburgh publisher, was Chairman of the Edinburgh and Glasgow Bank. Sir Charles Tennant, Alexander Crum of Thornliebank, Humphrey Crum-Ewing of Strathleven, John Leadbetter, William L. Ewing, Adam Black, and Charles Cowan, all commercial or industrial magnates, were at one time directors of the Union Bank.(68)

The Commercial Bank professed special intimacy with industry, and it is thus natural to find on its list of "Extraordinary Directors" such names as those of James Dunlop of Clyde Ironworks, Henry Dunlop of Craigton, Peter Denny of Dumbarton, Archibald Russell, coalowner, and Sir Nathaniel Dunlop, shipowner.(69)

The possibilities of geographical extensity even in the days of inadequate communications are indicated by the case of John Maberly; like Owen an incomer from South of the Border and originally a London draper with continental interests, he became M.P. for Abingdon. Early in the century he bought the Broadford linen factory in Aberdeen and another at Montrose; he also owned a bleachfield and a drysaltery. He established in 1818 an Exchange and Deposit Bank in Aberdeen, but this venture proved his undoing, and he failed in 1832. His properties were acquired by Richards & Co., who about 1860 were one of the largest firms in the linen industry, employing over two thousand hands; they "imported, spun, weaved, bleached, and calendered" the flax.(70)

William Dunn of Duntocher between 1818 and 1831 bought or erected four cotton factories in Dumbartonshire; a machine shop in Glasgow seems to have been his original venture, and he continued to make all his own machinery. He bought Dunottar Ironworks (1813) and also owned coal-pits, limeworks, and sheep grazings; he acquired the water rights of Lochs Fyn and Humphrey to ensure a supply of power for his mills; in 1835 he introduced steam engines. He employed many hundreds of workmen, and was deemed a good employer; he considered that factory legislation would benefit masters rather than employees, as it would reduce excessive output but involve a fall in wages. He died in 1849 at the age of 79, leaving a fortune of about half a million. Much of this was dissipated in litigation, and most of his enterprises were soon discontinued.(71)

George Macintosh (1739–1809) set up in Glasgow about 1770, and dabbled in a variety of trades; shoemaking was at first his main concern, but he soon devoted himself to dyeing; in this and in a speculative cotton-mill venture in Sutherland he was a partner of David Dale. His son Charles (1766–1843), starting with the advantage of paternal backing, was an outstanding example of the unusual combination of inventive skill and business capacity. He first undertook the manufacture of sal ammoniac, became a partner in the great chemical works of Charles Tennant at St. Rollox, and with Major John Finlay (brother of Kirkman) in the alum works at Hurlet; he joined J. B. Neilson in the exploitation of the latter's hot-blast process, and formed companies in Glasgow (1823) and in Manchester to produce goods in accordance with the best known of his numerous patents, that for the waterproofing which bears his name; the business was finally absorbed by the Dunlop Rubber Co. in 1895.(72)

The transition from textile to metallurgical industry, and particularly the evolution of shipbuilding, was responsible for some interesting associations. Glasgow early in the century became noted for its "millwright engineers,"(73) and from them were specialized the various branches of the engineering industry. With the use of steam power and of iron and steel vessels, shipbuilding was developed through the enterprise of engine builders, notably the Elders and Napiers; a large number of firms were the creation of men trained in their employment.(74) In Dundee also there were such enterprises as those of the brothers James and Charles Carmichael, who started as millwrights in 1816, specialized in flax machinery, and also constructed marine engines and locomotives.(75)

The classic example is that of the Houldsworths. Henry Houldsworth (1770–1853), also a Southron hailing from Nottingham, established cotton mills in Glasgow, and took to making machinery for them; this developed into the Anderston Foundry (1836). His son John (1807–59) abandoned cotton, continued the machine works, and with his uncle Thomas Houldsworth of Farnsfield, M.P., bought Coltness estate (1837) and commenced an ironworks there. This Coltness Iron Co., in which the family retained a predominant interest, subsequently acquired Dalmellington Ironworks, Ayrshire, Blairhill Colliery, Culross, and iron mines in Spain.(76)

This integration of kindred interests was common in heavy industry, usually on the initiative of iron and steel manufacturers. The old established Carron Co. possessed and worked coal, iron, and lime mines, and maintained canal boats and steam vessels to transport their products.(77) The Bairds had ironworks at Gartsherrie, Eglinton, Lugar, Muirkirk, and Portland—thirty-seven furnaces in all; they also held leases of coal and iron mines.(78)

William Dixon (the second, 1788–1863) inherited from his father William (the first, 1753–1824) a lease of Govan coalfields, continued ironworks founded at Calder about 1800, and established (1839) Govan Bar & Iron Works ("Dixon's

Blazes"). His son William Smith Dixon (1824–80) formed his ancestral business into a private company in 1872; its properties then included collieries at High Blantyre, Carfin, Cleland, and Wilsontown; ironstone mines at Fauldhouse; ironworks at Goven, Calder, and Wilsontown; and coal depots at Glasgow, Leith, and Edinburgh; the production and sale of by-products from blast furnaces was also undertaken.(79)

Colin Dunlop, M.P., of an old commercial firm (James Dunlop & Co., founded 1786), bought Clyde Ironworks (1810); with his partner John Wilson (1782–1851), who introduced Neilson's hot blast, he started Dundyvan Ironworks, Coatbridge, in 1833. On his death in 1837 his nephews carried on Clyde Ironworks; the firm became a Limited Company in 1886. Wilson became sole partner at Dundyvan, acquired coal and blackband measures at Arden, near Airdrie (1838), leased Kinneil (Bo'ness) from the Duke of Hamilton (1845), and set up blast furnaces; he was also first part (1846) then sole owner (1850) of Lugar Ironworks. On his death (1851) most of these enterprises were taken over by his sons, but soon passed into other hands.(80)

James Merry (1805–77), best known as a politician and sportsman, chief rival of the Bairds in these spheres as well as in business, was son of a small coalmaster, and first held a lease of old Carnbroe coalfields (1833–53). In 1838 he established blast furnaces there, and entered into partnership with Alexander Alison, and subsequently (1843) with Alexander Cuninghame of Craigends, of an old Renfrewshire family, thirteenth in succession from a sixteenth-century Earl of Glencairn. Their firm leased the minerals on Woodhall estate, and bought the ironworks at Glengarnock (1843) and at Ardeer (Stevenston, 1854). John C. Cuninghame (1851–1917), son of the co-founder, was long managing director of Merry & Cuninghame,(81) which became a limited company in 1872.

Interrelationship with shipbuilding, so noticeable in recent years, had some early anticipations. The Dennys of Dumbarton were responsible for several co-partnerships in engineering and shipbuilding; the interconnected firms of William Denny & Bros., shipbuilders, and Denny & Co., engineers,

E

were the survivors.(82) The separation and reunion of the kindred Napier firms has already been noted, as also the relations of their founder with shipping.(83) A further instance of the latter is afforded by the Hendersons; of four brothers, two were founders of D. & W. Henderson & Co., shipbuilders, Partick, two became prominent partners in the Anchor Steamship Line, which from 1872 to 1889 held an interest in the shipyard and gave it many orders.(84)

A still more definite tendency towards concentration, indeed a definite policy, becomes evident in certain spheres. Cotton, at first dispersed in search of water power, was already with the adoption of steam finding a larger unit more economical. Three Dumbarton Steam Boat Companies, after a period of bitter rivalry, realized that union would be more profitable (c. 1850).(85) The railways were established as relatively small-scale concerns with a conspicuous absence of "planning"; "it is in universal and ubiquitous competition that the keynote to the Scottish railway system is to be found." "The earliest lines were built . . . merely for local traffic . . . when some twenty years later the idea of through traffic first emerged, even then the railway magnates of the day contemplated nothing more than a series of allied companies forming separate links in a continuous chain."(86) They soon, however, found themselves driven towards combination. By 1870, the "Big Five" (Caledonian, North British, Highland, Glasgow and South-Western, Great North of Scotland) owned or controlled all but a fraction of Scottish lines; some of the smaller concerns preserved a nominal existence, but were leased or worked by the large combines.(87) The Glasgow and South-Western was itself for many years virtually "a Midland dependency," though amalgamation was strenuously opposed, e.g. by Provost Campbell of Greenock, on the ground of removing control outwith Scotland, and refused by Parliament (1873).(88)

The Paisley thread industry had gone far on the road to monopoly by the 'eighties; the Coats, dating from 1826, established in 1889 a central selling agency along with their only serious opponents, the Clarks, and amalgamated with them in 1896.(89) Bremner found a tendency to concentration in the cotton manufacture in the 'sixties, but that industry was already on the downgrade. In the new mineral oil trade, concentration was rapid; in 1871 there were fifty-one firms engaged, mainly small; by 1890 it was in the hands of fourteen relatively large concerns, and a combine to regulate prices existed till 1892; attempts at amalgamation did not finally succeed till 1918.(90) In 1890 the United Alkali Company absorbed the pioneer chemical firm of C. Tennant & Co., St. Rollox, and the Eglinton and Irvine Chemical Companies, Ayrshire.(91) The Distillers' Co., Ltd., united six whisky firms in 1877;(92) the United Turkey Red Co. (1898) brought together the chief dyeing firms of the Vale of Leven.(93) The other notable subsidiary of the cotton trade was unified by the formation of the Calico Printers' Association in 1899.(94) The tobacco trade was long in the hands of a number of small firms in Edinburgh and Glasgow, but three of the latter attained considerable dimensions; Mitchells provided Glasgow with its great public library before joining early in next century with F. & J. Smith and D. & J. Macdonald among the lucky thirteen component parts of the Imperial Tobacco Co. (1901).(95)

PATENTS

Patents occupy a niche in economic development sufficiently important to justify special notice. In their political aspect, they were a bone of contention in the seventeenth century; their value as an expedient of eighteenth-century Mercantilism is still debated by economists; the inventive genius of the nineteenth to an incalculable extent furthered industrial advance. Consequently, the legal protection of patent rights was frequently an important aspect of industrial ownership. Inherent difficulties of definition and enforcement, together with the ambiguities of legislation derived from the restrictive seventeenth-century Statute of Monopolies (for which a modern enactment was not substituted until the Patent Act of 1883), were responsible for much litigation.(96) Some outstanding cases may be cited.

Four generations of the Dundonald family contributed much to industrial science and took out many patents, e.g. for making soda at Dalmuir, but without much commercial success. The ninth earl indeed died in poverty, having dissipated the remnants of an encumbered estate in his experiments.(97)

Charles Macintosh had a successful lawsuit with one Edrington and others for violation of a waterproofing patent which he developed in partnership with Messrs. Birley of Manchester.(98)

James Beaumont Neilson, inventor of the hot blast, formed to exploit his patent a partnership including Charles Macintosh of waterproof fame, and Colin Dunlop and John Wilson the ironmasters; the two former like himself were each to receive three-tenths of the profits. Licenses to use the patent were granted at a charge of one shilling per ton of manufactured iron. After some time the Bairds in July 1832, declined to continue payment, but by legal proceedings were constrained to resume. In January 1840, however, in concert with the Househill Iron & Coal Co., Dixon & Co., and others, they resolved to ignore the patent, and the "objects of the confederacy" were embodied in a formal deed. A protracted legal case followed, which is said to have cost the parties about £20,000 each. Neilson won his claim against the Househill Co. (April 1842) and the Bairds (May 1843). In the former suit, Mushet of blackband fame, Houldsworth of Coltness, and Professor James Forbes bore witness on his behalf; while among those cited by the defence was David Elder, then an employee of R. Napier & Co. The wrath of James Baird at his defeat is commemorated in some of the legends that have gathered around his truculent personality. A compromise as to the future was negotiated, but Neilson received ample compensation, arrears of "royalties" being awarded at from 7s. 6d. to 15s. per ton. He is reported to have cleared some £90,000, and was able "to retire as a country gentleman"; he bought an estate in Kirkcudbright and his fortune helped to establish his family as ironmasters at Summerlee. At the expiry of his patent, granted on October 1, 1828, for the normal term of fourteen years, his process had been adopted by all but one of the Scottish ironworks.(99)

An action by James Brown of Eskmills against another paper manufacturer, Annandale of Polton (1842), occasioned the legal verdict that a separate Scottish patent could not be upheld for an invention unprotected in England; this was reaffirmd by the Patent Amendment Act of 1852.(100) Apparently, however, distinct registrations could be made by different people in England and in Scotland, as in the case of the vulcanization process of Charles Goodyear, who was thereby enabled to set up the manufacture of rubber goods in Edinburgh.(101)

James Young had frequent litigation against parties who had infringed his patent for the distillation of paraffin, notably one against the Clydesdale Chemical Co.; and successfully claimed a royalty of 3d. per gallon (1860). On the expiry of his patent in 1864, competition at once began, and the price of the oil soon fell from 2s. 6d. and 3s. 6d. to 1s. and 1s. 6d. per gallon.(102)

A. Orr-Ewing & Co. brought a successful action to restrain R. Johnston & Co., London, from infringing their trade-mark for Turkey red yarn (1879).(103)

Professor Sir William Thomson (Lord Kelvin) took out fifty-one patents between 1858 and 1900, and secured the commercial success of some of them by first finding capital for and later (1884) becoming a partner in a firm of opticians and scientific instrument makers founded by James White in 1849.(104)

Of Robert Napier it is affirmed by his biographer that he was not an inventor or mechanical genius; his "success lay rather in selecting the inventions of others, and . . . adapting these to the requisite needs." His cousin David and other members of the clan were more distinguished as applied scientists. His brother James, "perhaps the more able engineer of the two," invented the tubular boiler (1830), and also patented a steam carriage without commercial success; from fraternal dutifulness, he gave up his own business, the Swallow Foundry, to act for thirty years as commercial manager of his brother's Vulcan Foundry.(105) John Elder and his partner Charles Randolph took out a number of patents for marine engineering between 1853 and 1867.(106)

CHAPTER II

FINANCIAL ASPECTS

I. STOCKS AND SHARES

We now approach the kindred if not inseparable question of how industry was furnished with the capital which the growth in scale of production and marketing rendered ever more essential. In their early stages most businesses were presumably financed chiefly from the savings of their promoters, and subsequently by the reinvestment of their profits. The "cash credit" system of the Scottish banks, which permitted overdrafts on primarily personal security, was notoriously favourable to such individual ventures, and because of its dependence on moral character is regarded by Dr. H. M. Robertson as one of the very devious ways in which Calvinism facilitated capitalism.(1)

This private provision of capital persisted to a late date in some important industries, particularly in the textiles of the East Coast; in Dundee in the 'eighties a total investment estimated at two and a half million pounds in the jute trade and over two millions in subsidiaries had thus been effected. Even in the early twentieth century, almost the whole of its textile factories were privately owned; for this "the speculative nature of the industries" was suggested as the reason. So late as 1884 there were no limited liability companies in Dundee, and capital was thus difficult to realize. Surplus profits were put into shipbuilding or other local industries, and particularly into investment trusts, which are sometimes regarded as a native invention. Dundee also exported its capital in connection with its own speciality, the jute trade.(2)

Of some sixty large firms in the Clyde heavy industries, "rather lower than one-half . . . were limited liability companies before the War."(3) Conversions of old-established concerns into the limited form, with or without public subscription, was frequent in the 'nineties; e.g. Lothian Coal Company (1890), William Baird & Co. (1893), D. Colville & Sons (1895), Shotts Iron Company (1897).(4)

An indication of the complexity of financial organization is afforded by the growth of accountancy. It seems that the "profession . . . originated in Scotland. The Court of Session early adopted the practice of seeking the aid of professional 'accountants' to assist in managing the estates of bankrupts, lunatics, infants, and other persons not regarded as fit to look after their affairs. . . . In 1853 an Association of Accountants was formed in Edinburgh." It was incorporated next year, as were similar societies in Glasgow (1855) and in Aberdeen (1867).(5)

The opening of Stock Exchanges in Glasgow (1844) and in Edinburgh (1845) facilitated investment and speculation. The former was mainly the creation of James Watson (1801–89), a railway promoter and municipal reformer, subsequently Lord Provost (1871), and of Andrew Macewen (1812–66), its first Secretary.(6) Reid and Nicholson, founded by John Reid, author of the well-known *Manual of Scottish Stocks*, was one of the first Edinburgh stockbroking firms.(7)

These developments were associated with the growth of railways, which offered the first real scope for modern financial devices. "The interest of the stock market was definitely deflected from the debts of home and foreign Governments to the securities of private companies. The railway system was made by an outpouring of mass investments. . . . There came into existence a numerous investing public."(8)

The methods employed in the establishment of railway companies thus demand particular consideration. The usual practice was for a committee of local magnates to further a scheme by raising capital and promoting a Bill in Parliament. In 1830, for example, some Glasgow business men appointed a Committee to investigate a proposed Glasgow to Paisley route; the conversion of the canal into a rail track was meantime rejected, though later accomplished; in 1836 effort was renewed, and connections with Kilmarnock and Ayr were mooted. Among the objects in view were: the transport of Ayrshire minerals to Glasgow and to the Irish Sea, the carriage of handloom woven goods, and the facilitation of access to the rich agricultural soil and to the coast holiday resorts of the lower Clyde. The opposition of Road Trustees was bought off, and the line was opened in August 1840.(9) John Leadbetter, who besides being a linen merchant was Chairman of the Union Bank, was an active promoter, and also served a term as Chairman of the Edinburgh and Glasgow; and Glasgow, Dumfries, and Carlisle Railways.(10)

The brothers George and Peter Anderson, solicitors in Inverness (whose father had been responsible for starting regular stage-coach services in the Highlands early in the century), were concerned in several local railway enterprises. The Highland line project (Perth to Inverness) met with much opposition, and a Bill authorizing it was rejected by Parliament in 1846; though repeatedly agitated, it was not accomplished until 1863. The stock then issued was taken up within a week, three-fourths locally. Meantime a line from Inverness to Nairn had been opened in 1853, and extended soon afterwards to Aberdeen in terms of an Act secured in July 1856; this was also largely subscribed.(11)

It is not intended to give an exhaustive account of the establishment of the Scottish railway system, which has already been adequately done by other writers; it is merely hoped to illustrate some of the methods by which that enterprise was accomplished.

The Edinburgh and Glasgow Railway raised about one million pounds in £50 shares (1838); it cost £30,000 a mile to construct. Its stock was in 1841 held largely in England—over a third by Lancashire merchants.(12) Conversely, not only a capitalist like Duncan McLaren,(13) who was on the shareholders' committee which finally dethroned Hudson, the "Railway King," but the ordinary small investor was involved in English projects. The Glasgow and South-Western Railway Company had in 1854 about 1,400 shareholders in Glasgow and district, owning about two and one-third million pounds' worth, 400 in Edinburgh, holding £400,000, and 400 in London, with nearly half a million."(14)

Opposition on Sabbatarian grounds to Sunday running of trains introduced a non-economic complication into railway affairs. Sir Andrew Agnew, Bart., of Lochnaw (1793–1849) (15) had in the first Reformed Parliament been the spokesman of the "Lord's Day Society" in their efforts to enforce Sabbath observance by law. Later he became a railway shareholder with a view to promoting the stoppage of Sunday services; he was associated in this campaign with other aristocratic Evangelicals like Thomson of Banchory and John Hope, founder of the "Hope Trust." Motions to discontinue seven-day services were chronic at shareholders' meetings for several years, and on at least one occasion are said to have depreciated stock.(16) Under pressure from the Sabbatarians, the offending services were withdrawn in 1846, but restored twenty years later, when the directors were charged with truckling to Southern shareholders.(17)

Edinburgh Corporation took much interest in railway development, actively supporting or opposing various enterprises, by petition to Parliament, by giving evidence before Parliamentary Committees, and otherwise. In some cases they apparently took up stock.(18)

The potentialities of the railway were foreseen by Dr. James Anderson, the agricultural economist,(19) and proclaimed in the early 'twenties by Charles Maclaren, the first editor of the *Scotsman*.(20) Lord George Bentinck used the remarkable success of the Arbroath-Forfar Railway as an argument for railway promotion in Ireland.(21) During the 'thirties, twelve Scottish railway Bills were passed, under which nearly two hundred miles were laid down, and a capital of over three millions raised.(22)

It was in the mid 'forties that a railway boom ensued; in 1846, fifty-eight Scottish railways Bills were passed.(23) A speculative mania followed, with the usual accompaniment of fraud and sequel of widespread ruin, especially in Glasgow (1847).(24) Cockburn, who particularly objected to the "brutal inroads . . . on the most sacred haunts" made by the railways, poured scorn on the "island of lunatics, all railway mad";(25) and Professor W. E. Aytoun, who had experience as a counsel before Parliamentary Committees, commemorated the phase in his satirical "How we got up the Glenmutchkin Railway and how we got out of it," and in passages of his novel *Norman Sinclair*.(26)

The average price of railway stock declined about 20 per cent in the late 'forties.(27) The check was temporary, and development continued steadily for about twenty years. Some companies, however, notably the Caledonian, were in chronic financial difficulties, and required legislative relief.(28) The payment of inflated prices for land, and extravagant initial expenditure in promotion and litigation, burdened many lines from the start, and the haphazard method of their inauguration involved much overlapping and uneconomic competition. Amalgamation, though discouraged by Parliament, had gone far by 1870.(29)

By this date, street transport was developing, and after the passage of the Tramways Act (1870) which authorized procedure by Provisional Order,(30) tramways (at first horse-drawn) were introduced into urban centres. They were usually worked by private companies, who might hold a lease from the municipality—e.g. Glasgow, Edinburgh (1871).(31) The American G. F. Train was a chief promoter, and the British and Foreign Tramways Company, of American origin, controlled the Glasgow and other companies.(32) These were later municipalized—e.g. Edinburgh (1892),(33) Glasgow (1894).(34)

Water and Gas Companies also sprang up early in the century. "The whole water apparatus" supplying Edinburgh was "made over by the Corporation to a joint-stock company which was incorporated by Act of Parliament in 1819."(35) The Corporation was represented on the Directorate by the Lord Provost and two Councillors, and also till 1840 held shares.(36) In 1869 by the Edinburgh Waterworks Act, a Public Trust was substituted for the private company.(37) After the ingenious efforts of Mr. William Harley to supply the needs of the rapidly growing city, Glasgow relied for some decades on the Glasgow (1806) and Cranstonhill (1808) Companies, united in 1838, and supplemented by the Gorbals Company in 1846. In 1855, after long and violent controversy, the Council bought up the Water Company, and substituted its brilliant achievement, the Loch Katrine Works, also acquiring the Gorbals works as an auxiliary.(38) The establishment of private companies early in the century, and the substitution of some form of public control in the later decades, is a common phenomenon.

A somewhat similar tendency is seen in the provision of coal gas for lighting, though municipalization was less general. Reid included eighteen Gas Companies in his list of Scottish stocks (1842);(39) and those of Edinburgh, Glasgow, Paisley and Dundee figure in Fenn's Compendium (1869).(40) In that year the two chief Glasgow companies, dating from 1817 and 1843 respectively, were purchased by the city.(41) Gas Light Companies were established in Edinburgh in 1817 and in 1839; and an unsuccessful "Oil Gas Company," of which Sir Walter Scott was Chairman, at Tanfield in 1824. The surviving concerns were bought by the Town Council in 1888.(42) Electric lighting, introduced in the 'nineties, was in the two chief cities virtually a municipal monopoly from the outset.(43)

2. THE BANKS AND INDUSTRY

The oft-told history of Scottish banking will not be repeated here. Suffice it to note some points of particular relevance to the financing of industrial and commercial enterprise. In particular, from time to time attempts were made to direct banking policy to more "active" participation on Continental rather than traditional British lines. The Commercial Bank was formed in 1810 as the "Commercial Banking Company of Scotland," "professing to be the bank of the citizens" of Edinburgh, with the definite object of furthering industrial development.(44) Though perhaps less rigid than their English compeers, the established banks were too cautious in their granting of credit for speculative enterprise to please the more venturesome, to whom, however, the successive fates of the Western and the City of Glasgow Banks were held up as a horrid example.

The Western, founded in 1832 with 471 partners and £600,000 capital, was to some extent the victim of the U.S.A. crisis of 1857, in which it was involved by its establishment of a discount agency in New York and through other speculative

transatlantic business.(45) It had also made advances on inadequate security at home, especially against "indents," i.e. invoices
of goods; and had retained insufficient cash balances. Calls of
£50 per cent were made on shareholders, and creditors were paid
in full. More efficient management might have saved it.(46)

Not so much rashness as corruption was responsible for the
fall of the City of Glasgow; the notorious criminal proceedings
demonstrated that huge unsecured loans had been made by
several directors to their own insolvent firms. It was started in
1839 with 779 partners and a capital of £670,000; and survived
a suspension during the crisis of 1857–58. When it crashed in
1878 it had over 1,200 proprietors with unlimited liability, of
whom Robert Craig (1808–92), the Caldercruix paper manufacturer, was the largest holder. It had 133 branches, £8,000,000
deposits, and £1,000,000 capital. Its last dividend was 12 per
cent, and its shares stood at a considerable premium. Its investments were largely overseas; it had also financed much speculative building, hence its failure paralysed this already
over-expanded industry. Directly or indirectly, it intensified
considerably the local ravages of the Great Depression. Ultimately the depositors were reimbursed in full, at the expense
of ruining the majority of the shareholders by a call of 2,750
per cent. A relief fund of £400,000 raised by public subscription was some alleviation; and surviving resources were successfully administered by the Assets Company, formed in 1882 by
some shareholders. The ill wind blew good to the printing
trade, because of the litigation involved.(47)

A new type of investment bank had a somewhat hectic
career largely associated with the railway excitement. These
"Exchange Banks" were originated by George Kinnear of
Glasgow, who wrote pamphlets in their defence.(48) He
complained of the hostility of the orthodox banks, and with
some grounds; e.g. Charles W. Boase of the Dundee Banking
Company called them "a sort of society got up for promoting
the mania of the day." (49) The veteran author of the standard
history of Scottish banks, while critical of their management,
regards "the theory on which these companies were formed"
as "by no means an unsound one." (50)

Kinnear started the first, the Glasgow Commercial Exchange Company, in May 1845 with a capital of £1,000,000. Speculators received advances from it at 6½ per cent on the security of stocks, especially those of railways. This concern had several successors in Glasgow, and one in Edinburgh, the Exchange Bank of Scotland, which was managed (1845–49) by Duncan McLaren, the eminent Radical politician; it soon absorbed an "Edinburgh and Leith Investment Company." Several collapsed during the railway slump of 1847–48, including the Commercial, with a loss of £600,000. The Exchange Bank, after reorganization in 1849, survived till 1852. The North British Bank, established in Glasgow in August 1845, lost £92,000, but was still extant in 1872; it subsequently evolved into a bonded store.(51) The West of Scotland Exchange Investment Company, presided over by the commercial magnate Henry Dunlop of Craigton, appears also to have succumbed in 1848.(52)

Meantime the regular banks had devised a more or less competitive scheme in the British Trust Company (1847) with a million capital, to invest in Government and other approved securities, but to act as agents and trustees only. The provisional committee included J. T. Gibson-Craig of Riccarton, the Whig politician.(53)

The Scottish banking system, notably the device of "cash credits," had its admirers in England, and an ill-starred attempt was made, chiefly by Scots, to import it into the South. The Royal British Bank was founded in London in 1849, with John Macgregor, M.P. (1847–57) for Glasgow, who had some repute as a statistician, as chairman, and Hugh Innes Cameron, formerly agent of the National Bank in Dingwall, where he held a multiplicity of local offices, as manager. Its shares were rapidly taken up to a total of £1,000,000, and a Royal Charter was obtained. Partly owing to the failure of the Cefn Ironworks, Glamorgan, in which it was largely interested, it however closed its doors on October 3, 1856. Criminal proceedings were taken against the directors, who included two M.P.s, Humphrey Brown and John Stapleton, and also Henry Dunning Macleod, son of a Highland chieftain and son-in-law of

Cameron the manager. He had recently published a book on banking, into which he introduced a defence of the Royal British methods. Macgregor retired to the Continent, disavowing responsibility, and died before the trial. All the others were found guilty and sentenced, though participation in fraudulent transactions was not clearly brought home to all alike. Stapleton was virtually absolved, and against Macleod there was "no positive proof"; he soon rehabilitated himself, and acquired distinction as a writer on finance; he was once a candidate for the Edinburgh Chair of Political Economy.(54)

The Royal Bank first ventured on overseas investment in 1834 by purchasing at a low figure Pennsylvania 5 per cent stock and (through Rothschilds) half a million in West India Loan.(55) About the same time the Dundee Banking Company had about £200,000 invested in heritable bonds; during the lifetime of a century (1764–1864) it lost only £32,000 by such investments; of this total £22,000 was incurred on an estate in Harris, which depreciated considerably in value owing to the collapse of the kelp trade (1822–29).(56) The same bank (which amalgamated with the Royal in 1864) in 1864 bought the Tay Ferries for £27,498 19s. 5d. from the Public Works Loan Commissioners, in order to prevent the loss of a claim for £10,000, and sold them within ten days to the Scottish Central Railway Company at the buying price plus the amount of debt due.(57) Investment in Colonial, Indian, and American Government securities, and dealing in real estate, were inaugurated by the Union Bank about 1874.(58) The Forth Bridge (1882–90) was financed through the Union Bank, of which the contractor, Sir William Arrol, became an Extraordinary Director.(59)

The Scottish banks generally facilitated small-scale saving by their ample provision of branches; in 1855, e.g.—surely a peak year—a total of ninety-five branches was opened.(60) The City of Glasgow Bank laid itself out to cater for the "small investor," opening at nights to receive deposits; hence the widespread panic and disaster at its collapse. Trade Unions which had patronized it were crippled.(61)

Trustee Savings Banks spread rapidly in the towns and

villages after the pioneer venture of Rev. Dr. Henry Duncan of Ruthwell (Dumfriesshire) in 1810.(62) In 1844 *Tait's Magazine* remarked that Savings Bank deposits were in inverse ratio to the price of bread (63); in 1854 the *Scottish Guardian*, an Evangelical organ, referred to the Glasgow "National Security Savings Bank," then eighteen years old, as "one of the most useful and prosperous of our local institutions." (64)

Other ventures, aiming at "investment," if not speculation, rather than mere "saving" on the part of the middle and working classes, emerged sporadically. The Edinburgh and Leith Bank (1838) was established "for the benefit of the industrious middle class." It was at first popular and successful, and amalgamated in 1844 with the similar Glasgow Joint Stock Bank (founded 1840) and the "Edinburgh and Glasgow Bank"; its directorate included Lord Provost Sir James Forrest, and it drew on Williams Deacon & Co. Latterly it suffered from internal dissension and incompetent management, particularly that of John Thomson, who had been "sacked" from the cashiership of the Royal Bank (1845). The 1857 crisis proved fatal to it, partly because of the lockup of much of its assets in a bridge-building project on the Thames, and after writing off half its capital, it was glad to accept incorporation in the Clydesdale (1858).(65)

The Dunedin Bank issued a prospectus in Edinburgh (1844); it was to have no branches, but to act as agent for local banks; it promised a fixed rate of interest and discount, and invited small cash tranactions.(66) The Money Order Bank, designed to compete with the Post Office by issuing "stamped papers" for sums of a few pounds, was formed in 1881 under the ægis of the Union Bank. It established over 400 agencies, but lost £3,500 in its first year, and went into liquidation in January 1883.(67)

The People's Bank, Edinburgh, was established in 1888, at the instance of an East of Scotland Co-operative Conference, and was registered under the Industrial and Provident Societies Acts. One of its main aims was to assist in the purchase of dwellings, and it became banker to St. Cuthbert's Co-operative Association, the Trades Council, and other working-class organizations. It thus built up "a modest but successful business." (68)

Robert Ewen, while Provost of Hawick in 1875, established there an "Investment Bank" as a limited liability company with a capital of £12,000 in £10 shares; it shared trustees, staff, and premises with the local Savings Bank, which was suffering at the time from defalcations. It apparently made small advances to local people, and about 1890 was allowing 3½ per cent to depositors and paying 10 per cent to shareholders; it had paid off in ten years a deficiency of £2,000 incurred by the Savings Bank. It still exists.(69) Ewen advocated the general extension of such "Industrial Banks" on the analogy of Germany; savings banks "should be turned into regular banks for the industrious classes," and lend their savings for productive uses rather than hoard them. He commended the Dumfries and Greenock Provident Savings Banks for so doing, and deplored the restriction of the powers of Savings Banks in this respect by an Act of 1891, which limited them in future to investment in Government securities. He had promoted in Glasgow a bank of the type proposed—apparently designated "the Mercantile Bank of Scotland Ltd."; this prospered though Ewen retired from participation owing to friction over its policy.(70)

3. MIGRATION OF CAPITAL

The investment of "foreign" capital was no novelty in Scotland, as the well-known instances of the "Darien Scheme"(71) and the York Buildings Company (72) sufficiently demonstrate. The evolution of financial technique permitted the holding of shares in industrial concerns by non-resident investors. Apart from whatever may have been held thus by individual "absentee capitalists," there are a few notable concerns alien in extraction or control.

The makers of the Singer sewing-machine, a U.S.A. patent, established on the initiative of their manager, George R. MacKenzie, a Scots emigrant (afterwards head of the firm), an agency in Glasgow in the 'fifties for the sale of their products. They soon set up a local manufacture, situate in Bridgeton (1866), and in 1884 transferred the factory to the world-famous site at Kilbowie (Clydebank).(73) Another American firm, the Howe Machinery Company, engaged in the same industry in Glasgow in 1873, and later introduced the production of cycles.(74)

The North British Rubber Company, Castle Mills, Edinburgh, was organized by "an enterprising American gentleman," Charles Goodyear, inventor of the process of vulcanization. He established himself in Scotland to avoid the monopoly secured in England through registration of a patent there by a rival, Thomas Hancock (1856). Control gradually passed to local shareholders, and the Company was reconstructed in 1888.(75)

The British Dynamite Company was formed in 1871 by Alfred Nobel, the Swedish inventor, and some Glasgow financiers, the former holding half the shares; it opened works at Ardeer (Ayrshire) in 1873. In 1876 Nobel's Explosives Company was formed to take over the British patent for a later invention; shares in this were issued in payment of the assets of the former, whose value had increased tenfold in four years. In 1886 the Scottish and other enterprises were merged financially in the Nobel Dynamite Trust.(76)

The Cassel Gold Extracting Company was similarly formed in 1884 by H. K. Cassel of New York, inventor of a process for extracting gold and silver from ores, along with Tennant and other Glasgow magnates. Friction soon ensued, and Cassel's patent was superseded by that of J. D. Macarthur, a local chemist, who became manager. The patents held by the Company were much utilized in mines throughout the world, and a factory was erected in Glasgow (1887) to supply the increasing demand for "cyanide".(77) The activity of American entrepreneurs in promoting the introduction of street tramways was noted in an earlier section.

Conversely, foreign investment attracted a considerable share of Scottish capital. The part played by Dundee in facilitating the ultimately dangerous rivalry of the Bengal jute manufacture was decisive. The first jute spinning machinery was erected near Calcutta in 1855. A second venture in 1859 went to Dundee for its plant and its manager. The latter, Thomas

Duff, after his retirement floated with some fellow citizens the Samnuggar Jute Factory Co., Ltd. (1873), "the success of which encouraged them in 1884 to establish the Titaghur Jute Factory Co., Ltd." A third company, the Victoria, was established about the same time by other Dundee interests. The capital of these three amounted to about one and a third million pounds, which was reckoned about one-eighth of the total investment in Indian jute.(78)

Investment in American and Australian real estate, mining and railways was also popular, because of "the opportunity of investing surplus capital at a high rate of interest, combined with security of the investment." (79) Several American estate companies dated from the 'forties, including two domiciled in Aberdeen, the Illinois and the Galena Investment Companies.(80) With the opening up of the Western territories, American "land and cattle companies" became the object of a speculative "ranching" mania in the late 'seventies and early 'eighties. "Scotland revels in foreign investment," said *Blackwood's*; "three-fourths of foreign and colonial investment companies are of Scottish origin." One Rufus Hatch of Wall Street was a chief promoter; a satirist speaks of their establishment by "Yankees with a cattle ranch in one hand and a timber limit in the other"; while in Edinburgh "every s.s.c. had his own little syndicate at his back"; landed gentry like Sir George Warrender of Bruntsfield and Colin Mackenzie of Portmore (son of Forbes Mackenzie of the Licensing Act) were conspicuous on directorates. Their capital amounted to some six millions. Dundee also had its share, including two noted cattle companies and an ill-fated Oregonian Railway, wound up after long litigation with its lessees (1884–89).(81)

The vaunted security proved deceptive, and serious losses were incurred. Their undue reliance on debentures and small proportion of paid-up capital evoked criticism from financial authorities; uncertainties as to title in American law and difficulties of effective control contributed to ill-success. Some, like the Swan Land & Cattle Company and the Arizona Copper Company, were reconstructed with good results, and most of the survivors enjoyed an uneventful career till the

Great War. Lumber and mining companies usually led a precarious existence.(82)

Australasia had special connections with Scotland. The Scottish Australian Investment Company, established by deed of copartnery in 1840, adopted limited liability in 1856; it included mines and pastures in its properties.(83) In 1877 the Scottish and New Zealand Investment Company was floated with half a million capital to finance the development of the Southland area.(84) The City of Glasgow Bank at its collapse owned 40,000 acres freehold in New Zealand, and shares in the New Zealand and Australian Land Company, registered in Edinburgh the preceding year, to the nominal value of nearly a million pounds. The latter company was carefully cherished "from virtual bankruptcy to a favourable investment." (85) In sum, Australia attracted large deposits from Britain, "an investment in which Scotland through its legal firms took more than its share." Heavy losses were incurred in 1893 through land speculation and bank suspensions in the Antipodes.(86)

That now popular form of financial mechanism known as the Investment Trust was in the first instance closely associated with American real estate. Its origination has been attributed to Robert Fleming (1845–1933), a well-known Dundee merchant and philanthropist, but anticipations have been found in Belgium in 1822 and London in 1863. To Fleming the popularity of the device was admittedly due.(87) He visited the United States in 1870 in the service of Baxter Brothers, and was thereby inspired to form in 1873 the Scottish American Trust Company, which later split into three; of these he acted as Secretary.(88) He subsequently established a house, latterly centring in London, which was virtually "an operating corporation for a number of leading investment trusts." (89)

In 1873, too, also as a result of a visit to America, William J. Menzies (1834–1905), an Edinburgh w.s., registered the Scottish American Investment Company, which invested half a million in selected land and railway mortgages, Government stock, etc., in U.S.A. and British America, on the basis of not more than one-tenth in a single security.(90) Fifteen such companies were established in Scotland, chiefly in Dundee and

Edinburgh, before the end of the century. As they flourished in much larger proportion than those across the Border, it is inferred that they attracted considerable English capital.(91)

4. SPECIAL TYPES OF INVESTMENT MECHANISM

Two types of enterprise, of some importance as media of investment as well as in other respects, call for notice. These are the Building Society and the Insurance Company.

(a) *The Building Society*.—As defined by Sir Edward Brabrook, the agencies thus commonly misnamed "ordinarily . . . undertake no building operations, but . . . advance money to their members to enable them to build or buy houses or land;(92) in Scotland they have often adopted the more correct designation of "Property Investment Society." Though the earliest examples seem to have originated in Birmingham late in the eighteenth century, Scotland was soon to the fore with experiments at Hamilton, Stonehouse, Kirkcudbright (under the auspices of the Earl of Selkirk, 1815), and elsewhere early in the nineteenth. These societies were sometimes termed "menages," being based on the same principle as the sharing-out clubs of that name, and, like the Friendly and other similar societies of the period, were usually "terminating," or limited membership, and dissolved when "every member had received the amount agreed upon as the value of his shares." (93)

Later, they became permanent, e.g. Ayr Building Society thus changed its form in 1870.(94) At first operating under the Friendly Societies Acts of 1793 and 1834, they obtained specific legal status by an Act of 1836, amended in 1874.(95) The first so registered in Scotland was founded by Reid, a Glasgow bookseller, in 1845.(96) The early societies in that city were rather unsuccessful, perhaps because of the "depressed money market"; in one case, misappropriation was responsible.(97)

About the middle of the century, such societies were recognized as an important factor in facilitating occupying ownership, and as such were commended by Dr. Begg and other housing reformers. In a lecture delivered in 1851 Begg estimated that shares to the value of £12,000 were owned in

Edinburgh, largely by working men.(98) His somewhat optimistic financial calculations received posthumous criticism from his more canny biographer, Rev. Dr. Thomas Smith. Begg realized that the savings societies must be supplemented by organizations which actually undertook building, else the increased facilities for purchase merely drove up prices while supply was limited and stationary.(99)

Here we are concerned with the financial aspect, and must leave the provision of housing to a later section. The functions of the "building society" as a means of accumulating small savings, indeed more and more overshadow its original purpose of fostering house-owning; an enquiry of 1860 states that they "now subside into their proper position of affording excellent investments."(100) This Dr. Blaikie attributed mainly to "their not having had affiliated to them as in England land societies for the purchase of suitable sites."(101)

The Property Investment Companies, which were distinguished by being "proprietary," as opposed to "mutual," were the "first notable craze of the Scottish investor" in the 'seventies, and through them much speculative building was financed. Seventeen companies domiciled in Edinburgh had in 1877 a quarter of a million paid-up capital, and loans of nearly four millions;(102) the insecurity attributed to this disproportionately small basis was censured by critics. "Heritage companies," which invested or speculated on their own account instead of merely lending money to others, were particularly insecure, and several failed in the 'eighties. By the end of the decade, however, the position was retrieved.(103)

The Registrar of Friendly Societies in his Report for 1892 shows sixty-eight Scottish Building Societies with 13,000 members and about one million pounds in funds.(104) Conversely to Investment Trusts, Building Societies in Scotland have not kept pace with these across the Border, and societies domiciled in Yorkshire, the stronghold of the movement, notably those of Halifax, Leeds, and Huddersfield, have opened offices in Scotland, and along with other large English societies such as the "Co-operative" have absorbed considerable Scottish savings. The Scottish Amicable Building Society, founded in

1892, claims to be the largest native association; it is one of the only three Scottish bodies affiliated to the National Association of Building Societies which was instituted in 1869. The others are two old provincial concerns, the Kilmarnock Building and Investment Society (1864) and the Clydesdale (Glasgow, 1871), (105) which in its first twenty-five years paid a dividend averaging 7 per cent.(106) The oldest survivor of note is the Standard Property Investment Society, established in 1857, under the headship of Sir John S. Forbes, Bart., of Pitsligo, Chairman of the Union Bank, in which his well-known ancestral firm had by this time been absorbed. The "Standard" instituted life insurance schemes for borrowers; its advertisements are ubiquitous.(107) Other old Edinburgh societies are the Improved Edinburgh Property Investment Building Society (1847), the Scottish Building Society (1847), and the Dunedin Investment Building Society.(108)

(b) *Insurance Societies.*—Insurance, as a medium of investment, rather than a social service, also demands mention. Its early history is bound up with that of Friendly Societies and kindred bodies. As a commercial enterprise, insurance against fire preceded life assurance; the Friendly Insurance Company, probably the first in Scotland, dated back to about 1720, and about 1840 was paying 70 per cent, while its stock exchanged at thirty years' purchase.(109) The first Life concern was the Scottish Widows' Fund and Equitable Assurance Company, which commenced business in 1815, under titled patronage; its tables were founded on Dr. Price's "Northampton Observations." It was a "trading organization on mercantile principles," and at first made slow progress.(110) In the 'twenties the practice of life assurance received a fillip from the investigations of the Highland and Agricultural Society into Friendly Society activities; these had the aim of encouraging tenant farmers to take out policies.(111)

The North British Fire Company (1809) added life assurance to its purposes in 1823, as did the Insurance Company of Scotland (1821) in 1825; it became the Standard Life Assurance Company in 1832. In the same year the Edinburgh Life Assurance Company was founded by Edinburgh legal bodies;

it returned nine-tenths of its profits to policy-holders. The Scottish Amicable (1826) and the Scottish Equitable (1831) were formed on a "mutual" basis. Nine new companies were started between 1826 and 1845; none of these failed, though some were absorbed by more successful rivals.(112) Some fraudulent undertakings of English origin, however, did some havoc, notably the "West Middlesex," exposed by Peter Mackenzie, the Glasgow Radical journalist (1839).(113)

A survey of early development is given by William Fraser, a Friendly Society expert. He asserts that premiums are generally too high, thus the proprietary companies reap excessive profits, and friction and inequality are occasioned in the mutual societies. He holds that in view of their popularity there is room for a new venture, apparently designed for those of moderate means; and winds up by displaying the prospectus of a new company, whose founders had Friendly Society experience. The premiums proposed were compiled by an actuarial authority, James Cleghorn (1779–1838). Fraser's *Essay* was first published in the Highland Society's Transactions for 1831; it reached a second edition in 1840, by which time the "Scottish Economic Life Assurance" had been successfully launched (1837) and soon re-named the Scottish Provident Institution.(114)

Among other leading figures in the early insurance world were William Spens, a Glasgow lawyer and a chief promoter of the "Amicable," (115) and James Mitchell, LL.D. (1787–1844), appointed in 1824 Secretary of the British Annuity Company; he was also active as a writer and lecturer for the Society for Promoting Useful Knowledge, and served on the Handloom Weavers Commission.(116)

Tait's Magazine interested itself in the subject. In 1839 it published an article proposing a Government mutual insurance scheme.(117) In 1849 it undertook an inquiry into alleged defects of life assurance, and sent a questionnaire to various companies, afterwards publishing the returns, which seem on the whole to have been satisfactory.(118) It subsequently gave publicity to the reports of the principal companies.

In the 'fifties Scottish assurance policies totalled about

thirty-three million pounds.(119) The North British Insurance Company in 1860 absorbed an important North of England concern, the Newcastle Fire Office, instituted eighty years earlier.(120) In the 'seventies there were sixteen Scottish insurance companies, which acquired about one-third of the new business in Great Britain, held three-tenths of the policies and owned over one-fourth of the funds.(121)

CHAPTER III

INTERNAL ADMINISTRATION

IN businesses of the smallest scale, the "one man" and comparable units, no real administrative problem arises; efficiency depends simply on individual capacity and fortune. As trade expands, an amorphous interconnection evolves, wherein the bounds of effective control are hard to demarcate. Attempts have been made to classify such intermediate conditions under designations like the "merchant middleman," "domestic" or "verleger" system, by laying stress on different aspects. Functions become specialized, and in some cases, once specialized, they are again integrated under a single control.

At the beginning of our period, the intervening stage is conspicuous. A well-known form of middlemanship is that which, naturally, long survived in the "domestic" processes of textile handicraft production. Hand-loom weavers of cotton goods in particular, scattered in villages throughout the South-Western Counties, worked in more or less relation to and dependence on firms established in Glasgow or Carlisle. In several Dumfriesshire villages, e.g., the weavers were mainly in the employment of Messrs. Dickson and Fergusson, Carlisle, by whom yarn was "brought regularly every fortnight and distributed." (1) "Agents" connecting Ayrshire handloom weavers, e.g. at Maybole, with Glasgow manufacturers were "generally very prosperous through the practice of keeping shops and paying in kind"; a similar practice is indicated at Carstairs and at Lochwinnoch.(2)

Members of a Hand-loom Weavers' Union were in 1860 still engaged by an "agent" at Lesmahagow, when the recently-formed Glasgow Trades Council negotiated with him on their behalf.(3) Weavers of Paisley shawls worked in shops containing four to six "harness" looms, which were rented by the workman who received the material.(4) The introduction of the Jacquard loom destroyed the independence of the Paisley weavers, of whom some 6,000 to 7,000 came to be subordinate to about 750 loom owners.(5) Five per cent less was paid to country weavers "on the pretext of the extra expense of the agency to the manufacturer." (6)

The Paisley shawl industry, introduced early in the century as an outcome of the Napoleonic invasion of Egypt, through which the Oriental fashion was introduced to Western Europe, was largely controlled by Edinburgh Quakers, such as the Wighams, noted also as Temperance advocates.(7) The status and function of the designer in the textile trades is graphically depicted in *Alfred Hagart's Household*, the sole novel of Alexander Smith of *Dreamthorp*—one of the best specimens of the domestic fiction of Victorian Scotland.(8)

A primitive variety of middlemanship was known as the "small cork" system; these entrepreneurs were represented to the Maxwell Committee as the villains of the piece; they were self-made men, who sold at cut prices to warehouses and to commission agents, and thus depressed earnings. They were further accused of reset, and an illicit trade was alleged to exist in Bridgeton and the Saltmarket; its prevalence, under the name of "Bowl Weft" (because hawked under pretext of selling crockery), was deplored in a "Report on Crime in Glasgow" read to the British Association in 1840; the law was incompetent to suppress it.(9)

Analogous conditions were found in the linen and woollen industries. In Dunfermline and Hawick, linen and hosiery wares respectively were at first woven in the home, then weavers were aggregated in hand-loom shops, under the employer's direction; finally, power looms were gradually substituted, within the experience of men still working.(10) A contract system in vogue in the linen mills of the Dundee area was responsible, according to James Myles, author of an autobiographical novel, for excessive child labour under brutal conditions (*c.* 1830).(11) The "hecklers" who prepared the flax for spinning held a key position in the industry, and made full use of the privilege; from their political proclivities, the name of the craft has acquired its second and more familiar connotation. Their pretensions stimulated the employers to seek an alternative, and a mechanical device invented by John Sharp ultimately destroyed their preroga-tive.(12)

"Tambouring"—i.e. "decorating with needlework muslin or other stuff previously stretched on a 'tambour' or circular frame for the purpose of being embroidered, so called from its resemblance to a drum"—was a distinctively feminine accomplishment; it was introduced by one Ruffin at Dalkeith in 1790, and long survived as a home industry. About 1860, "the needlework, although partly done in Scotland and particularly in Ayrshire, was chiefly executed by the female peasantry of Ireland." (13)

In the early development of the heavy industries, a contract system was prominent, and may be regarded as a survival from pre-capitalistic conditions. In such cases the operatives were engaged, directed, and paid by an intermediary, himself dependent on one or more employers. Illustrations of this periodical or permanent letting out of jobs to a sub-contractor are afforded by coal mining, iron manufacture, railway construction and operation, and dock labour.

In collieries the practice was usual, and is not extinct in the Western counties, but by the 'nineties was rare in Fife and seemingly not found in the Lothians. Contractors sometimes had fifty men under them, and usually got twopence to fourpence per ton. Iron and coal cutting was in the 'sixties sometimes contracted for at so much per yard.(14) In the iron trade contractors were paid by the piece, and were chiefly responsible for boy labour—e.g. at Falkirk; partly on this account, the expansion of iron mining was regretted by moralists.(15) In the steel works—e.g. at Parkhead—the majority of the owners let out melting shops by contract, Colvilles being an exception. "The contractors being responsible for the payment of workmen's wages, they usually received a contract on an overhead basis at so much per ton." At Parkhead in the 'seventies the forehand puddler was responsible for paying underhands. Contracting was abolished after presistent pressure by the Trade Unions, on the score that it depressed wages; a rise of 30 or 40 per cent is said to have resulted from the change; the Steel Company of Scotland took the initiative.(16) Many pits

belonging to the Carron Company were long wrought by contractors, with their own employees.(17) The notorious evils of
tax-farming were to some extent reproduced under these
conditions.

Railway construction was at first usually let out by the
companies to contractors, who subdivided and sublet the
job; "it was in a large number of small contracts that the first
railways were built. Engineers came to rely increasingly upon
one or two contractors . . . to be sublet in smaller units. . . .
The contractor acquired a dignity and prestige independent of
the companies that employed him"; of such standing were
Brassey and Peto.(18) Their nearest equivalent in Scotland
was John Waddell (1828–88), who from about 1860 executed
important contracts for the Peeblesshire, Caledonian and
Edinburgh Suburban Railways, and also for the Mersey
Tunnel, the Putney and other bridges, etc.; he was interested
in coal, oil and tramway companies.(19) Sidelights on the
methods of railway construction are afforded by the autobiography of John Taylor, an early "navvy poet" (1876); he
was engaged on the Highland line in the 'sixties.(20) A pamphlet
on the condition of navvies written by Edwin Chadwick evoked
a Parliamentary Committee of Inquiry (1845).(21)

Much of the operation of railway services was also at first
devolved; "the original conception of a railway company was
not that of a carrier at all, but simply of a company owning a
road and charging a certain toll for the use of it";(22) the
private ownership of coal trucks may be regarded as a survival.
On the Edinburgh and Glasgow Railway, "the engineer acted
as manager, the agents as superintendents; afterwards a general
manager and a passenger superintendent were appointed."
Similarly on the canals the transport of passengers and goods
was assigned by the proprietor to a contractor; e.g. Hugh
Baird, c.e., Kilsyth, for twenty years put his boats on the
Union Canal from Edinburgh to its junction with the Forth
and Clyde Canal.(23)

In the Clyde Docks, stevedores were licensed by the Clyde
Trustees and competed for contracts from shipowners to load
and unload ships; they employed labour by the day; and

provided tools. The Allan Line loaded and discharged cargoes by direct labour, which cost less; but did coaling by contract.(24)

Peculiarities of two minor industries may be noted. In the Edinburgh plate and jewellery trades "small masters" worked for merchants by contract or otherwise, not being bound to any one.(25) Tobacco spinning in Edinburgh and Glasgow employed much casual juvenile labour; the boys were hired and paid by the journeymen, with the exception of those working along with an apprentice.(26)

Some further data relative to the technique of buying and selling and kindred business functions may be added; there was considerably diversity with regard to purchase of supplies and sale of the finished product. Selling agents, independent or subsidiary, direct sale by the producer, and the establishment of wholesale markets, are all represented.

Paisley muslin manufacturers in their early prosperity produced high-class goods chiefly for the London market, and disposed of them through salaried agents and branches established in the metropolis and elsewhere. By the 'forties, goods were not "entrusted exclusively to agents in London or at a distance. . . . Partners in the respective concerns have periodically gone forth to the great marts of commerce, to be their own salesmen, or agents in their pay have been duly commissioned"—e.g. the three partners of Robert Sinclair & Co., shirt manufacturers, Londonderry, Glasgow, and London.(27)

Dunfermline linens, formerly sold to visiting merchants, were at the same period chiefly disposed of through visits of the manufacturers to London and other English centres.(28) The Baxters of Dundee were quick to establish connections with foreign houses (instead of dealing through English Factors).(29)

Professor James Mavor, writing of Glasgow in the 'sixties, says that a wide range of drysalters' goods was imported in cargo lots or bought at London dock sales, chiefly by dyers and calico printers. Of the latter, some had warehouses in Glasgow, some shipped to foreign agents, some worked to order.(30)

The Border tweed industry developed from the 'thirties

[argely through its cloth being "pushed" by wholesalers such as Archibald Craig, Edinburgh, and James Locke, Regent Street. About 1880, the foreign trade done by manufacturers was about a half of their total; it was effected partly through London woollen houses, such as Holland and Sperry, Bond Street, and H. Mead & Sons, St. Paul's Churchyard; partly by direct communication with French and German merchants, who sent buyers twice a year. Their customers also bought competitive foreign goods. There was no overproduction, as all goods were made to order. Wool was sold at auction through brokers.(31)

In two important trades, details of more highly organized wholesaling are available. Dundee flax spinners attended a daily mart in the Cowgate and transacted much business in the street. Stocks were usually kept in the mills or in public calendars. One Alexander Easson erected new offices about 1860, apparently to facilitate selling arrangements, but according to Warden the open air remained more popular.(32)

Developments in the Glasgow iron trade are described by Professor J. G. Smith in his study of "Organized Produce Markets." "For about seventy years the Scottish ironmasters sold notes to whoever would buy them. These were merely promises to deliver a certain quantity of iron to the bearer on presentation of the note and on payment of the accrued charges for storage. After a time it was found necessary to provide security, in addition to the maker's name; for firms in difficulties often raised money on notes for iron that did not exist. Therefore, arrangements were made to hand over the iron to railway companies or to a store owned and managed by an independent firm which issued warrants undertaking to deliver the iron to the bearer. The firm of Messrs. Connal & Co. secured the bulk of this business, with the result that their warrants became a marketable security all over the world. One penny per ton per month was charged for rent or storage. Having thus been rendered negotiable, iron warrants were readily accepted by the banks as security. . . . It was possible to obtain advances on them up to within a few shillings of their market value, with the result that dealers were enabled to hold a large number at a very small cost. The Glasgow Iron Market was established specifically to deal in these warrants";(33) it was constituted by the Pig Iron Brokers' Association, which dated from 1881.(34) The depot became a "focus of wild speculation." The warrants, being "accepted as good security for cash advances" served as "a useful channel of finance" but also enabled mere speculators to indulge in "bulling and bearing." (35)

The firm of Connal & Co., formed in 1864 as an offshoot of one of the oldest Glasgow houses, and long conducted by eminent citizens, William Connal and his son of the same name, found this enterprise extremely profitable.(36) Another wholesale business of note was William Jacks & Co., founded by a one-time M.P. for Leith; the late A. Bonar Law was a member of the firm until he retired on the proceeds to take up politics.(37)

As to the other extreme of distribution to the final consumer, evidence is scanty. Apart from the normal retail store, the early existence of instalment purchase is noticeable. It was in vogue in Lanarkshire in the 'forties, and was regarded as an alternative to truck; agents of Glasgow firms were apparently supplanting the old-time packmen.(38) The use of "club tickets," when workers clubbed to guarantee each others' debts, was another contemporary expedient. In Heiton's *Castes of Edinburgh* (c. 1850) the prevalence of "those peripatetic *menages* called the 'club trade' or middlemen, who stand between the shopkeeper and the poorer customers, who can only pay a shilling per week or month," is noted; it obtained particularly in Glasgow and Dundee.(39)

Along with or consequent upon the specialization of manufacturing, marketing, and other processes, their integration is also to be observed. James Finlay & Co., probably now the doyens of Glasgow enterprise, have retained throughout their twofold character; they still own the famous mills at Catrine and Deanston, though long since chiefly interested in Oriental commerce, as will subsequently be described.(40) At Deanston in the 'thirties, cotton spinning, power weaving, ironfounding and machine-making were all carried on in the same establishment. The latter department was introduced by the manager, James Smith (1789–1850), to utilize his own patents; but was abandoned after his death, doubtless because of the specialization of engineering then attained. Smith was also noted as an agricultural "improver," having devised a reaper, and initiated "thorough drainage" and "deep ploughing." (41)

Another veteran firm, the Carron Company, besides the original ironworks controlled 3,500 acres of coal-fields near by and long obtained all the ironstone they required from their estate at Cadder; they also acquired large hæmatite ore mines in Cumberland. They transported their goods in their own vessels from Grangemouth to London, and brought return cargoes of groceries, dyestuffs, etc., for Scottish Midland consumption; thus they came to own bonded warehouses for teas, wines, and spirits in London, and to act as public carriers on steamers from the West coast of Scotland to the South-East coast of England.(42)

Cox Brothers, jute manufacturers, Dundee, "completed every process within the gates of their own works, including weaving, bleaching, and dyeing"; they had a jute store in Calcutta and a branch railway from the docks; they also made and repaired all their own spinning and weaving machinery, as did the other great local firm of Baxter Brothers.(43) Corsars of Arbroath (1823), makers of "Reliance" sailcloth, combined "importing, hackling, spinning, bleaching and weaving." (44)

Pollok, Gilmour & Co., timber merchants, developed their own shipping; the Burnses of the Cunard Line were originally produce merchants, and the Smiths of the City Line were at first warehousemen in Glasgow and Belfast.(45) The Anchor Shipping Line evolved from the business founded by the Handyside Brothers as shipbrokers and Baltic merchants in 1838; they became shipowners in 1852. Under the control of the brothers Thomas and John Henderson, the firm devoted itself to Atlantic and Mediterranean shipping, and established a branch in New York (1856), and emigration agencies in Scandinavia (1869), besides holding for some time an interest in a Partick shipyard.(46)

Of the highly organized self-contained business unit, Messrs.

Collins of Glasgow offer an excellent early example. William Collins the first, a schoolmaster, started a publishing business in 1819; his partner for some years, Charles Chalmers (who retired in 1826 and founded Merchiston Castle School in 1833) was a brother of the eminent divine, whose works were among their staple and lucrative publications. Collins had a separate printing works in Candleriggs. At first specializing in theological literature, he later undertook the publication of cheap reprints, school-books, etc. The business expanded greatly under the direction of William Collins the second, sometime Lord Provost, and like his father conspicuous as an advocate of total abstinence. A London branch was opened in 1839, at which date only one traveller was employed; in the same year the firm was licensed to print Bibles. The manufacture of stationery was undertaken in 1843, and the various departments were concentrated in 1861 at Herriot Hill, where printing and binding were done. The scholastic connection was an outstanding feature; at first arranged with John Burnett, a Glasgow bookseller, it evolved into the Scottish School Book Association (c. 1860), which allowed 12½ per cent discount to teachers; this was bought out by the firm in 1875. A large colonial trade was also developed.(47)

Messrs. Maclehose of Glasgow likewise combined printing, binding, publishing and retail bookselling, and concentration of processes became common in the Edinburgh trade—e.g. Chambers, Nelsons.(48)

William Love, bookseller and newsagent, of St. Enoch Square, Glasgow, whose shop was a howff of mid-century Radicals, in twenty years built up the largest wholesale trade in printed matter outside of London, coming to receive a weekly parcel from London weighing four to five tons. The wholesale business is still carried on by his collateral descendants.(49)

The co-ordination of wholesale and retail trade is most notably illustrated by J. and W. Campbell, started in the Saltmarket of Glasgow in 1817 by (Sir) James Campbell (father of "C-B") and his brother William, afterwards a Free Church leader. They carried on a retail business as soft goods merchants until 1856, and also manufactured for some years.

G

In the early 'thirties they had sales of nearly half a million a year, and produced goods to the value of seventy or eighty thousand pounds. They dealt largely in tartans, sewed muslins and baby linen. They are claimed as pioneers of early closing, of "occupying the upper flats of a tenement for the retail of soft goods," and of the elimination of "prigging" or haggling over the price of wares retailed (50)—an honour asserted in Edinburgh for Duncan McLaren in his early days as a draper.(51) Being latterly confined to the wholesale trade, the firm ultimately amalgamated with its chief rival, Stewart & McDonald, founded in 1826 by R. B. Stewart and John McDonald.(52) Fleming, Reid & Co., hosiery manufacturers, Greenock, established their own retail stores in 1883 (53) (Scottish Wool and Hosiery).

The Niddrie & Benhar Coal Company commenced direct sale to Edinburgh domestic consumers in 1889, and later introduced their own carting service.(54)

John Anderson, who had opened a small shop in Glasgow in 1837, eight years later "introduced the general store idea into his establishment," at Pelham Street, Gorbals, soon transferred to Argyle Street. He laid the foundations of the fortune of the "Royal Polytechnic" by such coups as a consignment of "genuine Hoyle's prints which he retailed at a penny a yard under the lowest wholesale price in the city," seven tons of books from the Religious Tract Society, and six hundred barrels of St. Vincent arrowroot. He also bought up goods at knockdown prices after the "Forty-Eight" in Paris, and after the abdication of Napoleon the Third.(55) His example was followed towards the close of the century by Walter Wilson of the Colosseum, Jamaica Street, and the Treron, Sauchiehall Street, who relied much on "stunt" advertising.(56) Wylie and Lochhead, upholsterers and funeral undertakers, found a grim path to fortune through the cholera epidemic of 1832; they became general house furnishers, and in 1855 "took possession of one of the most superb buildings in the kingdom erected by themselves in Buchanan Street, Glasgow." They were also "the first to introduce omnibuses, both for the town and suburban districts in Glasgow." (57)

CHAPTER IV

COMMERCIAL DEVELOPMENT

UNDER this head we propose to discuss the expansion of Scottish trade, particularly overseas, and to illustrate the sources from which industry was supplied with its raw materials, and the markets in which its products were sold.

The beginnings of Scottish overseas enterprise have been illuminated by Dr. George Pratt Insh in his two epoch-making volumes.(1) The effects of the opening up of the American Colonies by the Treaty of Union (1707) are a commonplace, and the part taken by Clyde merchants, such as Patrick Colquhoun,(2) in the tobacco trade of what have come to be the Southern States, is an oft-told tale. The rapid development of cotton after the American revolt created a renewed interest in importation of transatlantic produce, and the introduction of Eli Whitney's "gin" (c. 1794–96) (3) enlarged the output of raw material. Later, the stoppage of supplies by the Civil War (1861–65) was probably the final blow to Scottish competition with Lancashire; a plea by the noted manufacturer, Henry Dunlop, then President of the Glasgow Chamber of Commerce,(4) that the growth of cotton within the Empire should be fostered (1862), had not sufficiently timeous effect to assist the Scottish industry.

1. SCOTTISH "SPHERES OF INFLUENCE"

For the marketing of cotton and other finished goods, as well as for the import of Oriental wares, trade with the East was cultivated. For some time it was conducted, partly through the participation of individual Scottish "nabobs," whose share in the domination of India was augmented by the patronage of "King Harry" Dundas, partly by "interlopers" in illicit rivalry with the East India Company. Glasgow merchants such as Kirkman Finlay and James Ewing of Strathleven were leaders in the agitation against "John Company's" monopoly, and gave it prominence in their Parliamentary candidatures. Complete abolition was attained in 1833.(5)

Finlay was himself a pioneer of the Eastern trade. He was the first to send a vessel direct from the Clyde to India (1816), and to China (1834); he gave evidence to the Committee on Manufactures (1833), describing the large consignment of Scottish goods to South America and the East Indies; bills in advance were discounted in London.(6) Offshoots of his firm, notably Finlay, Clark & Co., domiciled in Bombay, with houses in Liverpool and London—long headed by a former employee James Clark (1813–76), who became a partner in 1847— developed the Indian trade.(7) The original firm, dating from the mid-eighteenth century, still survives as James Finlay & Co., retaining possession of the famous mills at Catrine and Deanston, and carrying on a large mercantile business in India as nucleus of the "Finlay Group." (8) Sir John Muir, Bart., of Deanston (d. 1903) was the predominant partner in the latter part of the century; eight separate houses were associated under his control, including tea estates and jute factories.(9)

On the expiry of the East India Company's monopoly (1833), Melrose & Co., Edinburgh, imported tea direct from Canton to Leith on boats of the London & Edinburgh Shipping Company;(10) next year the *Camden* brought a consignment to William Mathieson of Glasgow, a partner of Ewing of Strathleven. (11) The tea trade was quite small till the 'forties, and after the repeal of the Navigation Laws (1849) British merchants were faced with the competition of American firms, with their then supremacy in swift sailing vessels.(12) In 1847, according to William Law, a wholesale and retail merchant, most Edinburgh supplies were imported *via* Liverpool or London.(13)

Findlay, Duff & Co., colonial produce merchants, had a bonded warehouse for Indian tea, carried on shipping services with India, and became interested in West Indian sugar— successfully until the competition of Continental beet emerged in the 'eighties. Its onetime head, William Connal (1789– 1856), formed the firm of William Connal & Co., to specialize in the import of tea; he was an original partner in the Cunard Company. After his death the firm split (1864), one branch being devoted to the iron trade, the other dealing in colonial produce, particularly in sugar, regarding which they issued periodical reports,(14) now preserved in the Mitchell Library, Glasgow.

Several other eminent West of Scotland firms were primarily associated with the economic development of the Indian Empire, and of the Orient in general. Robert Hastie & Co., long headed by Lord Provost Alexander Hastie of Carnock, M.P. (d. 1864), were "merchants in Glasgow trading to the East Indies and America." (15) Buchanan, Hamilton & Co., whose head was Walter Buchanan, M.P. (1797–1883), were East India merchants with depots at Singapore and Shanghai; their chief business was the carriage of goods from the East Indies to China, from which in return they exported tea.(16)

A long-lived and far-flung firm was William Graham & Co., which originated in the Lancefield Spinning Company, founded by the first William Graham (1762–1836) of Burntshields. His son of the same name (1786–1854) added to cotton manufacture the importation of Portuguese wines and East Indian produce. His son, William the third (1817–85), M.P. for Glasgow 1865–74, and his younger brother John of Skelmorlie (1797–1887) controlled the firm in the latter part of the century. It is still conducted by descendants of the latter, numerous offshoots being reunited in 1924 under a holding company headed by his son Sir John H. N. Graham, Bart., of Larbert (1837–1926).(17)

J. Nicol Fleming & Co., of Calcutta, with the allied firm of Smith, Fleming & Co., John Innes, Wright & Co., East India merchants, together with Glen, Walker & Co., Melbourne, were the concerns most deeply involved in the City of Glasgow Bank debacle.(18) Donald R. Macgregor (1824–89), a shipowner, afterwards M.P. for the burgh (1874–78), promoted trade with local capital between Leith and the Far East after the opening of the Suez Canal.(19)

Among businesses more definitely planted abroad may be noted Todd, Findlay & Co., Rangoon, Government contractors, exporters, shipbuilders and shipowners; it was founded about 1850 by James Cameron Todd (1821–64) of Anstruther, Fife.(20) Of still greater repute is Mackenzie, Mackinnon & Co., Calcutta, of which Sir William Mackinnon (1823–93) was an original partner (1847). He founded in 1856 the Calcutta and Burmah Steam Navigation Company, re-named the British East India Steam Navigation Company (1862), and thus established communication with Zanzibar (1871), as a result of which he became a pioneer of Empire there as head of the British East Africa Company (1888). The Netherlands Steam Navigation Company (1866), designed to serve the Dutch East Indies, was an associated firm.(21) He and a partner James M. Hall were both natives of Argyll;(22) of his Indian enterprises, James Lyle Mackay (1852–1932), a native of Arbroath, afterwards Lord Inchcape, at first a junior clerk, ultimately became head.(23)

In the opening up of China to economic relationships with the West, the Scottish founders of the gigantic firm of Jardine, Matheson & Co. took an outstanding part.(24) Dr. William Jardine (1784–1843), surgeon on an East Indiaman, in accordance with the license accorded to employees by the Company, began trade on his own account in Canton about 1820, through the agency of H. Magniac, a Swiss. He entered into partnership with James Matheson (1796–1878), a younger son of the Chief of the clan, about 1827, and retired in 1839, becoming M.P. for Ashburton. Matheson returned to Britain three years later, and became M.P. for Inverness-shire, and as proprietor of the Lews, one of the largest landowners in Scotland.(25)

The firm traded *inter alia* in tea, of which they sent the first "free" cargo to England in 1834, and in opium; they claimed £50,000 in compensation for stocks of the drug surrendered to the Chinese Government (1840). They were the first firm to establish a warehouse at Hong Kong, and laid out £50,000 on buildings; they employed regular salesmen to dispose of shirtings and other wares retail to the natives; they formed connections with several Chinese *hongs* (trading guilds) and with the Bombay firm of Jejeetboy. Among their vessels were some of the famous China clippers, built for the purpose by Alexander Hall of Aberdeen.(26)

The business was continued by nephews of both founders, Andrew Joseph and Robert Jardine, and Alexander and Donald

Matheson. Of these Alexander (1805–86) became a Director of the Bank of England and a Baronet, and was an M.P. from 1847 to 1884;(27) Donald (1818–1901) retired, owing to conscientious scruples against the opium trade, as was elicited by Gladstone as a member of a Select Committee investigating the China Trade;(28) before this body Dr. William Jardine denied the sincerity of the Chinese Government's objections to opium.(29) Donald Matheson long survived to enjoy his inheritance of his uncle's Highland estates. Andrew Jardine of Lanrick (1812–81) and Sir Robert Jardine, Bart., of Castlemilk (1823–1903) became large landowners in their native Dumfriesshire; they were successively heads of the allied London firm Matheson & Co.(30) Latterly William Keswick, M.P. (1835–1912), who also owned an estate in Dumfriesshire, was predominant partner. (31)

In other areas Scottish overseas trade followed a traditional course. The West India connection is further illustrated by James Richardson & Co., who were long in the sugar trade, and also undertook dealings with Mauritius.(32) Lord Provost Andrew Galbraith of Glasgow was partner (c. 1850) in a mercantile house trading with Havana and Honduras.(33)

Commercial dealings with the Baltic were of long standing, and received only a temporary setback from the Crimean War.(34) Several Dundee houses were engaged in the import of flax for local manufacture, e.g. David Martin (1777–1863), who had connections with Riga, and was a partner in the London Shipping Company.(35)

Leith was a natural centre for North Sea and Baltic shipping, and was headquarters of the London & Edinburgh Shipping Company, James Currie & Co., and several other concerns.(36) A notable firm was that of James Miller & Sons, long headed by Sir James Miller of Manderston, M.P. (1809–87), which exported herring to Russia, imported thence hemp, tallow, etc., and owned breweries and shipping there.(37)

The oceanic steamship lines naturally had branches or agencies in the chief centres which they served. The Allan brothers were at first distributed among the terminal ports (notably Montreal) and under the direction of Sir Nathaniel

Dunlop, the Canadian connection was maintained.(38) The Cunard Company (1839) was formed by a combine of American (Cunard), Liverpool (Maciver), and Glasgow (Burns) shippers.(39) Henderson & Co., ship and insurance brokers, Glasgow, of which James Galbraith (1818–85) became managing partner (1867), opened up shipping in New Zealand (the Albion Shipping Company), and founded the Irrawaddy Flotilla and Burmese Steam Navigation Company, which received a Government contract for conveyance of troop stores and mails (1865).(40) Dennys of Dumbarton obtained an interest in the latter company, Peter Denny becoming principal partner.(41) They also gained a footing in the River Plate in the 'eighties; They first built vessels for a French firm, La Platense Flotilla Company, and on its going into liquidation bought it up in 1885; later, they took over a rival firm, the Messageries Fluviales, after prolonged and difficult negotiations, which are said to have precipitated the premature death by his own hand of William Denny the younger (1887).(42)

Of one of the most notable firms a detailed account has been given by one of its members.(43) Pollok, Gilmour & Co., founded in 1804 by Allan Gilmour and the brothers John and Arthur Pollok, all of Mearns parish (Renfrewshire), commenced business in Glasgow as timber merchants with a capital of £3,000 and imported wood from the Baltic and Canada, tar, hemp, and flax from the Baltic. They established several branches in Canada between 1812 and 1838, and entered into shipowning. Most of these branches and others subsequently formed were organized as separate firms, with complicated personal interrelations—e.g. Gilmour, Rankin & Co. (1812) had a ship-building yard; Gilmour & Co., Montreal (1841) conducted a wholesale dry goods and grocery store, and acted as a financing house for the kindred concerns. About 1840 the parent firm owned twenty-one ships, with a tonnage of 12,000, manned by 500 sailors; they shipped over six million cubic feet of timber per annum, and employed 15,000 men. In 1847 they were the "largest timber importing establishment in the world." (44) The senior partner retired in 1838 with a fortune of £150,000. The firm, however, had a large capital outlay and were much affected by the successive financial crises of the "trade cycle." About 1860 they curtailed their foreign connections, and most of the agencies were gradually closed. The original firm was dissolved in 1874, and the principal offshoot, Rankin, Gilmour & Co., domiciled in Liverpool since 1839, has survived there as a firm of shipowners; it has given to public life the families of Gilmour of Montrave and Rankin of Hereford.

The White Star Line, Aberdeen, was initiated in 1825 by George Thompson. He first conveyed emigrants to the St. Lawrence; his captains acted as supercargo, buying timber, furs and wheat for return freight. Services were later extended to other parts, notably Australia, in connection with Gibbon Wakefield's settlement scheme. Thompson's "wool clippers" were renowned, and were built by the local firm of Walter Hood & Co., in which he held large interests.(45)

Arthur Anderson (1792–1868), an Orcadian, first employee and then partner in a London shipowning firm, acquired for it in 1837 a Government contract for the Gibraltar mails, and in 1839 for those to Alexandria, thus constituting it the Peninsular and Oriental ("P. and O.") Company.(46) Subsequent Chairmen included three noted Scottish magnates, Sir James Matheson of Lews, M.P. (Jardine, Matheson & Co.), Sir Thomas Sutherland (1880–1914), and Sir James Mackay (Lord Inchcape).(47)

In the "Partition of Africa" in the 'eighties Scotsmen had a notable part in securing the British share. The activities of Sir William Mackinnon in East Africa have already been mentioned; partly owing to German rivalry, the venture was not a financial success, a total loss of nearly £200,000 being incurred; the Company finally, after Mackinnon's death, sold its rights to the British Government for a quarter of a million. His efforts, however, constituted a political triumph; "to the judgment, foresight and patriotism of Sir William Mackinnon British East Africa practically owes its foundation." "Sir William and his colleagues were largely animated by humanitarian motives —the desire to suppress slavery and to improve the conditions of the natives. With this aim they prohibited the drink traffic, started industrial missions, built roads, and administered impartial justice." The recognition of their work as "the greatest philanthropic achievement of the latter part of the century," may have afforded some consolation to the shareholders.(48) Alexander Low Bruce (1839–93), son-in-law of Livingstone and a partner in Younger's Brewery, was an active promoter of this venture, and of that in Nyasaland described below.(49)

This enterprise is of peculiar interest in that it seems to evince a throwback in a new environment to the ideals of Calvinistic Geneva. The pioneering work of David Livingstone, the onetime Blantyre factory boy, excited popular interest in "Darkest Africa," and the perennial zeal for foreign missions revived in a new form of Christian imperialism.

The essential facts in a tangled situation appear to be these.(50) Settlements of a definitely religious character were established in the late 'seventies at Lovedale and Blantyre in the Lake Nyasa region, under the auspices of the Established Church and of the Livingstonia Committee (an *ad hoc* body) of the Free Church. "From its first inception the Livingstonia Mission was designed upon industrial lines;(51) in that environment trade seemed at that time to be a suitable instrument of missionary policy."(52) The African Lakes Corporation was formed in 1878, primarily to assist the mission in respect of transport and supplies (1878). Its capital of £20,000 was largely supplied by Glasgow commercial magnates associated with the Free Church; of these James Stevenson, F.R.G.S., of Hailie, Largs, was Chairman from the start till his death in 1903; and Alexander Stephen, shipbuilder, Linthouse, and James Young, founder of the shale oil industry and fellow-student of Livingstone, were directors, as was for a few years Professor Henry Drummond, who described a visit to it in his *Tropical Africa* (1888). Its agents, such as Monteith Fothering-ham and the brothers John W. and Fred L. M. Moir, were "practically missionaries" as well.(53) It built roads, notably the "Stevenson Road" between Lakes Nyasa and Tanganyika (1881–85), ran steamers, established coffee and tobacco plantations, and carried on a general business, exclusive of liquor and fire-arms. It thus "sought to advance the Kingdom of God by honest trade," with such success that "philanthropy and large dividends lay down in peace together." (54) The enterprise became associated financially with the British South Africa Company, and was reconstructed in 1893 with a capital of a quarter of a million. Latterly it engaged in banking, and still flourishes.(55)

Meantime, in the absence of organized government, the missions under the guidance of Dr. Robert Laws and Dr. Alexander Hetherwick acted as "administrators and lawgivers of the native community,"(56) ruling on theocratic principles as a benevolent despotism. No more troubled than their Covenanting forefathers by pacifist scruples, they exercised penal discipline, aided in military conflict with Arab slave-raiders, and eventually pressed annexation upon a reluctant Cabinet, in order to forestall the Portuguese. The British Central Africa Protectorate was proclaimed in 1891, and as Nyasaland became definitely a part of the British Empire in 1907, an asset of which admittedly "the missionaries were the real founders." (57)

To turn to West Africa, the connection of Scottish traders and missionaries with the opening up of Nigeria is well-known;(58) differences of climatic conditions and economic opportunity, perhaps also the somewhat different social outlook of the U.P. Church, precluded analogous development. Some pioneer work was done in the 'fifties by the explorers William Balfour Baikie (1824-64), an Edinburgh medical graduate of Orcadian origin, who established a settlement on the Niger (1857),(59) and Macgregor Laird (1808-61), a native of Greenock, partner in a Birkenhead shipping firm, who first participated in and latterly financed expeditions, including that of Baikie. The venture was abandoned after their deaths,(60) but their unfinished labours were resumed some twenty years later, and brought to fruition by such men as Sir William Wallace (1856-1916),(61) a native of Arbroath, under the auspices of the Royal Niger Company (1886), whose political rights were transferred to the Crown in 1900.(62) The later economic transformation of these regions has been the subject of a research study by an Edinburgh graduate, Dr. Allan McPhee.(63)

2. SUPPLIES

The cotton industry was for climatic reasons necessarily dependent on imports from the tropics. It consumed in 1846 some 120,000 bales.(64) During the time of its prosperity in the West, the Southern States of the American Union were the chief source of supply; in the 'fifties the average importation to Glasgow from U.S.A. was thrice that from the East.(65) The suspension of supplies by the Civil War seems to have been a main cause of the decline of the Scottish manufacture.(66)

The novel jute industry was likewise based on import, and established a new link with India. At first imported *via* London or Liverpool, the trade became in the 'forties virtually a Dundee monopoly, and required the services of seventy to eighty vessels.(67) Thomas Neish (1789–1864) was one of the first importers,(68) and Cox Brothers, Lochee (1841), were the real founders of its manufacture.(69) When Warden wrote (1867) the annual import of jute to Dundee averaged some 65,000 tons.(70) Complaints were then made of speculation in jute in London because of the "terms of sale." "Were prompt cash payment in ten days made the rule the trade would be more in the hands of consumers." (71) An incidental result of the expansion of jute production was the revival of whale fishing, to obtain the oil required in the preparation of the fibre.(72)

Of the older textiles, linen had since about 1770 been drawing upon foreign sources, and during the century came to be manufactured chiefly from Russian flax. Efforts were made to encourage home growing. Robert Brown, factor to the Duke of Hamilton, was an active propagandist in this cause, and in a pamphlet published about 1850 gives details of various schemes.(73) Besides individual efforts by Highland lairds and others, organized attempts were made from time to time. A Flax Spinning Company projected in 1835 by a solicitor, John Young, received the blessing of Edinburgh Town Council;(74) a flax company in Airdrie proposed to raise a capital of £30,000 and manufacture home-grown flax;(75) in January

1848 a flax-growing association was formed in Aberdeen under the presidency of Alexander Thomson of Banchory, a landowner and Free Church leader, best known as a patron of Industrial Schools.(76) Over 400,000 tons of flax, to the value of four and a half million pounds, were imported in 1845.(77) The abnormal demand arising through the American Civil War taxed the available supplies, yet even high prices were inadequate to stimulate the European flax farmer.(78) Later attempts by the Baxters and other Dundee manufacturers to encourage local growth were unsuccessful.(79)

With the expansion of the Border woollen manufacture, the local production of wool became insufficient. The first import in the 'thirties was chiefly of fine merino from the Continent, but the Colonies, commencing with Tasmania about 1833, soon supplied nearly all the requirement from overseas, which constituted about four-fifths of the total. George Thomson of the Aberdeen White Star Line was a pioneer of the Colonist trade (c. 1840).(80) So early as 1846, 119,000 bales of colonial wool were consumed in Scotland.(81)

Local mines at first supplied all the ore utilized in iron manufacture, and received a fresh lease of life from technical improvements both in extraction and in treatment—notably David Mushet's successful experiments in smelting the "blackband" seams of ironstone and J. B. Neilson's invention of the "hot-blast" method.(82) "The hot blast was the making of the iron trade in Scotland," and in the 'forties "iron was everywhere on the aggressive." (83) The "most valuable deposits" were in Lanarkshire and Ayrshire, and iron manufacture was largely concentrated in these counties.(84) The output of iron ore from Scottish mines reached its maximum in 1857, with about two and a half million tons.(85) By the following decade such native ores as could be profitably mined were beginning to be exhausted, and by 1876 "large quantities of hæmatites and other ores (were) imported from England, Spain and elsewhere, for smelting with the native ores."(86) Home production, though relatively declining was, however, well maintained till about 1880, but had fallen to under a million tons per annum by 1900. Foreign imports rose during the same period from about 40,000 to nearly one and a half million tons.(87) "The ironmasters of Scotland owned their own iron ore fields from the inception of the industry," and now bought mines in Spain—e.g. the Coltness and Langloan Companies were joint owners of Spanish mines.(88)

The wide ramifications of the typically scientific chemical industry founded by the Macintoshes and the Tennants involved the use of foreign supplies, though Macintosh himself protested against the competition (which he alleged to violate a treaty) of Sicilian brimstone with Scottish alum.(89) Local supplies of alum shale became exhausted about 1880, and his successors, the Hurlet & Campsie Alum Company, diverted their efforts to the production of ferro-cyanide from crude coal gas.(90)

Kirkintilloch foundries imported iron ore from New Caledonia, smelted it and despatched it to refiners in England and on the Continent. The Nickel Company (1880), with a factory in the same burgh, had its head office in Paris, owned mines in New Caledonia, and had refineries in Birmingham, Le Havre, and Iserlohn.(91)

Scientific methods in agriculture demanded chemical manures and for this purpose Alexander Cross & Sons, founded in 1830, imported mineral phosphates chiefly from America, and prepared them at Port Dundas from 1872.(92) Peruvian guano was first used in the 'forties, e.g. by George Hope of Fentonbarns, progressive in private business as in public activities.(93) "The first mercantile fleet which participated in the guano treasures of Ichaboe was fitted out (1844) by Alexander and John Downie, a Glasgow house. They possessed themselves of the secret of the whereabouts of this then supposititious island, and fitted out an expedition regarded at the time as a mysterious one, which returned in due course laden with these fertilizing deposits."(94) The discovery saved the situation for Pollok, Gilmour & Co., providing steady cargoes after several years of shipping depression.(95) South American guano and nitrates together with North American cotton and tobacco, being non-perishable goods, of which large stocks could be maintained in the importing country, while speed of transport was of little account, remained the standby of the sailing vessel in its competition with the steamship.(96)

Aberdeenshire farming became dependent on Canadian store cattle, U.S.A. and Egyptian feeding-stuffs, and River Plate manures; disagreement as to rates for transport of guano occasioned a lawsuit between the Aberdeen Manure Company and the Great North of Scotland Railway.(97)

Among other industries which came to depend on foreign materials were porcelain manufacture, paper making and sugar refining. The first-mentioned developed rapidly in Glasgow about the mid-century; Cornwall was its chief source of supply, and its progress was attributed to "the demands of the Clyde foreign trade for bulky freight" as inward cargo—as had been the case in Liverpool with the corresponding industry.(98)

Aberdeen paper mills came to use Swedish pulp, finding the local product too resinous.(99) Milton paper mills, Dumbartonshire, used esparto grass from Southern Spain and North America as their staple material, supplemented by rags from the Continent, old ships' sails from British ports, wood pulp from Norway, and straw pulp from Germany and France.(100) Midlothian paper manufacturers imported *via* Leith linen rags from Central Europe, esparto grass from North Africa, and wood pulp from Scandinavia.(101)

The sugar refineries of Glasgow and Greenock were long associated with the West Indian sugar plantations. The trade is described in the 'sixties as almost a monopoly of Greenock, having been quadrupled within a decade. Of the import nearly one-half came from Cuba and a fifth from the British West Indies; beet sugar chiefly from France, though still small in quantity, was rapidly growing.(102)

In the depression of the early 'eighties, sugar prices were halved, and beet production was largely expanded in Germany by Government bounties, being nearly doubled in four years.(103) Beet sugar was imported chiefly *via* Leith and Grangemouth;(104) imports to the Clyde increased more than six-fold between 1868 and 1884, while cane imports fell in a few years by nearly one-half. The American market afforded better openings for West Indian produce, while Java canes from their quality and cheapness captured most of the Scottish demand.(105) Their success was short-lived, and by 1890 imports were negligible. Greenock refineries were still further injured by the development of the Continental beet manufacture, and prices continued low, with compensating advantage to the jam and confectionery trades.(106) The leading wholesale firm was William Connal & Co., a distant descendant of the Virginia house founded in 1722 by Provost Andrew Cochrane. After the failure of an offshoot, Findlay, Duff & Co., in the "black year" of 1826, a junior partner, William Connal the first, set up as a produce broker (1828), dealing chiefly with sugar and tea, and built "a great bonded tea store, the finest privately owned in Europe or America." After his death the trade in tea and general produce was practically dropped, and after 1864, the firm of William Connal & Co. was devoted to sugar, under the nominal headship of Sir Michael Connal (d. 1893), who "gave himself up to philanthropical and educational matters," and virtual control of William Wilson. With the falling off of West Indian imports the firm "had to enter the Continental trade, and suffered by the speculation of agents in Antwerp and Magdeburg." It languished for some time before its extinction in 1929.(107)

Dundee marmalade factories were in the 'sixties importing about 6,000 boxes of Seville oranges per annum, and also utilized during their four months' season some one and a half million jars of Newcastle manufacture.(108)

3. MARKETS

Among markets, the Government, principally through its "defence services," was an important factor. Naval contracts were responsible for an appreciable proportion of the tonnage built on the Clyde, averaging one-sixth between 1893 and 1914,(109) and for much of the prosperity and renown of Robert Napier. He received his first order in 1838, and thereafter built many war vessels for Britain and for Continental Powers; he maintained "intimate personal relations" with the Admiralty.(110) Messrs. Elder also "executed various large contracts for marine engines for the Admiralty." (111)

As regards naval equipment, Baxters of Dundee provided almost the entire requirements in sailcloth; they also supplied "tent duck" to the War Office.(112) The Inchholm Works, Whiteinch, after some experience as sub-contractors, held from 1875 a contract for brass fittings for the Admiralty.(113) Messrs. Thomas Shanks & Co., Johnstone, supplied machine tools to H.M. Dockyards, and to those of several foreign Governments.(114)

The Crimean War was specially welcome to trades interested in armaments who had more reason than poets for rejoicing that the "long, long canker of peace" was over. New factories were opened in Angus to manufacture sacks and sandbags;(115) the Falkirk Ironworks supplied 16,000 tons of shot shell;(116) Napiers, now a prominent name in naval estimates, built in three months an iron floating battery for the Crimea.(117) The American Civil War also offered opportunities; "in 1864 the Clyde shipbuilders did a lucrative business in constructing swift and handy steamers for running the blockade of the Southern States of America." (118) As for textiles, "the experience of the linen manufacturers of Dundee goes to prove that the calamity of war may directly promote the arts of peace, for they profited largely by the demand created for their goods, first by the Crimean and subsequently by the American War. . . . The American War was the most fortunate event that ever occurred for the linen manufacturers of Dundee. Both armies became extensive customers, and for three years the factories were kept fully employed. Great wealth was realized, and the stability of most of the firms well secured by the accumulation of capital." (119) They suffered, however, after the restoration of peace from the Nemesis involved in over-expansion.(120) Arbroath production of sailcloth also received a temporary stimulus.(121) The cotton manufacture was precluded by geographical circumstance from a like lucrative impartiality, and, as already indicated, shared in the defeat of State Rights and Slavery.

The arts of peace provided more permanent and stable outlets for these and other Scottish industries.

Cotton was essentially an export industry. Perth made a

kind of coloured cotton fabric called umbrella cloth, and sent much of it to England; imitation Indian shawls were exported thence to Turkey, handkerchiefs, scarves, etc., to America and the Indies.(122) Kirkintilloch wove a special kind of muslin known as "lappets," "with raised flowers in imitation of tambouring," chiefly for the East Indian trade; it was in 1840 worth noting that "letters are often received in two months" from consignees.(123) Paisley, after the ruin of the shawl industry, exported to South America "ponchos" modelled on the native garment of that name.(124) Dalglish, Falconer & Co., calico printers, Campsie, sent most of their wares to India, so felt bound to suit Oriental tastes by making the designs peculiar and the colours lurid.(125) Exports of cotton manufactures were in 1867 valued at £5,000,000, in addition to nearly one million pounds' worth of cotton yarn.(126) Aberdeen in 1886 was exporting all its cotton to India; half its products were sent abroad.(127)

Fife linens were largely exported to the United States, West Indies, and South America.(128)

There was much export of coal, especially from Forth ports; the new harbours of Granton and Burntisland were developed largely for this purpose.(129) The harbour of Grangemouth, commenced in 1777, and much extended in the middle of next century, with the support of the Caledonian Railway, was used for the export of local iron and chemicals.(130) In the East, in the 'forties, coal was "wrought almost exclusively for family consumption"; in the West, ironworks absorbed a large proportion, the Old Monkland furnaces as much as all Glasgow.(131) In 1831 half a million tons were brought to Glasgow, of which 120,000 were exported. In 1854, two and a half million tons were used in the manufacture of iron, at an average price of 7s. 6d.; about one million tons were exported.(132) In 1866, fully half a million pounds' worth of coal was sent all over the world; Bo'ness, Leith, Ardrossan, Kirkcaldy, Glasgow, Grangemouth, and Greenock shared the major portion in the order given.(133)

In 1854 about 700,000 tons of iron were manufactured in the West of Scotland, of which over 400,000 were exported at about £4 per ton.(134) In the 'sixties, export averaged five to 600,000 a year, chiefly to American and Rhenish ports.(135) A falling demand, and consequently lowered price for steel rails, caused manufacturers to turn to plates, bars, etc., whose use was adopted by the Admiralty in 1876.(136)

Among engineering products may be mentioned exports of nearly half a million pounds' worth of sugar machinery from the Clyde to the East and West Indies in the mid-century;(137) with the decline of West India sugar production, South America became the chief market.(138) The wares of the Falkirk Iron-works "ranged from bridges of the largest size to ornamental inkstands and fancy castings of the most delicate patterns possible in cast iron." Among their notable contracts were those for the provision of columns for the Solway Viaduct, of castings for bridges in India, Italy, and Spain, of fountains for the Calcutta Water Company, and of tubular telegraph posts for South America. Machine-made pipes were sent by Glasgow firms all over the world; the largest order in this line then known was one for 80,000 tons of pipes worth £1,000,000 for Rio de Janeiro.(139)

In the latter part of the century, "Clyde-built" vessels became the outward and visible sign of Scotland's new-found place in world economics. "The building of tea clippers on the Clyde laid the foundations of that river's supremacy in ship construction." (140) Within ten years the North German Lloyd Company of Bremen had twenty-six vessels built at Greenock, and within twenty years the Hamburg-America Steam Navigation Company had twenty-one. For the Austrian Lloyd's Steam Navigation Company of Trieste fifty-seven vessels were built up to 1876.(141) About 1890, approximately one-fourth of the tonnage launched on the Clyde was designed for foreign owners.(142)

Regarding other trades, it may be noted that about three million fire-bricks were sent abroad per annum, two-thirds going to the Continent;(143) and that Ushers' whiskeys, to which Edinburgh owes its greatest public hall, became popular in Japan.(144)

CHAPTER V

COMBINATIONS OF CAPITAL

WE have already reviewed aspects of the process by which independent units of business were brought under a common control. We can now ask how far the traditional competitiveness was modified by joint action among concerns which maintained a separate existence. Various instances of temporary combinations of the cartel type in the early industrial age are familiar, such as those in the coal trade (1790, 1813-17) and in the iron trade in the first quarter of the century, of which Dr. Hamilton has given detailed accounts.(1) Some later cases may be cited; they range, without any clear dividing line, from highly organized cartels to loose informal associations of a mainly consultative character.

The coalowners of the Lothians frequently combined (e.g. 1837, 1874), though in ephemeral organizations. A Mid and East Lothian Coalmasters' Association existed in 1890, but the existing body was not definitely established till 1907.(2) A scarcity of fuel in Edinburgh (1836) was attributed to a combination of coalmasters, and led to the formation of a local association which by working seams reduced prices.(3) It was denied that owners acted in concert to reduce wages; some were reported to the Royal Commission on Employment of Children (1842) as favourable to legal regulation of hours and working conditions.(4)

Coalowners' Associations were in active operation in Fife and Lanarkshire. The former originated in 1868, and set a precedent by meeting representatives of miners in conference.(5) Nearly all the local owners were members; the Fife Coal Company, with about half the total output, became the predominant partner in this and in a "Price Association" (c. 1894) which fixed "not the actual prices . . . but the standard differences between them."(6) The Lanarkshire body included only one-fourth of the local industry, and similarly decided, not on the actual rate of wages, but on a general advance or reduction.(7)

An Association of Mine Owners of Scotland gave evidence (1866) on the Master and Servant Act through its Secretary and law agent, William Burns, Solicitor, Glasgow. Burns, well-known as a champion of Scottish nationalism, was also on the Executive of the "Mining Association of Great Britain."(8) The "Scottish Mine Owners' Defence and Mutual Insurance Association" sent a return to the Commission on Mining Royalties in 1890.(9)

The shale oil producers of the Lothians, though at first intensely competitive, formed a Mineral Oil Association, to discuss trade questions (1871). Under the menace of the great and growing output from Pennsylvania, regulation of production and prices was accepted in May 1887, and common action towards labour undertaken. In May 1888, an agreement with American producers was negotiated, and lasted till 1892; (10) its lapse left the Association only nominal.

The "iron interest" is said to have been strong in Parliament, and to have forced concessions from the Clyde Trustees on a Navigation Bill, obtaining reductions in the rates for iron and corn. This was a burning issue in Glasgow in the General Election of 1847, when William Dixon of Govanhill was an unsuccessful candidate.(11)

A temporary price-fixing arrangement among Scottish iron-masters was brought to an end in September 1882, by the withdrawal of Messrs. Baird, who produced about one-fourth of the output.(12) An Iron Manufacturers' Association in Lanarkshire had a sliding scale wage agreement with employees (c. 1892).(13)

A Scottish Steelmakers' Association was intermittently active in the 'eighties in an attempt to control the local market; it comprised the four leading firms.(14)

The Clyde Shipbuilders and Engineers' Association was formed by employers in 1886 as a "defensive" association; it submitted its rules to the Royal Commission on Trade Unionism (1868).(15) It was apparently this body which after the Employers' Liability Act of 1881 formed an Employers' Liability Expenses Fund.(16) A Clyde District Employers' Association, presumably a reincarnation, was formally constituted in 1888, and formed the nucleus of the national Engineering Employers' Federation.(17) The shipowners in Leith and in Glasgow had their local organizations affiliated with a national Shipping Federation founded in September 1890.(18)

The Glasgow Cotton Spinning Employers formed a "protective combination" about 1830 to withstand the pressure of the operatives. This Association has what Bremner terms "a somewhat mysterious character," it dispensed with rules and subscriptions, and met only at need, but maintained a Secretary by a levy on members proportionate to the number of their spindles.(19) Charles R. Baird, who made the Sanitary Report for Glasgow in 1839, was "legal adviser" to employers' associations (1833-35), apparently in the textile trades.(20) The Association in 1837 established a new price list, withdrawing an advance of 16 per cent granted the previous year; this precipitated the strike which was rendered notorious by the trial of its leaders. (21) The Glasgow cotton-mill owners took joint action with regard to the administration of the Factory Acts, sending a deputation to the Government in March 1854.(22)

A Board of Arbitration was formed for the Hawick hosiery trade in 1867.(23)

Collective action was also characteristic of the building trades. In Glasgow, Master Brickbuilders' and Masons' Associations were formed in 1860 and 1861 respectively; the former laid down rules as to wages, and inflicted a fine for their infraction. (24) An Edinburgh Builders' Association was involved in the famous Nine Hours' Strike of 1861.(25) During this year the possibility of a national organization was canvassed, and in 1867 there was stated to be such a body, whose three or four Scottish branches enjoyed local autonomy.(26)

Of a more general and semi-political character were the Scottish Trade Protection Society, formed in 1852 with Charles Cowan, M.P., the paper manufacturer, as Chairman,(27) and the Traders' Defence Association of Scotland, formed about 1887. The former appears to have originated in an agitation against the Excise Laws, shared in by licensed victuallers as well as paper manufacturers, which contributed to the defeat of Macaulay by Cowan in the election of 1847; in its first year it obtained 300 members.(28) The latter comprised wholesalers, retailers and manufacturers, and professed to "inform" the public against co-operative and civil service stores, and to oppose "the credit system, unjust taxation," etc.; it appealed specially to commercial travellers.(29)

Here may be noted also two abortive movements aiming at trade regulation, of interest as indicating some persisting tility to *laissez-faire*. An early scheme of "Empire Trade" was fostered by George Troup, an erratic journalist then editing the *Glasgow Daily Mail*, who formed in 1849 the "West of Scotland Reciprocity and Native Industry Association," of which his paper became the short-lived organ. Sir John Maxwell of Pollock, the veteran "hand-loom weavers' champion" who throughout his life naïvely let himself be identified with a curious variety of enterprises, was secured as figure-head; Hugh Tennent of Wellpark, head of the well-known brewery, and other Glasgow business-men were among its chief promoters. The platform comprised a form of colonial preference and trading agreements with foreign countries. The Association seems not to have survived Troup's departure from Glasgow on the failure of the first Glasgow daily.(30)

An outcome of the Protectionist revival encouraged by the Great Depression was the Glasgow Committee for the Preservation of British and Irish trade (1888), headed by two leading ironmasters, John Cuninghame of Craigends and James Neilson of Mossend.(31)

Permanent local organizations to further general business interests were constituted by the Chambers of Commerce. The Glasgow Chamber dated back to 1783, and was one of the numerous achievements of Patrick Colquhoun, merchant and statistician.(32) That in Edinburgh followed two years later, and at first consisted largely of bankers.(33) Of later origin were the Dundee (1835) and South of Scotland (1860) Chambers; the latter comprised chiefly the woollen manufacturers of the Borders, and partially superseded a Galashiels "Manufacturers' Corporation" existing since 1777 among master weavers.(34) The Chambers expressed their views on legislative and other proposals relating to industry, and furthered such objects as technical education; all were strongly represented at a conference on the subject in Edinburgh in 1868 and on the Committee set up to prosecute its decisions.(35)

The Glasgow Chamber criticized the Bankruptcy and Limited Liability Acts (Jan. 1854),(36) and in 1862 sought an investigation of the currency and banking laws.(37) Led by men like Adam Black, Duncan McLaren, and Charles Cowan, the Edinburgh Chamber was a protagonist of Free Trade, and claimed to have inspired improvements in commercial law and in postal and harbour facilities; it opposed in 1859 a proposed railway combine. About 1860 it promoted evening meetings for social and educational purposes, having e.g. lectures on "Judicial Remedies" by Sheriff Substitute Frederick Hallam and on "Naval Longitude" by Professor Piazzi Smith. The Chamber had then between 300 and 400 members and was open to any "merchant, manufacturer or trader."(38)

CHAPTER VI

SURVEY OF DEVELOPMENT: FLUCTUATIONS OF TRADE

THE development of Scottish industrial organization in the nineteenth century does not lend itself to facile generalizations. Some points, however, seem to emerge from the foregoing narrative.

In the first place, Scotland becomes more interdependent, as regards trade and finance, with England and also with the world at large. Effort is more and more concentrated on those constructional or instrumental heavy industries—steel manufacture, engineering, shipbuilding—together with the older textiles, which cater largely for foreign markets, and draw much of their supplies from overseas.(1) Hence Scottish conditions are increasingly affected by the environment of world economy, notably by the recurrence of the trade cycle, and Scottish industrial prosperity comes to depend essentially on the retention of Victorian principles of economic internationalism.(2)

Other aspects emphasized by recent economic study perhaps find particular exemplification in Scotland. In the staple industries at any rate, a regime of pure individual enterprise and unrestricted competition was rather an economic ideal than a description of current practice at any time. The tendency to combine, as indeed was indicated by Adam Smith himself,(3) is now recognized as a recurring phenomenon in economic development;(4) there was indeed a sharp reaction against the arbitrary, inefficient, and even corrupt control associated with the agencies of government; the freedom sought was freedom from state intervention; *laissez-faire* implied "liberty to act" by way of combination as well as of competition.(5)

Further, the growth of the joint-stock system may be interpreted partly in terms of technical change in certain industries. The increase of fixed capital was hardly compatible with such frequent withdrawals as were common on the expiry of the normal short-term co-partnery. The transferability of shares was thus of growing utility, and the limitation of liability enormously increased the range of investment.(6)

Finally, the long-drawn-out character of the "Industrial Revolution" is now generally accepted. It is possible to argue that because of its previous economic backwardness, the initial stages were more catastrophic in Scotland than south of the Border, but its subsequent course was evolutionary. The survivals of an earlier stage, in the technique of handicraft production, in the paternalist methods of factory control, in the extension of the practice of a landed estate to extractive industry, make it impossible to fix a termination of the movement before the later decades of the century. Perhaps we may regard the "Great Depression" as in part the process of final adaptation to the new order.(7)

The main fluctuations of Scottish trade during our period may now be briefly outlined.

In the early 'thirties, the political crisis centring round the Reform Bill combined with a visitation of cholera to depress trade.(8) A premature boom in company promotion had arisen in Edinburgh in 1824, with a consequent and more lasting slump from 1826 onwards.(9) Argument regarding the "Hungry 'Forties" tended to revolve round the Free Trade issue, but, then as now, there were writers who essayed a financial diagnosis. Peel's Bank Acts of 1844–45 came in for much Scottish criticism, on the ground that they hampered the native banking system. Sheriff Alison, from the High Tory point of view, condemned Peel and all his works, regarding Free Trade and restricted currency as twin evils of liberal industrialism.(10) From another angle, the Act was assailed, on the strength of his experience of country banking as an accountant in Cromarty, by Hugh Miller the geologist.(11) "Currency cranks" like John Crawford of Paisley (1802–74), a disciple of Attwood, and William Cross of Aberdeen advocated inflation by the issue of paper.(12)

Financial factors of a somewhat different type had undoubtedly much to do with two later crises which fell with special severity on Scottish industry. The failure of the Western Bank

(1857) was precipitated by dislocation in America and by the bankruptcy of D. & J. Macdonald & Co., muslin producers, and of two similar firms which had expanded excessively on very small capital; their debts to the bank totalled two millions.(13) An older and more reputable firm, J. & A. Dennistoun & Co., with affiliations in England and U.S.A., suspended payment for a year, while 41 furnaces went out of blast.(14)

The downfall of the City of Glasgow Bank (1878) was the inevitable result of fraud, quite irrespective of the commercial situation, but it much intensified the prevailing depression by the losses inflicted on shareholders and depositors.(15) In the early 'seventies, economic expansion had been temporarily excited by the recovery of the U.S.A. from the Civil War, and consequent railway construction there, while the war between France and Germany for the moment eliminated their competition; shipbuilding was stimulated by an advance in freights. The joint-stock company with limited liability had now established itself in the confidence of investors, and there was considerable flotation, some of a highly speculative nature. Capital was thus largely attracted to the mineral oil industry and to urban real property, in both of which rather indiscriminate expansion took place. In this period also, as improved transport opened up the food-producing resources of Australasia and West America, investment in ranches and railways, estate and mortgage companies overseas, sometimes of a precarious nature, became a favourite outlet for Scottish financial enterprise. The attention given by the Press of c. 1878–87 to such developments indicates the importance and novelty of the phenomena.(16)

Under conditions of such instability, a reaction soon set in, contributed to by a railway crisis in U.S.A., disastrous speculation in Australia, and the effects of the French indemnity.(17) Thus came the Great Depression; among causes alleged were also Continental and American tariffs and bounties, the competition of Indian textile mills, the decline of agricultural purchasing power, and a general excess production. One outcome was a general reduction of wages, which again occasioned a number of unsuccessful defensive strikes.(18)

By the last decade of the century, equilibrium had been

meantime restored, and the close of our period leaves Scotland in a relatively stable and undisturbed economic position.

The growth or decay of some notable branches of enterprise may finally be considered.

The manufacture of cotton was in 1838 still reckoned "by far our most important branch of trade";(19) a few years earlier, Glasgow cotton operatives were estimated to constitute one-seventh of those in the United Kingdom.(20) The special restrictions imposed upon it by Factory Legislation were complained of, as by Kirkman Finlay in his "Letter to Ashley" (1833).(21) Its decline, however, as already indicated, seems attributable mainly to the competition of Lancashire, and was accelerated by the difficulties of supply occasioned by the American Civil War.(22) Cotton weaving held its ground better than spinning, and became "more and more exclusively a women's industry"; the number of men employed was halved between 1871 and 1881.(23)

While printing and dyeing of fabrics prospered meantime, another subsidiary, that of tambouring, fell on evil days. There were few industries "into which individual labour enters more deeply," hence it was a stand-by of many a female home-worker. Its gross value amounted to about a million pounds in 1856, and it was marketed equally at home and abroad. This was its apex; by 1861 it had fallen to one-third by reason of the glut of 1856–59, the American War, and the "capricious fickleness of feminine fashion," especially as the glut had "vulgarized the manufacture and tended to render it unfashionable among the better and wealthier classes."(24)

The dramatic and decisive reversal of fortune of the hand-loom weavers has made their fate almost proverbial. Once the aristocrats of labour, they were doomed by machine competition, most rapidly and completely in the case of cotton, at first far-flung throughout Lowland villages; perhaps with less suffering in the older and more localized woollen and linen manufactures, where factory production of a stabler type was more gradually substituted. The cause of the hand-loom weavers received publicity from the efforts of such sympathizers as the

Maxwells of Pollok, father and son, who obtained the appointment of successive Committees of Inquiry (1831-41) and advocated Wages Boards, alike without avail.(25)

One specialized branch, the Paisley shawl industry, enjoyed a brief prosperity. Introduced early in the century, it was declining after a generation of success, apparently in the main through a change of fashion. Its decay contributed to make Paisley the most chronically depressed of Lowland industrial centres. Between 1841 and 1843, 67 out of 112 manufacturing firms in the locality failed,with losses totallingthree-quarters of a million. Parochial relief to the unemployed had to be permitted, in violation of the law, and employment was afforded by the provision of looms and of allotments, while some £50,000 was subscribed in charity.(26) Small wonder that Paisley was a stronghold of Chartism, and even a parish minister (Patrick Brewster, of the Abbey "second charge") found among its leaders.(27) The weavers have their memorial in the writings of David Gilmour, Matthew Blair, Provost Brown of Underwood, and Rev. Dr. Metcalfe; the *Edifying Information Concerning the Working Class* of the blind evangelist Daniel McCallum contains some reminiscences of the last stages of decay in Glasgow.(28)

The Fife linen industry, after twenty years of great progress, stagnated in the 'forties, and took some twenty years to revive.(29) Later, the flax trade, after the artificial stimulation due to the American War, was said to be hit harder than other textiles by foreign competition (1883).(30) The manufacture of canvas,e.g. at Arbroath, wasinjuredbythe growthof steam navigation.(31) The fine linens of Dunfermline, however, withstood better than most trades the hard times of the 'eighties,(32) and the progress of the Border Wool manufacture was steady.(33) Dundee jute firms were already beginning to feel the effects of subsidizing Indian mill production.(34)

The rise of shipbuilding and engineering, contemporary with the decline of domestic textiles, provided alternative employment for labour and capital, especially in the Clyde area, and was chiefly responsible for the general prosperity and rising standards of the middle decades (*c.* 1850-75). "The periodic fluctuations in the shipbuilding industry. . . . correspond closely to the general trade cycle. . . . It was invariably in the years of depression between 1865 and 1905 that a revival of sail took place. In times of bad trade, merchants having cargoes to ship were looking for the cheapest rather than the speediest mode of transport; whereas during a boom in trade time became an important factor."(35) The successive inventions of the Bessemer (1856), Siemens (1861), and Gilchrist (1878) processes "were events of first-class importance to the Clyde area, and made possible the rise of the steel shipbuilding industry on the river."(36) The prosperity of 1880 was said to have attracted too much capital to shipping.(37)

The coal trade was faced in the 'thirties by a temporary excess of demand owing to its increased use in blast furnaces and for gas manufacture and steamships; there was also a shortage of labour due to a drift to the iron mines; hence an increase of prices, relieved by the opening of new pits.(38) The course of the industry was marked by considerable irregularity throughout the century. The centuries-old mines of the Lothians and Forth valley were considerably supplemented; from the 'fifties, there was considerable expansion in Fife, especially after the formation of the powerful Fife Coal Company, in 1872.(39) In Lower Lanarkshire there was rapid development in the later decades; e.g. in 1888 it is observed that while "in 1870 Blantyre was a country parish prettily and quietly rural, it is now a district of pits, engine houses, chimneys, railways, crowded groups of miners' houses, smoke, and grime."(40) A similar transformation befell the neighbouring parish of Bothwell. Limited public companies such as the Omoa and Cleland (1872) and the Clyde (1876) superseded in this area small-scale working of single pits.(41)

The most spectacular rise was that of the iron industry, following upon the general adoption of the hot-blast process. The annual output of iron in the West increased from 40,000 to three-quarters of a million tons between 1830 and 1854; that of malleable iron, commencing about 1839, had by 1858 reached an annual value of well over one million pounds.(42) In 1861 it was surmised that the "enormous profits of cotton speculation" would be turned to iron as "the most attractive and likely investment."(43)

The railway boom brought with it a variety of demands; e.g. it is credited with having saved the Glasgow brick industry by its requirements for arches and tunnels.(44) The Glasgow & Ayr Railway Company during the construction of its lines crowded lodging-houses with labourers, "whose expenditure must be felt in a considerable degree"(45) (a rare recognition of "working-class purchasing power").

The establishment of the shale oil industry in West Lothian provided a livelihood for the survivors of hand-loom weaving in Bathgate and neighbourhood.(46) The lapse of James Young's patent (1864) was followed by the "Scottish Oil Fever." The original "torbanite" was exhausted by 1873; kindred coal substances were utilized also in Fife and the West.(47) Many small crude-oil works succumbed to the competition of American petroleum, and the Protectionist revival found in their fate a favourite illustration. The extraction of sulphate of ammonia and improvements of technique restored profitableness, and a new group of companies was organized in the 'eighties, of which the Pumpherston, formed in 1883 by William Fraser, had most enduring success and was the nucleus of the existing combine.(48) The companies in operation were reduced to seven by the end of the century, and were mainly self-contained, comprising shale mining, refining, and manufacture of finished products.(49)

Sugar refining, the staple of Greenock, based originally on West Indian slave-produced cane, suffered towards the end of the century from the competition of subsidized Continental beet.(50)

Improving standards of life stimulated the growth of industries catering for domestic consumption. Among these may be noted those providing for sanitation, such as the Tubal Works, Barrhead, which took the lead owing to the inventions and patents of its co-founder John Shanks.(51) The factory production of such commodities as soap, shoes, underwear, furniture, bread, and biscuits is also noticeable in the later years of the century.(52) The contemporary expansion of retail trading and in particular of the consumers' co-operative movement should be borne in mind in this connection. "Bargain sales" on the part of, e.g., such prominent Edinburgh stores as McLaren, Oliver & Co. and Kennington & Jenner become a feature of Press advertising. In general the democratization of purchasing power is a factor of growing importance to the state of trade.

PART III

LIFE AND LABOUR

CHAPTER I

LABOUR SUPPLY AND MIGRATION

It has become the established practice to treat of "consumptive" activities and conditions under some such title as "Life and Labour." The economic aspects are hard to demarcate; they shade off into the rather vague phenomena of "social history," as delineated for this period by Professor James Mackinnon and Miss E. S. Haldane.

By way of introduction, a few words may be said as to the distribution of population. As already indicated, the Forth and Clyde valleys continued to be the most densely peopled, but in both, and especially the latter, numbers grew phenomenally. The factors affecting the growth of population in Great Britain during the Industrial Revolution have been intensively studied by Dr. Mabel Buer and Mr. G. T. Griffith; and Dr. Arthur Redford has demonstrated that migration from rural areas to urban centres was mainly of a short distance character. Similar studies for Scotland are not yet available; it is, however, possible to show that a large immigration into the industrial districts was derived from two main sources.

The depopulation of the Highlands from the late eighteenth century, intensified if not occasioned by the clearance policy of the new type of landlord, contributed to Lowland industrial development as well as to overseas expansion. Dale's mills at New Lanark provide a well-known early example;(1) David Livingstone's forebears at the Blantyre cotton mills were of similar stock,(2) as were the inhabitants of Deanston model village (3)—which of course was virtually on the Highland border. Workers in the early bleachfields almost always came from the Highlands,(3) as did original employees of Clark's thread works in Paisley.(4) Hence a considerable percentage of the urban population of the Clyde was of Highland ancestry, as is witnessed to-day by the survival of Gaelic churches and clan societies; Greenock is traditionally noted for its Celticism as for its rainfall. The passivity if not servility often noted in regard to the Clearances was perhaps also in evidence in industrial disputes; Dr. Norman Macleod's hero in *Mary of Unnimore*,(5) who professed religious scruples against striking, probably had models in real life.

Though retaining in some cases their language and religious outlook and customs, these settlers were in the main absorbed with comparative ease. A more difficult problem, still unsolved, arose with the immigration of Irish Catholic labourers. Here the trouble was partly "racial" and sectarian, but still more economic, in the sense that it frequently involved the most cut-throat form of competition, that between two standards of life.

The Irish, with worse conditions, were more contented, and were "the main cause of pulling the Scotch down after them."(6) The rivalry was at times embittered by the deliberate introduction of Irish as strike-breakers; e.g. in the 1837 coal strike in Lanarkshire, when "off-handed men, Irish labourers, etc., required to be protected night and day."(7) They were probably also more prolific than the native Scots, and did not lose their fertility under urban conditions. Hence even without a fresh invasion their percentage of the population tended to increase, and in the main they settled down to the lower-paid types of unskilled labour. The heavy industries "owed their rise in a great measure to the supply of cheap labour which was thrown upon the market as the result of the Irish famine in 1847";(8) between November 1847 and March 1848, 42,800 destitute Irish landed in Glasgow;(9) the "venality of the shipping companies" and the payment of passages by Irish Poor Law Guardians were held responsible. The incursion somewhat earlier must have been considerable; Professor R. Cowan, in 1840, estimated the Irish inhabitants of Glasgow as probably one in four, compared with one in ten in 1819 and one in five in 1831.(10) "By 1856, however, the flow of Irish immigration to Glasgow (had) greatly diminished,"(11) and in 1861 about 16 per cent were of Irish birth, though considerably more of Irish parentage; and the migrants or their offspring were becoming distributed throughout the Lowlands, e.g. Dundee.(11)

Irish female labour was used on the "domestic" system by West of Scotland cotton manufacturers, on both sides of the

Channel; e.g. Robert Sinclair & Co., shirt-makers, employed Derry women (*c.* 1844–55).(12) Messrs. D. & J. McDonald of Glasgow, who did a huge trade in sewed muslin till their bankruptcy in autumn 1857, at one time used the services of over 20,000 needle-women in the West of Scotland and North of Ireland, paying sometimes £15,000 a month to their Irish employees. From about 1830 Irish work competed successfully with that of Scotland; a leading Ulster firm then transferred their headquarters to Glasgow. The trade declined considerably after the crisis of 1857–58.(13) Kilmarnock bonnet-making, until the introduction of knitting machines about 1870, also employed through agents much female labour in the North of Scotland and even the North of Ireland.(14)

The ironworkers of the original stock were once in semi-hereditary grades; many emigrated or took to other occupations; skilled labour for malleable works was introduced from the English Midlands, and the unskilled were substituted by Irish.(15) Some of the novels of "George Woden" cast sidelights on the development of this industry.(16)

The social habits of the Irish are frequently censured, despite the utility of their labours. Bremner attributed the greater prevalence of industrial conflict in the West to the great influx of the Irish element (*c.* 1830–50)— "a very rough type" as compared with the native Scots of the Lothians.(17) "Irish riots" are reported, e.g. among "navies" (*sic*) on the Caledonian Railway at West Calder,(18) and in the Cowgate of Edinburgh,(19) which became one of their haunts. Dr. George Bell, describing Edinburgh slum conditions about 1850, calls the Irish "a pestilence as well as a pest; this country both desires and deserves to be protected from them."(20) "Two-thirds of the tramps are Irish—a most dissolute class," says the Hand-loom Weavers' Report;(21) while an Ayrshire contributor to the New Statistical Account opines that their improvidence was a factor in perpetuating truck.(22) "A great number come (to Greenock) from Ireland and the Highlands with the express purpose of making a settlement,"(23) i.e. qualifying for poor relief.

A few voices are, however, raised in their favour. Mr. C. R.

Baird, in a Sanitary Report for 1839, says that "Glasgow reaped immense advantage from the exercise of their lusty thews and sinews";(24) while Professor R. Cowan, M.D., in his *Vital Statistics of Glasgow* affirms that the Irish "appear to exhibit less of squalid misery and habitual addiction to the use of ardent spirits than the Scotch of the same grade."(25) Later, the journalist Robert Gillespie, in his *History of Glasgow*, deems them "remarkable chiefly for steady industry . . . and just as peaceful as the Scots"; many had established themselves as small dealers.(26)

Towards the end of the century, Poles and Lithuanians appeared, especially in the coal mines and ironworks of Lanarkshire. Glasgow and Edinburgh Trades Councils in 1887 raised objections to their importation by Messrs. Merry & Cuninghame.(27) Less than 500 were however recorded in the census of 1891.(28)

Apart from the two main streams, there was a regular trickle of labour to the rising heavy industries from the agricultural and domestic workers. It is noted at Cumbernauld that the fluctuating nature and small remuneration of domestic textile work "induced many weavers to relinquish the loom and have recourse for employment to the coal and iron-stone mines,"(29) and this was paralleled elsewhere, e.g. at the commencement of the oil industry in the Lothians, and in such one-time textile centres as Hamilton, Blantyre, and other Lanarkshire villages.(30) The careers of John Hodge and Keir Hardie afford examples at a later date of a similar preference for the steelworks and coalpits; Hodge went to the former from a petty clerkship,(31) and Hardie, the son of a ship's carpenter, was a baker's errand boy before descending a pit.(32)

There were various local and temporary cross-currents. A curious example of a seasonal occupation arose in the Stirlingshire weaving trade. Since the decline in the demand for shawls and tartans, and exclusion by tariffs from American markets, activity was limited to a few months per annum, and weavers generally sought work for the winter in the Borders.(33)

During the depression of hand-loom weaving, employment in the Howe of Fife was temporarily found in harvesting (1861).

(34) Weavers at Carstairs (c. 1840) on "customary work" for Glasgow firms were "as often found handling implements of manual labour in the field as on the loom-board, the former employment being found more pleasant and more profitable."(35)

Criticisms were made that the establishment of factories in rural areas might not only occasion loss to the promoters, but introduce many paupers into the parish. "Such factories can only exist advantageously where numbers of persons in manufacturing employments are congregated together; such a population and that of a rich agricultural district have never been found to harmonize."(36) The labour "turnover" in the Lothians collieries was abnormally high, owing to migratory habits.(37)

The outward flow by emigration abroad must also be noted. The earlier and largely enforced displacement and colonization effected as part of the Clearance policy have been described from different angles by propagandists like Donald Macleod and Alexander Mackenzie and by scholars like Miss M. I. Adam and Miss M. M. Leigh. Lord Selkirk's Red River Colony is a familiar example of organized transportation. During the nineteenth century there were similar expedients.

After the potato famine (1846) a Highland Emigration Fund was established to finance the transplanting of the surplus population; it co-operated with the Colonial Land and Emigration Commissioners (appointed 1840) in providing a free passage to Australia and outfit for settlement there.(38) The Scottish Patriotic Society (1846), whose patrons included Professors Alison and Gregory and Dr. Robert Lee, sought to improve crofting conditions, stimulate fisheries, and assist emigration.(39) Sir Michael Connal and Sir James King, Glasgow commercial magnates, were among the promoters at a later date of State-aided emigration from the Highlands, when its economic difficulties again secured public attention(40) The Crofters Commission (1883) strongly recommended this policy. In 1888, the Government promoted a small scheme for settlement from the Western Highlands in Manitoba, and handed over control to an *ad hoc* body, the Crofters Colonization

Commissioners, which existed till 1904 without much result; powers granted to County Councils on their creation in 1889 also remained unused.(41)

With the evolution of the trade cycle, emigration also came into vogue as a means of disposing of surplus industrial labour. About a hundred emigrants from the Clyde participated in an organized settlement in New Zealand (Oct. 1839), and were speeded on their way by a public dinner in Glasgow and a discourse from the loquacious Sheriff Alison.(42) Paisley, the most chronically distressed of Lowland industrial towns, besides raising charitable funds and organizing relief work, collaborated in assisted emigration schemes to Australia and Canada (e.g. 1840–41, 1862–64).(43) Repeated but ineffective appeals were made to Edinburgh City Council for assistance in financing such ventures.(44)

The settlements at Otago (New Zealand) from 1847 onwards were made under the auspices of the Free Church.(45) The close of the Civil War was followed by a large efflux to the United States, whose industrial progress is said to have owed much to the technical skill and business ability of Scottish immigrants, from Andrew Carnegie downwards. Emigration from Glasgow in 1865 showed a 100 per cent increase over two years earlier.(46) Between 1875 and 1884, over 260,000 left from Clyde ports, of whom three-fourths were bound for the United States.(47)

Patrick Edward Dove, the advocate of Scottish nationalism, was bred to farming with a veiw to settlement in Australia, and in later life made a disastrous attempt to recover health and fortune by emigrating to Natal.(48) George Troup, his fellow in journalism and in misfortune, took part in founding a colony in New Brunswick in the 'seventies.(49)

Emigration was recurrently favoured, and sometimes organized, by Trade Unions, as a means of relieving the labour market. The ambiguous phrasing of rules on the subject by the Cotton Spinners was one cause of suspicion as to their ulterior motives and aims (1837).(50) It was not a popular expedient with the hand-loom weavers, though some emigration societies were formed among them.(51) The "financial schemer," John

Crawford, with some Trade Union endorsement, recommended large-scale loans for colonial settlement as a productive national investment.(52) Alexander Macdonald fostered the policy among the miners, and visited the U.S.A. to see the results.(53) So late as 1886, Aberdeen Trades Council petitioned Parliament in favour of "voluntary state-aided emigration."(54)

CHAPTER II

THE EMPLOYMENT OF CHILDREN

THE labour market was also swollen by the entrance of large numbers of children, probably increasing annually for some time with the rise in the effective birth-rate. It is hardly practicable to determine how far the proportionate contribution of minors to productive capacity was affected by their transference from the home to the factory; considered in relation to standards of life and indeed to long-run productivity, their employment has latterly been condemned, on economic as well as on humanitarian grounds. It was, however, either taken for granted or expressly approved by current sentiment, with significant exceptions. It may be borne in mind that the treatment of children of all classes at this period would be adjudged by modern standards as frequently brutal; Miss Haldane quotes instances of the ultra-Spartan upbringing of aristocratic progeny. (1) Sir David Barry, in his Medical Report to the Factory Commission (1833), while advocating reduced hours and a minimum age limit, is impressed by the general humanity of employers.(2) Dr. Andrew Ure, the indefatigable champion of the new industrialism, found child labour one of its assets and glories,(3) and he finds echoes in the New Statistical Account.

In the latter are, however, to be found protests such as that of the minister of Neilston (Renfrewshire), who voices a criticism of factory life, clerical rather than humanitarian in tone. He demands "a radical change of system throughout all branches of the cotton trade." This resolves itself into the requirement that "children must be taught, and none permitted to enter into any of these works below the age of 12 or 14 years, and until they have learned to read their Bible and say their Catechism."(4) Half a century earlier the minister of Avendale (Strathaven, Lanarkshire) had deplored the domestic employment of boys in weaving and of girls in tambouring, on grounds of injury both to health and to morals "by rendering them too soon independent of their parents."(5) A rare voice from the workshop (*crede experto*) is that of James Myles, whose *Dundee Factory Boy*(6) appears to be in part autobiographical. In the flax and jute mills conditions appear to have been particularly oppressive. Mr. Johnston gives corroborative evidence based on the Factories Bill Commission of 1832.(7) Kirkman Finlay had some warrant for his complaint that early legislative interference was concentrated on the cotton mills (1833).(8)

The coal mines are notorious for the repulsive conditions under which women and children were engaged, though here the worst features were condemned and avoided by enlightened employers and publicists like the Duke of Buccleugh and Robert Bald,(9) and largely eliminated by the Act of 1842.(10) There were cases in the East of children who commenced in the pits at five or six years of age; it was usual to begin at the age of seven or eight, though some employers excluded those under ten or twelve. A 14-hour day was common in the East, and was sometimes exceeded; in the West, eleven to thirteen was the maximum, but normally not more than nine days per fortnight were worked.(11)

The persistence of the "family group" as a productive unit was held to induce the early employment of children and their long hours;(12) the same objection as is still heard was made by parents to any interference with their children's capacity as wage-earners. The employment of children in Glasgow cotton mills, usually by the male operative spinner as "piecers," for hours and at wages in violation of the law, was described and condoned by witnesses at the Select Committee on Trade Unions (1838).(13)

The Ten Hours Act of 1847 brought relief to many factory workers, but exploitation continued in such industries as the printworks and bleachfields. In calico printing, children of from eight to nine years had a 58-hour week; 6 a.m. to 6 p.m. on weekdays, with two intervals for meals, 6 to 3 on Saturdays, while "over hours" were frequent. The "outby departments"—bleachers, packers, etc.—worked still longer; Glasgow calenders voluntarily restricted hours to twelve. Increasing competition gave a stimulus to lengthening of hours. Injury to the hands by machinery and to the lungs by the fetid atmosphere were additional evils.(14) Calender works were at last brought under the Factory Acts in 1863.(15)

In Glasgow, "child labour abounded wherever the Factory Act is not in operation." In the tobacco trade, over 500 boys worked an 11-hour day, at 1s. to 3s. a week. The half-time system was rare except in the cotton mills of Bridgeton.(16) George Anderson, a Radical M.P. and a flax spinner, who favoured national unsectarian education, considered the half-time system an educational failure.(17) It survived compulsory education in some localities, and was in vogue for "light" labour in the Angus linen and jute mills about 1890 for children of eleven and upwards.(18)

In ironworks, boys started at the age of seven or eight, working a 12-hour day for a wage which rose from 2s. 6d. to 12s. a week. They were usually short-lived, and "old at fifty."(19) Two well-known Edinburgh public men, Cowan the paper manufacturer and Chambers the publisher, employed child labour under what were then deemed humanitarian conditions, providing educational and other facilities at the end of a ten-hour day.(20) In the 'sixties, investigation showed that about one-fifth of the children of school age were receiving no formal education; consequently the Act of 1872 made attendance obligatory up to 13(21) and thus imposed the most effective check on the commercialization of childhood.

CHAPTER III

APPRENTICESHIP

APPRENTICESHIP was a cardinal feature of the older economy, and was preserved in form in the skilled trades, though sometimes deteriorating in substance. In some of the newer industries, it was never of great moment.

The hand-loom weavers sought to the last to maintain the system; about 1840 there were still over 700 apprentices in the Paisley trade.(1) Boys in the tobacco-spinning workshops were apprenticed at 14 or 15 after some years of casual labour.(2) In ironworks they were "bound" for 12 years at the age of 12 or 14 if they had given satisfactory service for five or six years previously.(3) In Glasgow potteries boys though not indentured were deemed apprentices, and received first half and then two-thirds of journeymen's wages (c. 1865).(4) In Anderston, the shipping quarter of Glasgow, the better educated boys "went mostly to offices instead of following their fathers' occupations, this being looked on as a rise in social position."(5)

Ironmoulders had a nominal seven years' apprenticeship, but were usually not "bound"; it was complained that while they formerly served their time in one shop, in the 'eighties they "get plain work to do . . . regardless of learning the trade."(6) At the same period, an apprenticeship of five years was usual among engineers, patternmakers and shipwrights; and one of three years among boilermakers, who prescribed a limit of one apprentice to five journeymen.(7) The Carpenters' Union deplored the prevalence of jerrybuilding; while a four years' apprenticeship was assumed, some adolescents were used as "improvers" at a low rate of pay; some years later, the Union professed to maintain a five years' "servitude."(8)

The Typographical Association, representing one of the most highly skilled and best organized crafts, insisted on a seven years' apprenticeship, and had chronic disputes over the introduction of machinery and of female labour. It maintained "houses of call" in the larger towns.(9)

The Edinburgh Trades Council reported (1884) that apprenticeship was lessening in that city,(10) and the miners, that the stipulation of the Mines Regulation Act for a two years' apprenticeship was ignored.(11)

CHAPTER IV

WAGES

ANY effective comparison of wages over differences in time and space is recognized as one of the most difficult problems of economics. As a guide to standards of life, monetary wages are vitiated by fluctuations in purchasing power, by varying composition of the standard, by the existence of "net advantages or disadvantages"; and by purely subjective variations of appreciation. The distinction between wage RATES and EARNINGS, and that between time and piece rates has also to be noted. Bearing these warnings in mind, we may examine some illustrative data for the period.

Consider first the textile industry. The hectic prosperity of cotton was already disappearing, and the hand-loom weavers bore the brunt of the depression. On this the Reports of the successive Committees and Commissioners are the best authority. The Commissioners reported in 1841 that the weekly earnings of weavers of pullicates (Lanarkshire) and of plain muslins (Glasgow) averaged 4s. 6d. to 7s. 6d.; of shawls (Renfrewshire) and of fancy muslins (Renfrewshire and Lanarkshire) 6s. to 10s. 6d. Where three of a family assisted the parents, the total income might reach 16s. or even a pound; the wife usually wound the "pirns."(1) Dr. Metcalfe gives a specimen of a typical fluctuation in the annual earnings of a Paisley weaver between 1810 and 1838: 1810, £70 8s. 0d.; 1826, £11 7s. 0d.; 1830, £40 7s. 0d.; 1836, £40 6s. 0d.; 1838, £32 5s. 0d.(2) "The bitterness of the contrast between past and present times"(3) intensified suffering. McCallum's reminiscences—those of a working-man—speak of an average for Glasgow hand-loom weavers of 11s. about 1840.(4) Those working in rural areas presumably had more chance of supplementary income from agricultural labour; the pay of hand-loom weavers is stated to have been in 1834 9s. a week at Earlston, 6s. in Coldingham, villages in Berwickshire—in both cases employed by Glasgow merchants.(5)

Fictitious but realistic descriptions of the hand-loom weavers' life and labour are to be found in the contemporary didactic story by Rev. Dr. Henry Duncan of Ruthwell, *The Young South Country Weaver* (1821), a polemic against Jacobinism and infidelity, and in the later melodrama of the Glasgow journalist William Freeland, *Love and Treason* (1872), where they furnish a background to reforming politics and sensational romance.

The Maxwells of Pollok have received some credit from recent historians as the "hand-loom weavers' champions," but their activities have not been clearly distinguished or specifically outlined.(6) Sir John, seventh baronet (1768–1844), an old Whig aristocrat of the school of Fox, and his only son John (1791–1865), who had already given active support to Owen's employment schemes, were both elected to the first Reformed Parliament (1832) for Paisley and Lanarkshire respectively. Both took part in public demonstrations in favour of Wages Boards to fix minimum rates. With the resignation of Sir John in March 1834, Parliamentary championship was left to his son. A minimum wage bill which he introduced in 1835 was opposed by the Whig Government and defeated by 129 against 41. He however twice secured the appointment of Select Committees of Inquiry (1834, 1835) and acted as Chairman. He gave evidence before the Commission of 1838–41, to which he recommended the establishment of Boards on the model of the Spitalfields silk manufacture. The Reports were, however, inconclusive, and no official action was taken. Maxwell abandoned his political career in 1837, and the weavers declined to gradual extinction.(7)

Turning to the cotton factories, we find that in those in the West of Scotland operatives earned "nearly double" what the domestic workers had at the same period, but that more than half of them wrought on the lower-paid fabrics.(8) Baird's figures for 1836-40 are: spinners, 25s.; weavers, 6s. to 11s.; tenters, 22s to 25s.(9) Ure in his *Cotton Manufacture* gives rates applicable to different ages: under 11, 2s.; 11–16, males 4s. 7d., females 3s. 9d.; 16–21, males 9s. 7d., females 6s. 2s.; over 21, males 16s. to 21s., females 6s. to 7s.(10) At a cotton-spinning mill in Kilbirnie, men earned 10s to 25s., women 5s. to 8s., children 2s. 6d. to 5s. (c. 1840).(11) Glasgow cotton spinners had in 1837 an average of 23s. to 24s., when a reduction of 3s. was demanded; strike pay began at three shillings a week, and was reduced to one and sixpence and then to ninepence; work had finally to be resumed with cuts of 30 to 40 per cent.(12)

Wages subsequently rose somewhat. Between 1841 and 1856, power-loom weavers improved from 7s. to 8s. 3d., cotton spinners from 21s to 28s., but in the depression of 1857 there was an average fall of 20 per cent.(13) The Report of the Factory Inspectors for 1883 shows that in the surviving Glasgow factories the average wage of female operatives had risen to 7s. for spinners and 9s. 6d. for weavers, as compared with 3s. 7d. and 6s. 9d. in 1856; the latter had touched a high-water mark of 10s. 3d. in 1870. (14)

The linen manufacture of the East coast, elaborately described by the Dundee mill owner, Alexander J. Warden, was also originally a "domestic" industry, and as such was investigated for the Hand-loom Weavers' Commission by Dr. J. D. Harding. His rather cursory account implies less severe dislocation than in the case of cotton.(15) The woes of William Thom of Inverurie, author of the *Rhymes of a Hand-loom Weaver*, may be partially attributed rather to his poetical temperament than to the conditions of his trade.(16)

As linen became a factory industry, it depended largely on female labour, and thus maintained low rates of wages. Jute on its introduction followed the same course, hence Dundee notoriously became a centre of women's work and of probably the only Scottish Trade Union where women predominated.

According to Myles, Dundee spinners (1832) were paid 6s. or 6s. 6d. per week; children rose from 1s. 6d. to 3s. or 4s.(17) Arbroath weavers fell 20 per cent between 1836 and 1841; in 1843 they ranged from 4s 6d. to 9s. In the same industry fully thirty years later, flax dressers had 20s., women spinners 10s., women weavers 13s., men weavers 17s. or 18s., mechanics 24s. to 26s., foremen 28s to 32s.(18)

It was noted that the introduction of machinery virtually

K

compelled general advances in wages, as compared with the individual variations of handwork.(19) The average wages of adult mill workers when Warden wrote (1866) were: Linen: women spinners 8s. 6d. to 14s. 6d., men hecklers 21s., women weavers 8s. to 15s., men warpers 20s. to 25s.; Jute: women spinners 10s., weavers 13s.(20) In the latter case a contemporary Report of the British Association credits skilled men with rising to 35s., while children got 4s. to 7s.(21) Hutchins and Harrison, comparing the position in 1860 and in 1892, show a rise of women's wages from a range of 6s. 9d. to 8s. 6d. in the former to 10s. 2d. to 16s. 4d. in the latter.(22) Average figures given to the Royal Commission on Labour in 1892 were: women 10s., men 15s. to 31s.; different factories had a variety of rates.(23) In the 'nineties, jute spinning was paid chiefly by the piece.(24)

In the woollen industries of the 'forties, the Borders provided a wage of 11s. to 16s. 6d., though for "Thibets and tartans" only 5s. 6d. to 7s. could be secured. Kilmarnock carpets rose as high as 18s.; "course heavy woollen fabrics" earned higher rates than linen; wages were higher "where strength is required."(25) The local historian reckons the average wage of Galashiels weavers at this period as 14s. 3d.(26) A generation later, Bremner was impressed by the variability of the rates of wool workers, and by the liberality of their remuneration, especially in that woman's wage almost equalled the man's.(27) Towards the end of the century, men and women were paid the same rates on piece work, and were obliged to earn a minimum wage on pain of dismissal.(28)

The building trades began the period under relatively prosperous conditions; the expansion of population and of industry necessarily involved a demand for their labour and encouraged their own organization. From the records of one such body we learn that the carpenters in 1836 regarded 14s. as the minimum weekly wage; this was the rate in Kirkcaldy, Dundee and Dunfermline had 15s., Leith 17s., Edinburgh 18s., while Glasgow claimed to have reached one pound.(29) At the same period, Glasgow bricklayers had 18s. to 21s., joiners 20s., and masons 22s.(30) In Edinburgh by 1840 masons had fallen to 14s. and 15s.(31)

Between 1846 and 1866 there was a considerable rise; averages given by the Glasgow civic statistician are: masons, from 22s. 6d. to 32s. 6d.; joiners, 22s. to 30s.; bricklayers, 24s. to 33s.; plasterers, 22s. to 30s.; painters, 27s. to 26s.; glaziers, 18s. to 26s.; slaters, 18s. to 27s.; plumbers, 20s. to 26s.; labourers, 15s. to 20s.; i.e. an average increase of about one-third in twenty years.(32) The bricklayers in the 'sixties prohibited piece work, claimed time and half rates for overtime work and double rates for Sunday labour.(33)

Later in the century, wages were commonly reckoned by the hour or by some multiple of it, a quarter-day equalling two and a half hours.(34) This method provoked considerable dispute, and made total remuneration very variable; because of loss of time through weather conditions, etc. Bricklayers had 5s. to 5s. 6d. a day in Glasgow in the 'sixties;(35) about 1890 they had 8½d. an hour.(36) About 1880 joiners had 6d. to 7d. an hour;(37) about 1890, carpenters had 6d. to 7½d., stonemasons, 6½d. to 8½d.(38)

The servile status of the coal miners in the eighteenth century, though legally abolished by the Acts of 1775 and 1799, left its influence on their conditions of employment and livelihood in the nineteenth. An advance of payment by way of bounty had been common, and in practice meant perpetual indebtedness;(39) this was prohibited by a clause in the emancipating Act of 1799, but apparently evaded.(40) Yearly contracts continued during the early decades, and a bounty of five or ten pounds was sometimes given and recovered by instalments deducted from pay, at least until the Truck Act,(41) (1831). In the 'thirties this yearly "bond" was giving place to monthly or fortnightly hiring; twenty years later "minute contracts" (in practice usually one day's notice) came into vogue, and by 1865 nearly three-fourths of the colliers worked on this footing.(42)

Owing to the peculiar dependence of the industry on the general state of trade, the fluctuations of remuneration were particularly great. Iron and coal getting were generally paid by the yard,(43) and sub-contracting was frequent. Mr. Johnston gives many detailed figures (44) which can be confirmed from other sources. One difficulty in computation lies in the variability in the number of days worked, wages being usually assessed daily in terms of output and paid fortnightly. The amount of "offtakes" has also to be taken into account in measuring "real wages." It seems that day rates were relatively high in the 'thirties—about 4s.; e.g. at the Haugh pit, on the estate of the philanthropic Sir John Maxwell (1836), miners received from 3s. 4d. to 4s. per day "with houses, fire, and gardens free of rent or other charge." At Loch Libo equal pay ruled and in 1837 reached 5s. a day for a 6-day week.(45)

Wages sustained a severe fall to about two shillings in the wretched early 'forties, and again in the 'forty-eight. During the 'fifties and 'sixties with minor oscillations they were steadily rising, and reached a peak of about 10s. in 1872. Thereafter they declined with the onset of the great depression to about three shillings, but were rising again about 1890.

Attempts at sliding scales were sometimes made, e.g. in Ayrshire in 1873, and in Lanarkshire, 1887–89, but these were ephemeral. References are made to restriction of "dark" (output) by Trade Unions, e.g. at Dunfermline in 1844, when a maximum of 32 to 46 cwt. per day was prescribed(46) in Lanarkshire, to reduce stocks in the depression, for 18 months virtually half-time working was insisted upon (1883–84); eventually the traditional 5-day week with Thursday idle was confirmed.(47) Boys from 12 to 14 were recognized as entitled to a "half-turn," those from 12 to 16 to a "three-quarter turn," those over 16 to a "man's turn."(48) In the East, wages were stabler; 10 or 11 working days per fortnight was normal.(49)

In the growing heavy industries, the burning question was time versus piece rates. In the pioneer establishment at Carron, in early Victorian days, moulders earned 24s., pattern-makers, 21s., wrights and blacksmiths, 20s.; labourers, 15s. At Camelon, nailmakers nearly doubled a previous average of 10s. 6d., but fell to 8s. or 9s. owing to London and American competition.(50)

In the iron and steel works, tonnage rates were usual from the beginning; daily or minute contracts were about the mid-century generally substituted for the previous weekly arrangement.(51) There was considerable class distinction in the earnings of the various grades. In West of Scotland ironworks

(c. 1840) moulders had 2s. 6d. to 6s. per shift, while puddlers and underhands had 8s. to 12s. 6d. a week.(52) In 1856 blast-furnacemen ranged from 4s. 2d. to 7s. 9d. per day, puddlers, 7s. 6d. to 10s., rollers, 10s. to 13s. 6d., labourers, 1s. 6d. to 2s.(53)

When steel manufacture became thoroughly established in the 'eighties a "first-hand melter" got 12s. a shift, a second hand 8s., a third 6s. The average weekly wage of a plate miller or roller was £7, of a heater £5, of a shearer £4; other semi-skilled workers gained 30s. to 50s., while a mere labourer, paid by day rates, could only touch 18s.(54) Wages were thus the highest attained by manual labourers, against which must be set the "net disadvantage" of the "severest kind of labour voluntarily undertaken by man" (to extend a phrase used by Bremner of puddling),(55) and relatively long hours (twelve) with periodic night shifts, owing to the technical necessity of continuous production.

Engineers, despite their highly skilled labour, only attained a maximum of less than £2 by about 1890, and pattern-makers were remunerated on a similar scale.(56) In the mid-century, "engineers and mechanics" had averaged 3s. 6d. to 4s. for a 10-hour day.(57)

In the shipyards "from 1830 to 1850 wages remained fairly constant. At times certain fortunate groups in the engineering industry rose to 30s. per week. The trend of prices was downwards, so that real wages were rising slowly." Engineers' wages on marine work averaged one pound odd (1851) and 24s. (1856), shipwrights', 24s. to 30s. (1857–58). The boom of the middle sixties brought engineers' wages up to 26s. (1868); in shipyard labour generally the height was reached in 1873,(58) though the uncertainty of a full week's work makes rates a deceptive measurement. Glasgow shipwrights reached 36s. in 1865, only to fall to 28s. two years later; depressed after a temporary rise in the early 'seventies they secured their old maximum in 1883, but in two years had to yield 6s. Marine engineering wages were usually paid by the hour or week.(59)

On the railways, general standards remained notoriously low, partly through backwardness in organization, right into the present century. In the early days of the Edinburgh & Glasgow

Railway, stationmasters had £50 to £130 a year, with free house, coal, and light; drivers, 27s to 42s.; stokers, 16s. to 20s.; guards, 18s. to 20s.; brakesmen, 20s. to 25s.; signal and points-men, 18s.; porters, 15s. to 19s.; platelayers, 15s. to 18s.; booking clerks, £20 to £70 a year.(60) In the middle years, engine drivers, the aristocracy of the craft, were gradually promoted after experience as cleaners and stokers, receiving ultimately 4s. 6d. to 7s. a day. Guards were selected among the station porters (paid 15s. to 18s.), and began by taking charge of goods trains; their earnings were 18s. to 30s. a week.(61)

DEDUCTIONS

Wages were in some industries in practice diminished by "offtakes" or "drawbacks" exacted in recompense for some equipment or contribution in kind. These seem to be originally derived from the paternalist regime hereafter described. At New Lanark (c. 1840) there was a drawback of 10d. for loom rent, 3d. for light, 2d. for carriage, imposed on hand-loom weavers.(62) At Peninghame (Wigtonshire) weavers hired looms at a rent of 6d. to 8d. a week, and the cost of carriage to Glasgow was deducted from the payment for their wares.(63) The hire of looms was common, at any rate in the later days of handicraft production.(64)

Miners in the 'fifties had deductions for blasting powder and oil, sharpening of picks, etc.(65) "Trade deductions" in the 'seventies averaged 9d. a week on a full-time wage of about 24s.(66) About 3d. a day was deducted for light, sharpening, etc., in the Lothians mines.(67) In 1892 a Lanarkshire colliery manager stated that offtakes had long been in force, and were not a violation of the Truck Act, under which indeed they were audited, "foreign material" being one legitimate item.(68)

Of similar character and effect were the fines enforced in some factories. At Deanston they were imposed by the over-looker for lateness, spoiled work, etc.; the rules were unwritten, and there was a right of appeal to the manager.(69) Fines for bad work and unpunctuality were levied in South of Scotland woollen mills (1890), but part was repaid as a bonus to steady workers, part went to a sick fund or to the Royal Infirmary in Edinburgh.(70) Dennys of Dumbarton handed over fines to an Accident Fund managed by the workers.(71)

ARRESTMENT OF WAGES

A peculiarity of Scots law which attained some importance as a factor depreciating real wages may conveniently be noted here. This was the practice of "arrestment of wages," i.e. a "process by which a creditor detains the goods or effects of his debtor in the hands of third parties till the debt due to him shall be paid."(72) The Cotton Strike of 1837 produced a crop of cases, thanks to supplies being given on credit to strikers, and the system was investigated by the Select Committee on Trade Unions whose appointment resulted.(73) It was severely criticized by several witnesses before the Select Committee on Payment of Wages (1842), among them Smith of Deanston, the noted inventor and "improver," who held that it encouraged shopkeeping credit, induced dismissals, and obliged Glasgow manufacturers to make daily wage payments. His condemnation was supported by Dixon, the Govan ironmaster.(74) Professor Robert Cowan, M.D., writing contemporaneously on Glasgow social statistics, held that the "law should be repealed" as constituting "an evil of the deepest magnitude."(75) About 30,000 citations a year under its terms occurred in Glasgow.

An agitation for its amendment was begun by George Anderson, a Glasgow flax spinner in 1852, and supported by Neale Thomson, a cotton spinner, and by the Trade Union movement. Anderson published a "very exhaustive and able pamphlet" (1853) and read a paper to the Social Science Association (1860). The Government commissioned Hill Burton, the historian, to investigate the matter (1853); he recommended abolition, but without practical result, "as under the ten pound franchise the small shopkeepers were too strong"; the Crimean War gave a pretext for shelving the matter.(76)

In 1868 Anderson stood as Radical candidate for Glasgow with the official support of the "trade delegates," and made reform of the law of arrestment a feature of his platform, as did the miners' leader, Alexander Macdonald, in his abortive candidature for Kilmarnock. On his election, Anderson pressed the question in Parliament, and in 1870 succeeded in carrying an Act by which "alimentary funds," which were not liable to arrest, were extended to cover wages up to 20s.(77)

CHAPTER V

HOURS OF LABOUR

It is familiar ground that "domestic" industry, whether in agriculture or manufacture, frequently involved extremely long hours of labour, not merely for the crofter or weaver, but for his family of all ages. Whether or how far this was compensated by a greater sense of freedom and "the feeling that they are their own masters"(1) is rather a matter of opinion. Varying verdicts are suggested by the comments of contributors to the Statistical Accounts. At Graitney (i.e. Gretna), "120 families or 600 persons" wove for a Carlisle firm. They "all work at the looms 6 days a week and 12 or 14 hours each day. . . . By diligent labour and punctual payments they are barely able to support their families by a mode of subsistence which appears to have a tendency to weaken the body, to depress the mental powers, and engender a spirit of improvidence and disaffection."(2) Of employees of the same firm in the same county it is, however, stated that "these individuals, not being crowded together in great numbers, suffer no very material injury either in their health or morals from the line of life which they follow."(3) Weavers for the Glasgow market at Torryburn (Fife) had a poor trade, but one easily learned and more independent, and therefore preferred.(4)

Certainly the position of the hand-loom weavers deteriorated in this as in other respects, as greater effort was required to maintain the same earnings in view of the fall in rates. At Kilbirnie, in brisk trade, they had made 11s. to 12s. in 12 hours; later they had to work 15 for 1s. 6d. to 1s. 8d.(5) In the 'thirties, working hours averaged 70 per week, including 5 to 10 hours on Saturday; Mondays were often "idle" as regards actual production, being utilized in "looming" new webs.(6)

Throughout the Victorian period the general tendency was towards a shortening of the time spent in wage labour. This was partly the effect of legislative restriction, the earliest form of modern collectivist enactment. As is well known, this control was first applied to the labour of women and children, especially in the textile factories. Scotland offers no peculiar features in this respect, although the first history of the movement was written by a Scottish Chartist, "Alfred" (Samuel Kydd);(7) it therefore seems unnecessary to deal in detail with the Parliamentary process. In the decade 1845–55, the ordinary working week fell from 69 to 60 hours.(8)

Miners in the Lothians about 1840 usually worked a 5-day week; the length of a shift varied considerably; on occasion, up to 18 hours might be worked at a stretch, though 8 to 12 was normal.(9) In Fife pits, hours averaged 10 till about 1870, thereafter about 8½.(10) Lanarkshire miners usually worked a 5-day week, to regulate output and allow repairs (c. 1890). The average hours were said to be 10 per day, though only 8 or even 6 might be worked if the day's job was finished. A double shift was worked at two Larkhall collieries.(11)

A 12-hour day and Sunday labour, associated with the double-shift system, persisted in the iron and steel trades till after the European War (1919).(12) The devout James Baird, however, stopped Sunday labour (1837), providing religious services in the works instead; "Gartsherrie fires don't burn on Sundays" proved a good electioneering slogan in his candidature for Falkirk Burghs (1851).(13) Iron-trade employers stated that the men's average attendance at the works was 11 hours, of which only 6 to 8 was actual working time (c. 1890).(14)

Bricklayers had a 60-hour week till 1864, then got a half-day on Saturday.(15) The shipwrights worked 60 hours before 1867; these fell as low as 51 in the early 'seventies, but rose to 54 in the depression.(16) Other figures supplied by Trade Unions to the Royal Commission on Labour in 1892 were: engineers, 54, ironmoulders, 54, pattern-makers, 54, boilermakers, 54, painters, 40 to 51, tinplate workers, 56, carpenters, 51, stonemasons, 51, printers, 51 to 57, jute and linen workers, 56.(17)

On the railways hours were exceptionally long; on the North British 2½ per cent worked over 18 hours, 14 per cent over 12 hours.(18) Intensity as well as duration of work, deplored in 1868 by the *North British Review* as a "crying scandal,"(19) together with a military type of discipline, were

other major grievances. A comprehensive demand for a 10-hour
day, limited to 8 in special cases, with annual holidays, and
payment of time and a quarter for overtime and time and a half
for Sunday duties, was rejected by the Companies, and
occasioned a bitter and disastrous strike (1890–91). Some
concessions, including reduced hours, were, however, soon after
accorded.(20)

A Shorter Hours Movement recurred repeatedly during the
period, and had two main phases. A reduction of the working
week for the industrial worker was pressed by Trade Union
action, coupled sometimes with a demand for legislative
restriction. There was also an Early Closing agitation, on behalf
of distributive workers, conducted mainly by sympathizers on
philanthropic grounds.

The latter comes first into prominence. The claim for a half-
holiday on Saturday evoked sympathy in religious circles for
Sabbatarian reasons, and secured the advocacy of Free Church
leaders like Drs. Begg and Guthrie (21) and of John Hope, w.s.,
the Temperance and Protestant leader, a champion of Ashley's
Ten Hour Bill.(22) The movement thus has its links with the
campaign against Sunday labour, especially on the railways,
carried on in the 'thirties and 'forties by Sir Andrew Agnew,
Thomson of Banchory, and other aristocratic Evangelicals, amid
the sarcasms of Radicals.(23) The *Witness* (the Disruptionist
organ) argued that Saturday evening payment of wages was
responsible for Sunday trading.(24) Chambers, the publisher,
took credit to himself for making payments on Friday evenings
to enable the money to be spent to the best advantage.(25) A
public meeting organized by the "Council of Trades Delegates"
was held in Edinburgh in October 1853 to demand a Saturday
half-holiday and Friday payment of wages, Hope being among
the speakers.(26) The bakers stood out against Sunday
labour.(27) Leisure for Volunteering was another plea which
appealed to mid-century military patriotism.(28)

A voluntary agreement as to evening "shop shutting" was
said to have been arrived at by Edinburgh drapers in 1832, but
by 1840 it had been broken down by newcomers. A normal
8 o'clock closing, with one hour extension on Saturday, was then

aimed at; and an undertaking by drapers to close at 7 o'clock after January 1, 1843, was reported.(29)

A Half-Holiday Association to encourage "moral elevation" during the new-found leisure was formed; winter courses of lectures were given under the patronage of the Town Council of Edinburgh and of clerical dignitaries (1854) and the Council was memorialized in favour of the opening of places of public interest.(30) A Drapers' Association with about 2,000 members was formed in the early 'fifties, and secured 7 or 8 as the usual closing time, with sometimes 5 p.m. on Saturdays; but in the 'sixties about one-half of the shops were open later, some till 10 or even 11 on Saturdays.(31) Demonstrations were held in Aberdeen and Glasgow as well as in Edinburgh (1853–54), and some advance was recorded.(32) *Tait's Magazine* strenuously supported shorter hours; e.g. in an article on the Forbes Mackenzie Act (January 1856).(33) In 1861 a deputation from the Drapers' Early Closing Association secured a promise of 7 p.m. closing.(34) Dr. Begg in 1863 read a paper on "The Early Closing Movement in Edinburgh" to the Social Science Congress. He pleaded for greater consideration on the part of the public, and a better sense of their own interest on the part of employers. To make the best use of leisure practicable, the School of Arts and evening classes should be encouraged.(35) Thirty years later a similar agitation appears in Glasgow, where the Scottish Shopkeepers' and Assistants' Union was formed in 1890 by Kenneth M. Milligan. Its spokesman asserted that local associations for early closing had secured only ephemeral concessions. The organization had several branches, and 1,700 members within two years; 10 per cent were employers. Membership was rapidly increasing; on the executive, employers and assistants were equally represented; over 1,000 employers subscribed as "affiliated members." The Shop Hours Act of 1886 (which set a maximum of 74 hours a week for "young persons" under 18) was largely inoperative, from insufficiency of inspectors. The Trades Council had refused to receive a delegation, but some ministers had preached on the subject, apparently in deprecation of the public proclivity for late shopping.(36) An amending Act of 1898, giving powers of

enforcement to local authorities, was forthwith applied by one
County and 18 Town Councils.(37)

To turn to the reduction of working hours in industry generally, the first phase was the humanitarian campaign associated
with the name of Ashley, and designed in the interest of women
and children in the textile factories. This, as already noted, seems
to present no features of special Scottish interest, and culminated in the Ten Hours Act of 1847. Oastler's tour of Scotland
in 1846, when he was supported by Dr. Chalmers and Sir
John Maxwell of Pollok, probably stimulated interest.(38)
Some similar agitation continued for the inclusion of operatives
still unprotected; e.g. a Short Time Committee for the regulation of hours in the West of Scotland bleachfields was established
in 1853; a proposed reduction to 60 hours was frustrated by the
recalcitrance of a small minority of employers. A petition in
favour by employees deplored their lack of time to participate in
Mechanics' Institutions or Church services.(39) An attempt at
legislative sanction was opposed by W. E. Baxter, the Dundee
millowner and Gladstonian M.P., on the ground of the dependence of the process on weather conditions.(40)

The Factory Extension Act and the Workshop Regulation
Act (1867) virtually completed Victorian legislation on the
matter, by extending the principles of the preceding Acts to a
variety of other occupations and in a modified form to smaller
non-mechanized establishments.(41). It met with some criticism, including a curiously intemperate and ill-informed attack
from the usually reforming Edinburgh Lord Provost, William
Chambers—perhaps because printing works were for the first
time embraced (December 1867). A meeting of "working men"
in support of the Act demanded its enforcement, and even
the Chamber of Commerce gave general approval to the
measure.(42)

A distinct development comes with the demand by organized
male labour for a reduction of the working day, enforced on
occasion by industrial action, and latterly coupled with claims
for legislative action. Cooke-Taylor regards the Act of 1874,
which "took half an hour a day off textile factories alone," as the
outcome of a "new agitation (which) marked the entrance on the

scene of the trade association in place of the beneficent out-
sider."(43) As regards Scotland, it is noted that Arbroath
millowners had voluntarily limited hours to 57 prior to the
Act.(44)

The phase of Trade Union action is clearly indicated in
Scotland in the 'fifties, when the brunt of the effort was at first
borne chiefly by the building trades. In July 1853 they demonstrated, with Brown Douglas, the Radical politician, in the chair,
in favour of the Saturday half-holiday.(45) About 1860 they
formed Nine Hours' Committees throughout the country, and
achieved that reform in Edinburgh (May 1861) after a notable
three months' strike. Their cause was supported by the Edinburgh Trades Council, and Trades generally, by Potter of
the London Trades Council, and by the journalist George
Troup, then editing the *Witness*.(46) "The Builders' Nine
Hours Movement of 1859–61 . . . was distinctly the starting-
point of a new phase of the labour question."(47) In Glasgow
the aim was not attained until 1866, and the joiners in that
city were again involved in a dispute on the same issue in
1870.(48)

The engineers took up the matter about 1870; their ideal
maximum was 51 hours, which was conceded with comparative
ease in most centres (1871–72), but afterwards withheld by the
North British Railway in its "shops."(49) One effect of the Great
Depression was a speedy reversion to longer hours, which by
1879 had on the Clyde generally risen again to 57. The Unions
accepted this under protest, and formed a "Recovery League"
to secure restoration when trade revived; John Burns the shipowner (Cunard Line) was described as the "John the Baptist of
the 54-hours movement." At the same time representatives of
the Edinburgh trades formed a "Fifty-One Hours Defence
Association."(50)

In an article on Social Legislation so early as 1856, *Tait's
Magazine* declared that the Saturday half-holiday had been
"long adopted in the manufacturing districts of Scotland with
admirable results."(51) About 1885 the normal working week
was 54 hours, against 60 in the 'sixties.(52) The long hours
worked under singularly unhealthy conditions in the Ruther-

glen chemical works of Messrs. White were brought to the notice of the Royal Commission on Labour (1892–94). A twelve-hour day and seven-day week was wrought by some 60 per cent of the employees, day and night shifts alternating. Attempts to form a Union had been unavailing, and three-fourths of the labour was of a "floating character," because of the effect on health. The witness, a former technical employee, then "Secretary of the Labour Literature Society," affirmed that one partner has left a million, another "settles the expenses of Evangelical tours."(53) No improvement, however, took place until the sensational exposure of Lord Overtoun by Keir Hardie during a strike at the works in April 1899.(54)

Opinion in Trade Union circles gradually veered round to legislative limitation of hours of labour, though against strong opposition. In 1888 a majority of Edinburgh Trades Council still preferred to rely on industrial pressure.(55) R. B. Cunninghame-Graham won renown among the miners by becoming Parliamentary champion of the cause (1888).(56) In the days of the Newcastle Programme there was an attempt to incorporate a statutory Eight-Hour Day in the Liberal platform. In the *Scottish Liberal* (1890) Keir Hardie was allowed to plead the case as it affected the miners, against the traditional dislike of State intervention voiced despite his Hegelianism by R. B. Haldane.(57) The Associated Carpenters and Joiners, claiming to represent some 10,000 journeymen, voted in favour of a Parliamentary Eight-Hour day (*c.* 1892).(58)

CHAPTER VI

SOCIAL PROVISION

THE survival of paternalism in the organization of industry has been demonstrated in an earlier section. Here we are concerned with its effects on conditions of labour. "The newer captains of industry," writes Mr. R. L. Hill, "were in the main new to the handling of men and the wielding of authority over large bodies of employees. They had for the most part retained the habits of mind of their pre-industrial fathers. In their relations with their men they went often to the extreme of paternalism. The Truck System, the close supervision of the moral and social relations of their workers, and a dozen other practices which later grew into the most flagrant of abuses took their origin from the farm, kitchen and parish church of an earlier day." (1) Mr. Hill is chiefly concerned with English politics, but his proposition can be amply illustrated from Scottish industry. The entrepreneur at first tended to continue or to imitate the devices and conventions of the agricultural regime. Coalmining afforded the easiest transition. As Professor Nef observes, "the proprietary attitude of the Scottish landowner towards his miners is evident. . . . The colliers are his servants; he provides them with a hovel, with meals, and with fuel. The mine and the salt work remained a part of the rural landed estate. . . . Actual slavery of the type developed in the Scottish coalmines appears to be the product of a rapidly developing industry in the hands of landowner proprietors."(2)

Heavy industry, textiles, and even railways often imitated these methods. Apart from traditional influences, the fact that new industries often sprang up rapidly in rural areas, lacking alike the amenities of town life and the care of efficient public authorities, almost enforced "welfare activities" upon employers. New Lanark is but the earliest and best-known example of benevolent despotism in the industrial sphere. The methods initiated by Dale and improved on by Owen were continued by their successors there,(3) and imitated by some of their partners and rivals in the nascent cotton industry. Monteith, the employer of Livingstone at Low Blantyre, Neale Thomson at the Adelphi Works, Bridgeton, and the successive managers of the Deanston Mills near Doune, where the model village still houses the employees, are outstanding illustrations (4) In the subsidiary branches of bleaching and dyeing, the Crums of Thornliebank and Robert Dalglish, M.P., at Campsie, were noted as philanthropists.(5) An early anticipator of modern ideas was the Earl of Mar, who in the first decades of the century in his coal mines at Alloa provided education, improved cottages, restricted female labour, and introduced self-government by "bailies."(6) In perhaps a majority of cases, however, the benevolence appears less conspicuous than the despotism.

The prevalence of paternalist methods well into the nineteenth century may be exemplified in detail under the heads of factory conditions and welfare activities, truck, medical and educational services, and the provision of housing accommodation.

(1) There appears to have been considerable variation in the HYGIENIC CONDITIONS of the early factories. Many of the early cotton and linen mills were buildings of a primitive type, sometimes crudely adapted to the purpose. While perhaps no more unhealthy than the home domestic artisan they were probably still more congested. The frequently insanitary condition of the Glasgow cotton mills was severely censured by Roebuck, the Radical M.P. (1838).(7) Many throughout the country were unimproved from their initiation, unless in the fortunate accident of a fire. In the printing and bleachfields the atmospheric conditions demanded by the technique were injurious to health.(8)

Dr. Ure glowingly describes the dressing-rooms and other conveniences at Deanston, and the ventilation and sanitation of the factory,(9) but fails to demonstrate that they are typical. The mill at Linwood (Renfrewshire) was conspicuously clean and roomy, though inadequately ventilated.(10) The new thread works erected by Dick & Sons in Glasgow in 1854 were commented on as a model factory.(11) The Border woollen mills, which were of later date, had a better reputation structurally and hygienically.(12) "Dry" spinning flax mills were much healthier than "wet."(13) The spinning mills of Dundee were much improved in structure about the middle of the century, and newer works built during the boom of the early 'sixties had "every modern appliance for the physical comfort of the operatives."(14) The Baxters at the Dens Mills (1836) introduced lighting from the roof, "a plan which conduces greatly to comfort and safety and has since been almost invariably followed in such works."(15) The carpenters complained of bad lighting and ventilation in workshops (c. 1890).(16)

As regards general welfare activities, an advance in the treatment of employees indicated by the Factory Inspector's Report is favourably commented on by the *Scottish Guardian* (July 1854).(17) The provision of canteens by Henry Dunlop at Broomwards Mill (Glasgow) exemplifies a new development. Messrs. Coats are also lauded for setting an example in the provision of shelter at meal hours. This policy was followed by the two great paper-making firms of Cowan and Craig, and by Fleming Reid, the Greenock hosiers, who also provided recreation grounds.(18)

In an article (1865) dealing with "welfare work" under the name of "Commercial Philanthropy," the *North British Review* apologized for drawing its illustrations from England on the ground that those existent in Scotland were not on "the same scale of magnitude" nor marked by the same "distinctive features of interest." Scottish businesses were generally smaller, and social conditions, education, religion, etc., afforded less scope. Without particularizing, it is added that employers sometimes catered for the welfare of their dependants by engaging lay missionaries and biblewomen, arranging lectures and Bible classes, promoting the circulation of books and the care of the sick, and organizing summer excursions and winter soirées.(19)

Buchanan of Catrine followed Owen in giving full time employment during depressions.(20) Much later, William Denny, the Dunbarton shipbuilder, held a competitive examination for offices, gave awards for suggested improvements, held conferences with workers, and contributed to an "accident fund" manipulated by them.(21)

Towards the close of the century, an idyllic picture is presented of the Border woollen industry. The workers joined co-operative and building societies, hired allotments, and conducted sick and benefit societies, to which employers often contributed.(22)

(2) TRUCK

In the case of works newly established in hitherto unpopulated areas, where ordinary retail stores were not available, the sale to employees of consumable goods such as food and clothing admitted of some defence as an emergency measure. It lent itself, however, to the abuses of the truck system, and provided an early occasion for Government intervention. Truck was definitely banned by an Act of 1831; Mr. J. R. Philip, discussing Scottish Labour Law, says that the abuse, whose earlier course he illustrates, was "struck at" by the Act of 1831 and "subsequent legislation."(23)

The first blow was not mortal. The prohibition did not apply to such enterprises as railway contracting, where the migratory character of the "navvies" (computed at some five to six thousand in Scotland during the railway age) gave a special pretext for the system; hence the greatest Scottish contractor, John Waddell (d. 1888), was able in the mid-century legally to cater for his 800 employees.(24) In the mines and ironworks and occasionally elsewhere, constant complaints of evasion if not violation were made, and were substantiated by several investigations, both public and private. A Select Committee of the House of Commons in 1842 examined *inter alios* four Scots witnesses, including Smith, of Deanston cottonworks, and Dixon, of Govan "Blazes," and reported a wide prevalence in Scotland, especially in non-urban areas; the law was circumvented by coercion to spend in stores controlled by the employers.(25) John Hill Burton was employed in a Government inquiry bearing on the matter in 1854, and addressed the Social Science Association on his findings (1860). He confirmed the allegations of evasion, which was almost universal in ironworks, and general in Western coal mines, being associated with advances of credit. He considered the profitableness to the employer illusory, and in the true *laissez-faire* vein deprecated legislative interference.(26)

The *North British Daily Mail* explored the position in 1869, and claimed partial responsibility for the appointment of a Commission of Inquiry by an Act passed next year.(27) Widespread infringement of the law, affecting 150 works with 36,000 employees, was revealed, especially in the coal and iron industries of the West, where it was of old standing; in the East the practice had considerably declined by the 'thirties.(28)

It was demonstrated that a chief contributory cause of its perpetuation lay in the custom of fortnightly or even monthly payment of wages; in Wanlockhead lead mines there was the remarkable device of an annual settlement. Men requiring goods before the expiry of the period could obtain them only through extension of credit at stores connected with the works; "lines" or tickets might be resold, thus constituting a localized currency; where an advance in wages was given at the intervening weekend ("Blind Saturday") a shilling in the pound might be deducted.(29)

In these shops the owners generally had some financial interest, at least as rent receivers. The store was sometimes conducted by employees of the firm; Merry and Cuninghame undertook to remedy abuses thus caused. In one case (Strathblane calico printing) a son of the proprietor, in another (Connell's shipbuilding yard) a brother-in-law owned the shop.(30)

The legality of company stores was affirmed in court, provided that the money was actually paid to the employee.(31) Thus an anonymous East Lothian colliery owner, who left a "large fortune," was enabled to keep a store at which he "sold provisions and whisky to his colliers, and used a coin peculiar to himself in his dealing in the shop with his men."(32) According to the *Mail's* commissioner, "£20 a month kept a large works operating, the wages passing from the pay office to the truck store, and from the truck store to the pay office, and sometimes the payment of wages was suspended until the first men who had been paid had purchased goods at the store and thus enabled the store manager to send the cash to the wages office again."(33) The behaviour of hand-loom weaving agents in Ayrshire, who paid in kind on the pretext of the improvidence of their clients (c. 1840), seems, however, to have been a flagrant violation of the law.(34)

In such cases as New Lanark, the claim that the food and clothing supplied were of the best quality was doubtless justified,(35) but accounts of others are reminiscent of those portrayed by Disraeli in *Sybil*. Parallel scenes are prominent in Mrs. Cranston Low's story of mining-life in the Lothians about 1840.(36) At the Glasgow Ironworks, Motherwell, and at Gartcosh, prices were high and quality poor; at Calder & Summerlee Ironworks intoxicating liquor was supplied; "the truck system always finds whisky for the men, we are not aware it ever provided intellectual and moral appliances."(37) Mr. Johnston, however, alleges that even Bibles were trucked.(38) An aggravation was the "slumping" of items in a bill to obviate the checking of charges for individual commodities.(39)

Blacklisting and intimidation of men who gave their custom elsewhere was also alleged—e.g. at Carnbroe & Summerlee Ironworks. Some employers professed anxiety for the abandonment of the system—e.g. Monkland Iron & Steel Co., Drumpellier Collieries—as causing or embittering strikes; Messrs. Hannay, on acquiring Blochairn Ironworks, put a stop to it. Truck shops were regarded as a safe investment, yielding large profits—e.g. Summerlee, 100 per cent., Monklands 50 per cent. (40) Such malpractices and extortion evoked the censure even of the usually complacent Bremner.(41)

A similar form of payment in kind was the allowance of a quantity of coal as a perquisite to miners, either free as at Gartsherrie, or at reduced rates.(42) Here the affinity with agricultural usuage is clear. Complaints were heard as to the quality. In Lanarkshire it was free till the middle of the century, by 1890 it is said to have been paid for at market prices.(43)

The abolition of truck was one of the reforms agitated for by Alexander Macdonald in his mid-century reorganization of mining Unionism,(44) but it was only in 1887, after a special report from the Chief Inspector of Factories, that the Truck

Act was extended to all manual workers.(45) Even in 1892 it was stated that in blast furnaces there was a store open to all but controlled by the employer, dividends in which were forfeited by leaving his employment.(46)

This may be held to mark a transition stage in which a semi-co-operative society was sometimes formed under the employers' patronage. The Bairds, through their nephew and manager, Alexander Whitelaw, took the initiative about 1856 at Eglington Ironworks; by 1867 there were retail concerns at five works which they had helped to finance. Stephens erected at their Govan shipyard at their own expense a building for the purpose.(47)

As the capacity for organization developed among the workers, the establishment of independent co-operative societies supplied the want more satisfactorily. The movement was encouraged by enlightened employers, who sometimes handed over the control of stores which they had themselves set up; e.g. the Crums at Thornliebank and William Denny the Dumbarton shipbuilder.(48)

(3) MEDICAL AND EDUCATIONAL SERVICES were frequently provided, sometimes "free," sometimes paid for by a form of "offtake."

The Factory Act of 1833 contained a clause which "authorized" the establishment of factory schools, and stipulated for daily attendance for at least two hours by child employees.(49) This, according to the Scottish Inspector, made little difference north of the Tweed, as few children under 13, and therefore liable, were employed, while many owners had previously established schools on their own account; as confirmed by evidence, he considered the Act beneficial in making attendance compulsory. At least fifteen schools attached to textile factories and maintained by the firms were enumerated, including three in Aberdeen; in other cases children attended the parish schools.(50) In 1850 it was asserted that less than 1,000 children in Scotland ($1\frac{1}{2}$ per cent of the total employees) were being educated under the Factory Act, which had rather discouraged their employment; the requirement of an educational certificate as a condition of employment was recommended as an alternative by George Anderson, millowner and later Radical M.P. for Glasgow (1857).(51)

In the collieries of the Lothians, one of the improvements due to the Mines Act (1842) was the foundation of first-rate schools; previously few children had attended. Even before the Act Sir John Hope provided a free school at Newcraighall;(52) the parish school at Newbattle was now supplemented by a "colliery school."(53) These schools were attended by miners' children up to the age of 10 or 12; twopence a week was regularly deducted from wages for fees.(54) In Lanarkshire, according to an account in 1860, there were 51 schools specially provided by masters or proprietors in the mining area for the children of employees; they retained control but usually welcomed clerical visitation. The verdict of an Inspector was that these schools compared favourably with the average parish school, both in the superiority of the building and in the emoluments of the teachers; the education given was similar, but the itinerant habits of the population led to irregular attendance, and only 10 per cent remained beyond their tenth year. The owners usually furnished a library; they subsidized a school of mining in Glasgow attended by some twenty colliers.(55) An official Report four years later states that there were 62 schools in the mining districts of the West under Government inspection and receiving grants from the Committee of the Privy Council on Education; schools existed in connection with all collieries of any extent; fees were moderate (usually twopence per week) and were normally deducted from wages.(56) Sir John Maxwell (d. 1865) bequeathed £20 a year for the education of the families of colliers and labourers "on that part of my property where the coal mines are situated, so long as the coal mines continue to be worked to profit" (Titwood, Renfrewshire).(57) In the coal pits around Dunfermline, a flat rate was usually charged to all employees, and an additional deduction made for each child actually at school.(58)

At Chapel Hill and Calderbank Ironworks, twopence a week contributed to the school fund entitled one child to education; a penny extra per week was charged for each additional child in the family.(59) At Dundyvan Ironworks (Coatbridge) a school was built by the Company; by day over 400 children attended; their fees were paid to the age of 13 (by which most had left) by the Company, which recouped itself by levies of fourpence per month on single men and ninepence on married men; evening classes were arranged for employees under 16.(60) At Coltness Ironworks, a school of high quality was carried on, thanks to the educational interest of James Hunter of Glenapp, long managing director.(61)

As indicated, the unmarried and childless had usually to pay for other folk's bairns. Rt. Hon. John Hodge records that he received the elements at a school at Muirkirk maintained by the Bairds, who "insisted upon the children of workpeople going to their school, school fees being a flat levy deducted from the wages of all workmen, married or single" (c. 1860).(62) In the West, where there was a large Irish element, one grievance was that this was exacted from Catholics who declined to send their children to Protestant schools, and sometimes provided their own, as at Carfin Wishaw and Mossend.(63) Sometimes, offtakes were paid over to an institution maintained from other sources; a Free Church school at Uddingston was thus subsidized, in respect of pupils connected with a local works who attended it.(64) At Tillicoultry, the proprietors contributed to the village academy, where most of the workers sent their children.(65) The Devon Iron Co. built a schoolhouse and a library.(66) Tennants of St. Rollox supported a school on their own premises for the free education of the children of their workpeople, and in 1858 erected a new building with accommodation for 2,000, to provide "an improved system of education."(67) Some Glasgow tobacco manufacturers gave financial aid to the Tobacco Boys School, founded as a charitable enterprise about 1810 by William Ford, a foreman; this apparently lapsed, but was revived about 1861 in imitation of one similarly established in Edinburgh about 1820 and remodelled in 1850. The "regular provision of evening schools was a feature of Edinburgh and Glasgow tobacco manufacture," which depended largely on casual juvenile labour; nominal fees were charged, and they were subsidized by employers and others in the trade.(68)

Some further details illustrating educational and other arrangements may be given. The works' schools, like the parochial, commonly laid stress on the religious basis of teaching; the Bairds, e.g., selected schoolmasters on the advice of the parish minister.(69) Dalglish of Campsie, however, went in for secular instruction. His firm erected at Lennoxtown a school-house containing infant and juvenile departments for the "numerous children in the locality," and accepted the aid of public sub-scriptions. Here one hour's teaching per day was given to relays of young operatives, with proportionate reductions of pay; additional employees were engaged to afford time for learning and prevent overwork.(70) The Buchanans, on taking over Stanley Cotton Mills, released children at 3 p.m. instead of 7, so that they might attend school.(71) At the model village of Deanston, there was a school-house at which children of from 5 to 9 years were full-time pupils; from the ages of 9 to 13 they worked an eight-hour day three days a week; from 13 to 16 they attended an evening class four nights a week. The school was financed and controlled by the firm, and was free to employees.(72)

The Barrowfield Cotton Works, Bridgeton, gave rent-free accommodation and an allowance of £20 to the schoolmaster. (73) At Blantyre, the Monteiths provided a library, with an extensive collection of volumes, erected a chapel, and paid half the emoluments of the incumbent; and bestowed on the school-master a salary of £20, plus house and garden.(74) David Livingstone paid tribute to the superior character of the education given, which included "some acquaintance with the Greek and Latin classics."(75) There and at Slamannan Colliery there was the exceptional device of selection of the teacher by the parents; in the latter case, a disabled miner was once appointed on charitable grounds.(76)

At Cowan's paper mills, Penicuik, there was from about 1818 an infant school and an evening school for those over 13, which was free and compulsory in the winter; the ladies of the firm supervised the education.(77) The Chambers, the publishers, gave gratuitous education to juvenile employees one hour daily, and established a library in their office.(78) J. B. Neilson, of hot-blast fame, established (c. 1824) at the Glasgow Gasworks, of which he was long manager, a workman's institute, containing a library, laboratory, etc.(79)

The education, like the more material goods similarly provided, varied in standard. "The educational system introduced by the enlightened and philanthropic proprietors of the Monkland Iron & Steel Works . . . affords educational advantages to the youth of a populous district equal to those enjoyed by children of the better class in Glasgow; as the workmen chiefly manage the school, the whole is conducted in a manner which is equally creditable to the employer and the employed."(80) The Factory Report of 1845 claimed that the factory owners in Forfarshire "maintained excellent schools . . . those in rural situations equal the best parochial schools."(81) The recent "debunking" of traditional estimates of the latter by Dr. J. C. Jessop, (82) with special reference to this very shire, suggests that this may have been no very exalted claim. The Reports of the Commissioners who investigated education in the 'sixties, prior to the passing of the Young Act, give statistical information as to the facilities afforded and at the same time demonstrate their insufficiency in quantity and quality.(83) In Glasgow only one-third of those between 3 and 15 were at school and there was accommodation only for one-half. Many works schools had only temporary occupation of their premises and were liable to be closed when these were required for other purposes. They were available for children of the general public but were not much utilized.(84) There were persistent but unsubstantiated suspicions that all the proceeds of the offtakes were not devoted to the educational or other ostensible purposes. The owners sometimes appointed inefficient teachers.(85)

Their experience converted the Factory Inspectors to State control of education.(86) The Bairds, however, being opposed on principle to a "national system" upheld the superior merits of their own schools which accommodated 4,500 children (1872), and prided themselves on spending £3,000 a year on education, supplementing the levy to make up reasonable salaries. They retained control of their schools even after the Young Act, to ensure religious instruction. The mineowners also objected to

public intervention; Merry and Cuninghame's schools cost them
£500 a year.(87) Bremner thought the Bairds' provision
"liberal and highly appreciated"; in general he was satisfied
that "abundant facilities existed," but that because of these
being "indifferently appreciated by parents . . . a little pressure"
was necessary, while the proprietors always made up the
deficit in fees.(88) The usual deduction of twopence a week was
retained, at the request of the employees of Young's Mineral
Oil Works, after the passing of the Education Act, and the
proceeds used in paying the fees of over 1,100 children.(89)
In 1892 the Dundee factory owners were paying twopence
per week to the School Board for each half-timer.(90)

Some provision for medical attendance was usually made on
similar lines, both in cases of illness and of accident; injuries
from machinery were frequent in early days, young children
being the chief sufferers; the Factory Commission (1833) gives
harrowing particulars.

A shilling a week for ten months was deducted from wages
at Craig's Flax Spinning Factory, Preston Holme, to establish
a sick fund; any balance outstanding was returned to those leaving the mills. Here and at Millport Mill, Dunfermline, injured
workers were treated gratuitously and retained in employment.(91) At New Lanark in the 'thirties, a doctor was paid by
the firm; from a sick fund constituted by a deduction of fourpence in the pound from wages, a weekly allowance was made
to the sick, supplemented at need by the Company.(92) About
1840, deductions averaging 12s. a year were commonly made
in Lanarkshire works for medical care of employees and their
families.(93)

In the 'seventies mineworkers everywhere paid into a fund
for the purpose; the employers often insisted on nominating the
club doctor, who was sometimes non-resident.(94) The Bairds
appointed one who did not give full-time service, but according
to Whitelaw, their Gartsherrie manager, there were no genuine
complaints of neglect.(95) About 1860 the Dunfermline mining
companies retained medical officers, remunerated by levies
on employees; Lord Elgin paid extra for attendance in case of
accident.(96) Blantyre colliers had in the 'nineties deductions

from their pay for a sick, accident and death fund, administered by the colliery cashier and a workmen's committee; the same method obtained in Ayrshire mines. The Dalmellington Co., with about 1,800 employees, had agreed deductions from wages for medical benefit of threepence, and for sick benefit of two-pence per week.(97) Bremner, with his usual optimism, asserts that one or two medical officers are attached to each colliery, and that the employers defray all extra charges on account of accidents.(98) The Tennants of St. Rollox for many years "retained the services of a medical gentleman . . . long known in Glasgow for his philanthropic and public spirit."(99) Dr. Robert Munro the anthropologist commenced his career as assistant to the doctor attending the employees of Messrs. Baird, at Lugar Ironworks (Ayrshire). John Elder, of Fairfield Shipyard, instituted an accident fund, jointly financed and administered.(100)

(4) HOUSING ACCOMMODATION

"Tied houses" were the rule in collieries as much as on farms and dated from the days of bondage. Houses and buildings were almost invariably built by the lessees but reverted to the proprietor at the termination of the lease.(101) About 1840, according to Tancred's Report, dwellings were mostly erected by the works, were deficient in numbers, and were let by the fortnight corresponding to pay-days.(102) The bad conditions common in miners' rows have been attributed to the shortness of mining leases, which were usually of nineteen years' dura-tion;(103) the lessee was thereby discouraged from laying out much capital on property of which he had no transient possession.

The provision of accommodation was regarded as part of the contract of service in Fife so late as 1892; most of the tenants paid rent, the houses being sometimes owned and sometimes leased by the colliery.(104) Elsewhere housing was regarded as part of the wage; in the 'forties rent was esti-mated at an average of 2s. 6d. per week.(105) Mr. Smillie thought the practice a good investment for Lanarkshire owners, and an instrument for controlling the workers.(106) Early in the twentieth century it was estimated that in the

Lothians and Ayrshire at least three-fourths of the miners'
dwellings belonged to the employers, in Lanarkshire and Central
Scotland between one-third and one-half.(107) The Duke of
Buccleugh provided a good class of house rent-free at Dalkeith,
and the Marquis of Lothian reconstructed his at Newbattle,
deducting rents from the pay (c. 1870).(108) Macredie of
Pearston, near Irvine, gave houses with gardens rent-free to
picked workers in his collieries. At the Portland Collieries,
Troon, there were annual lets. Prospectuses of coal and iron
mining companies usually include workmen's houses among
their properties.(109)

The kindred iron industry adopted similar expedients. New
and superior houses were built in the 'forties, e.g. at Lugar,
Kinneil, and Forth.(110) The Bairds had a virtual monopoly
of the accommodation within range of their works. They
practically built Coatbridge, previously a weaving hamlet,
in the 'thirties,(111) and after 1874 erected about 1,000 houses
in Lanarkshire, which yielded a return of $5\frac{1}{2}$ per cent gross
and $1\frac{2}{3}$ per cent net.(112) Eglinton Iron Co., which was under
the same control, built over 800 houses of two or more apartments at an average cost of £110; charging an average rent
of £5 10s. 0d. per annum, they obtained in the course of
twenty years a net return of under 3 per cent.(113) In 1892,
at Langloan Works, Coatbridge, the owner provided houses
at 5s. to 8s. a month.(114) Likewise, Dr. James Young, in
developing the shale oil industry of the Lothians, had to make
himself responsible for all accommodation. At Addiewell, "a
bed of clay was discovered on the property, a brickwork was
erected, and soon houses to the number of several hundreds
were provided, the building of the manufactory being at the
same time pushed forward"; additional houses were later
bought from other firms.(115)

Craigs the papermakers, on transferring their works from
Newbattle to Caldercruix, built houses for employees brought
with them (1890).(116) Messrs. J. & G. Thomson, on removing their shipyard from Govan, "built imposing blocks of
four-storey dwelling-houses for their workmen" and thus
began the burgh of Clydebank.(117)

In the textile industry, the principal illustration is found in the experiments of cotton magnates in model villages. Earliest and best known is that at New Lanark. Full descriptions of at least two others are available. "Immediately adjoining the works," at Deanston-on-Teith near Doune, "is a handsome little village built by the Company which contains about 1,200 inhabitants. The houses are neat, built in one long street parallel to the water-course, and are two stories [sic] with attics. They are most exemplary patterns of cleanliness, and to each house is attached a small piece of garden ground, and a range of grass plot for bleaching."(118) This village is still extant and occupied. Of the houses connected with Low Blantyre Works, the residue is preserved as the Livingstone Memorial, in virtue of being the birth-place of their most distinguished native. The village was "contiguous to the works, and pleasantly situated on a rising ground which overlooks the Clyde." The houses were comfortable and neatly built. "The village is kept clean, to ensure which the Company provide both watchmen and scavengers." They also built a public washing house, "supplied with hard and soft water for domestic purposes, by force pumps at the factory," "to which the householders have access in rotation"; and set apart ground for a large bleaching green. "Any worker known to be guilty of irregularities of moral conduct is instantly discharged, and poaching game or salmon meets with the same punishment. The general character of the population is moral, and in many instances strictly religious. Living in one of the fairy neuks of creation, religious and moral, well fed and clothed and not overwrought, they seem peculiarly happy as they ought to be."(119)

The Crums of Thornliebank owned most of the village, and improved its amenities in respect of gas and water supply, baths, gardens and halls.(120) Sir Archibald Orr-Ewing, founder of Levenfield printfield and dyeworks, erected and owned most of the house property in Jamestown (Vale of Leven); his works gave employment directly or indirectly to all its inhabitants. He furnished them with a hall and school, and bore half the cost of the parish church. Some of his structures are praised for their "substantiality and tidiness," but lacked "picturesqueness."(121) The suburb of Dennystown (Dumbarton) originated in a "cluster of workmen's houses" erected in 1853 by William Denny, founder of the shipbuilding firm.(122)

These anticipators of Lever and Cadbury were exceptional, and the housing conditions created alike by paternalist effort and by speculative enterprise were responsible for one of the chief social movements of the period, as narrated in a subsequent section.

In concluding this sketch of parentalist methods, we may briefly consider the factors responsible for their persistence. Apart from the immediate effects of the situation produced by the rapid expansion of industry in unpopulated areas, some weight must be assigned to the social heritage. Here one element consists in the "clannish" spirit which was traditional in the countryside, Lowland as well as Highland, and interacted with the earlier types of semi-rural organization in such activities as coal mining, salt refining, and timber cutting.

Another closely related influence is that of Presbyterianism. The rather specious and facile theory of Weber (123) and his school, which identifies the "spirit of capitalism" with Protestantism, especially in its Calvinistic form, and relies largely on rather forced interpretations of certain selected Puritan writings, has little substance as regards Scotland. Mr. Edwin Muir in his *John Knox*(124) and other exponents of the "Scots Renascence" have sought to make the identification, but with a singular dearth of evidence. The theory has recently been brilliantly refuted by Dr. H. M. Robertson, who devotes a few concise pages to Scotland. "Scotland remained more feudalized, less affected by the growth of the new state-system than most countries of Western Europe. The rise of rationalism in economic affairs was much slower in Scotland than elsewhere owing to the overwhelming power of a theological outlook enforced by the masterful Presbyterian Church. . . . It is forgotten how long Scotland was both Calvinist and poor before the remarkable economic progress of the later eighteenth and nineteenth centuries. . . . There is little reason why the Scots bibliolatry should have raised up a spirit of capitalism in Scotland. The doctrine of predestination . . . called for a complete subjection to the divine will; . . . in the economic sphere it resulted in a species of regulation of economic activity on moral grounds which was many times more thorough than any mercantilist regulation on political grounds."(125)

Mr. Carswell has perhaps more warrant for his attempt to correlate the rise of the Free Church with the development of capitalist industrialism in the early nineteenth century;(126) the two were at any rate contemporary. The great influence of Chalmers, however, while hostile in the main to State action, encouraged interest in social problems. "His conception of the gospel did not hinder him from giving attention to such commonplace things as land, labour, and capital. It rather urged him to the task."(127) Dr. Wilson Harper's presentation of Chalmers' teaching is perhaps somewhat idealized; in such matters as poor relief, notably in his famous controversy with Dr. Alison, he displayed a singular narrowness and blindness;(128) but Mr. Carswell also exaggerates in saying that "his social programme died with him."(129) While, as Dr. J. R. Fleming deplores, "not as yet was a social conscience generally aroused" in Victorian Presbyterianism, "there were men who saw further than their fellows,"(130) and such distinguished exceptions as Guthrie, Begg, and Blaikie may be considered more truly representative of the principles of their Church. It is true that from its inauguration many large capitalists—e.g. William Campbell of Tullichewan, James Stevenson of Largs, Henry Dunlop of Craigton, James Burns of the Cunard Line—were prominent as Free Churchmen; but to identify their Church simply on that score with a *laissez-faire* social ethic seems distinctly a *non sequitur*.

The impetus alleged to have been given to individualism by the evangelical revival of Moody and Sankey is doubtfully demonstrable. Even Moody, however exceptionable his theology, stressed the "social duties of our faith" and inspired Henry Drummond to social service.(131) The decline of the mid-century enthusiasm in Church circles as elsewhere may rather be attributed to the onset of the Great Depression.

It may then be affirmed that the patriarchal outlook was more in accordance with the traditional teaching of the Church than were the doctrines of *laissez-faire* individualism. In social outlook as well as in social conditions the Reformation in Scotland made much less difference than rival zealots would maintain. It is also a delusion to suppose that capitalism was universally associated with political Liberalism. The Monteiths and the Bairds were staunch Conservatives; the Whiggism of Kirkman, Finlay, and Ewing of Strathleven was much suspect to Reformers. A paternalist conservatism was the logical correlate of adhesion to the Auld Kirk, and might well harmonize with a theocratic objection to interference by a secular State with the liberties of the Christian man. The better side of this attitude has been sufficiently illustrated; its more unlovely aspects are summed up in the career of James Baird of Gartsherrie, a thoroughgoing exponent of industrial feudalism and ardent adherent to the Church of Scotland, to which he bequeathed half a million (132)—described by the irreverent as "the highest fire insurance premium ever paid"; it was at any rate in the tradition of the medieval baron, making his peace with the Church by endowing it. To take the most notorious instance from the Free Kirk, the Whites of Overtoun, its financial benefactors, could hardly be deemed to exercise much paternal care over their chemical workers, but it is difficult to deduce their negligence logically from their creed. It seems to illustrate rather that growth of Erastianism and secularism in substance if not in form which made the social witness of the Church obscure and its social sanctions cease to operate. By the end of the period the propagation of a social ethic has passed to the politician and publicist, though here in Scotland from Thomas Carlyle to Keir Hardie and Robert Smillie it bears the mark of its original religious inspiration.

M

PART IV

SOCIAL ORGANIZATIONS
AND MOVEMENTS

CHAPTER I

TRADE UNIONISM

FROM the conditions of life and labour arising out of the industrial system itself, we turn to consider movements of thought and action which arose to modify these conditions. Obviously most directly associated with industry is Trade Unionism.

Scottish Trade Unionism has never found its Webbs, and it may be that the opportunity has passed, so many of the records have perished by mischance or neglect. Those of the Glasgow Trades Council, e.g., were destroyed by a fire in the Albion Hall a generation ago (1909);(1) many old Minutes have been treated as scrap, and few odd copies survive of such "Labour" periodicals as the *Liberator* (*c.* 1834–38) and the *Glasgow Sentinel* (*c.* 1858–76). Mr. Thomas Johnston has collected some fragmentary data in his *History of the Working Classes in Scotland*; the Webbs make incidental reference, and Mr. R. W. Postgate in his *Builders' History*—an almost unique example of the history of a particular labour organization being undertaken by a professional historian—has commemorated the various sectional and often ephemeral Unions connected with that industry. Most of the existing Unions are of recent origin, and are merely branches of an English body. The artless reminiscences of such leaders as John Hodge (an up-to-date variant on the Smilesian self-made man) and Robert Smillie (a more consistent rebel) throw some light on their development. The Registrar's Return of 1892 shows 43 Scottish Trade Unions, with 52,000 members and funds amounting to £63,000.(2)

The main forms of Trade Unionism in Scotland may be conveniently surveyed under the four heads of Textiles, Building, Coalmining, Heavy Industries.

I. TEXTILES

Scotland shared in the efflorescence of Trade Unionism in the early 'thirties which followed the repeal of the Combination

Laws and the propaganda of Owenism. In the West of Scotland as elsewhere the relatively capitalized cotton industry was to the fore, and in the debacle of the grandiose projects sponsored by Owen (1834), a chief survivor was the "Association of Cotton Spinners of Glasgow and Neighbourhood." It was of the old-fashioned type, seeking to maintain a craft monopoly, and utilizing some of the methods of a secret society, inherited from the days of illegality. How far these methods went in the direction of sedition and violence was the chief matter in dispute at the trial of their leaders in January 1838, consequent on the great strike which won notoriety but little else for the Union. The rules of the Society were among the evidence produced in court. They provided for a body of delegates from each shop, and an executive of twelve "directors" meeting weekly, with four general meetings in the year. Entry money was demanded, and serving of time as a "piecer" insisted on by way of apprenticeship. "Idle" benefit and funeral money were paid, and an emigration fund was raised. A special "Supply Committee" had been set up (June 12, 1837) to function during the strike; it had published in the *Liberator* (a weekly partly financed from its funds) resolutions disavowing violence. About £1,000 was raised for the defence, and some leaders of the Bar retained. The verdict was indeterminate as to the nature of the Union, the accused being acquitted on the capital charge of murdering a blackleg, though transported for seven years on minor charges.(3) A pamphlet by their Chairman alleged unjust treatment; the plea of this "Rights of Labour" defended was voiced in Parliament by Radical spokesmen, and upheld by Lord Brougham, possibly from spite against his former Whig colleagues (Feb. 1838).(4) The whole matter was thrashed out afresh before a Select Committee of the Commons, at which conflicting statements on many points were made by spokesmen of employers and operatives.(5) *Tait's Magazine* offered sympathetic criticisms, stressing further Parliamentary Reform as the real solution of working-class discontents.(6) The Union, said Cockburn, was the "real mover of all combinations and strikes in the manufacturing districts of Scotland for about twenty years."(7)

Incidentally, "the innocence of mere combination" was judicially acknowledged by himself and his colleagues on the Bench in this case, thus definitely reversing the verdict in the Weavers' case (1813). The applicability of the Combination Laws of 1799 and 1800 to Scotland has been contested by Mr. J. L. Gray, who holds that here combination was throughout dealt with by interpretation of Common Law principles contemporary legal opinion seems to have agreed only that "the law of Scotland was rather undetermined with respect to combination."(8)

The Union, though suffering severely, survived, and thereafter, according to Bremner, "no serious strike occurred."(9) An agreed scale of rates of pay was introduced in 1846, and amended in 1853 (McNaught's List); the alteration was responsible for friction and rival charges of non-observance, culminating in a strike (Jan. 1854).(10) In 1870 the Operative Cotton Spinners' Union was resisting a 10 per cent cut and raising a levy to promote emigration, but had to surrender.(11)

The decline of their trade and the adverse judgment of 1813 had virtually destroyed combination among hand-loom weavers. A local union in Lanarkshire had been broken up by the Duke of Hamilton in 1832, after an unsuccessful attempt to buy up the stock of "revels"; by an extraordinary display of paternal authority, the Duke divided its funds among non-Unionists. It had obtained an agreed table of prices, but with its disappearance, combination, as was reported by the Commissioners of 1839 and 1841, was practically extinct.(12) In 1864, however, Henry Carrigan, of Bridgeton, gave evidence to the Children's Employment Commission as Secretary of a Hand-loom Weavers' Association, if only to affirm the destitution of his fellows.(13) The power-loom weavers in the factories established an organization, which conducted a strike in 1848.(14)

The block printers of Campsie also had a union in the 'thirties, which in 1834 had accumulated funds of £6,000–£7,000; they took an entry fee of £10 and a monthly levy of 1s. 6d. and regulated recruitment. The Union was ruined by an unsuccessful strike for increased wages, which was broken by the introduction of "nobs." (15)

These cotton unions, after their brief space of publicity and perhaps of power—somewhat exaggerated by the prejudices of writers like Dr. Ure and Sheriff Alison against "close corporations"(16)—passed into obscurity and insignificance. The spread of Chartism diverted attention to political agitation, among whose leading Scottish exponents were textile operatives such as Matthew Cullen and Abraham Duncan.(17) About 1890 the Glasgow textile trades were mainly staffed by women, who were unorganized; there were then six very small and exclusive men's unions, whose members performed subsidiary processes; these limited entry, and had high rates of subscription and benefit.(18)

In the linen and jute industry of the East, much of the labour was latterly also female. In earlier times, the domestic workers had been noted for their political independence; the term "heckler" is said thus to have been derived from a technical process in the industry.(19) An abortive attempt at industrial organization was made by mill employees in 1834, when after many preliminaries the Dundee and Lochee Factory Weavers' Union issued its statement of objects and rules. The owners forthwith combined to issue a pamphlet excluding Unionists from employment, and requiring repudiation of it as a condition of engagement.(20) Somewhat later, several operatives and also "Rev." John Duncan (a Chartist preacher) were charged at Dundee with criminal conspiracy in connection with a wage agitation.(21)

It was only in the 'eighties that effective organization was achieved. The Dundee Factory Operatives' Union, composed chiefly of women jute workers, embraced also some five hundred Perth linen workers. It was formed in 1885 in consequence of wage reductions, with the help of Rev. Henry Williamson, a Unitarian minister, who became Hon. President; it claimed to have raised wages by 30 per cent in a few years. In some degree competitive was the Forfarshire Federal Union of Textile Workers (1889), who favoured the abolition of half-time, and had locals in Brechin, Forfar, and elsewhere, including about half of the employees, of whom two-thirds were women. Their subscription was one penny a week.(22)

In the woollen industry of the Borders, largely owing to the survival of the patriarchal tradition, "Trade Unionism, if not a thing unknown, has seldom or never exercised its power for evil in the trade." Mr. Johnston by his silence seems to confirm the fact if not the opinion; a Weavers' Union existed in the 'fifties in Galashiels; organization in later days was initiated by power-loom weavers in Hawick (1887); and by the Yorkshire Textile Union in Galashiels (1895).(23)

2. BUILDING

The numerical expansion and technical conservatism of the building trades have been noted, especially by Professor Clapham,(24) as an important feature of the Industrial Revolution. Hence the prominence of a variety of specialized craft unions. These formed a strong constituent in the Owenite unions; a "Glasgow and West of Scotland Association for the Protection of Labour," later styled "the General Union of Glasgow" and subdivided according to trades, was initiated by the ardent Owenite, Alexander Campbell, himself a joiner by trade. Fragments survived for a short period in the different crafts.(25)

The bricklayers, though small in numbers, were in 1844 able to forbid piecework, and to regulate apprenticeship, having funds averaging over £8 per member.(26) To the Commission on Trade Unions (1867) it was reported that a Society dating from 1850 was nearly 100 per cent strong, prohibited piecework, and secured reckoning of wages by the day. They levied £1 entry money and dues of 3d. a week, and had a fluctuating influence on apprenticeship. Their funds amounted to about £1,400.(27)

Owing to the prevalence of stone building in Scotland the masons were here a more numerous and important body, and claim considerable notice in Postgate's *Builders' History*. The United Operative Masons of Scotland Society was formed about 1830 and was active in the decade, chiefly through several local lodges;(28) in 1836 they obtained in Court from Sheriff Alison a declaration of their legality and right to withdraw labour, if unaccompanied by intimidation.(29) This

appears to be the Union of which Hugh Miller gives so un-
flattering an account, being prejudiced against Trade Unions
by his experience of uncongenial company while working at
Niddrie House (c. 1828).(30) His views are to some extent
borne out by one John Wright, Vice-President of an Edinburgh
branch about 1833–34, and subsequently a Town Councillor,
who gave witness before the Poor Law Commission in 1844 in
the guise of a repentant sinner. He alleged that the Union
practised intimidation; it also had a funeral society and other
benefit activities, and combined with other unions to run a
journal edited by one Biggar.(31) Miller's biographer thinks
that the moral standards of Trade Unionists had much improved since his young days.(32) In 1845 the Glasgow branch
formed a mutual improvement class, sometimes cited as a
unique pioneer effort in Trade Union education.(33) In 1840
however the total membership was only 433, and in 1846 the
Union was reported to be "almost defunct." (34)

From 1847 onwards the stonemasons were reorganized with
English assistance, and in 1855 this Scottish United Operative
Masons' Association, centring in Glasgow, had thirty-one
lodges and some 3,000 members. They paid 6s. "idle benefit"
and awarded £3 as an "emigration bonus"; a feature of their
administration was the appointment of "collectors," or shop
stewards. They aimed at payment by the hour in substitution
for the usual fortnightly reckoning, and at shorter hours.(35)
The former claim had been decided against them in a notable
legal case at Dundee in 1840, when stoppage of work after a
week was held to forfeit the fortnight's wages.(36) Their
successful struggle for the nine-hour day in the 'sixties has
already been mentioned;(37) by 1870 it was almost universal
in the trade throughout Scotland. Membership continued to
rise during the building boom of the 'seventies, and reached
nearly 14,000 in 1877, when also the careful husbanding of
resources by the exceptionally able administrator, Matthew
Allan, secretary from 1867 to 1883, had built up reserves of
over £18,000 and achieved greater unity. The bulk of the funds
were, however, lost in the failure of the City of Glasgow Bank
(September 1878), and the depression which it intensified at

the same time produced unemployment and wage reductions in the building trades; consequently in 1883 membership had fallen to about 6,000 and capital to £1,800, while in 1889 there were little over 2,000, and funeral and sick benefits were abandoned. In the early 'nineties there was a revival though organization remained very feeble; in 1892 the Union claimed to have over sixty branches and nearly 4,000 members in Scotland, and thus to be about 50 per cent strong.(38)

An obscure society of carpenters and joiners, with which Alexander Campbell was connected, is believed to have existed till about 1838.(39) In 1827, the "Friendly Society of Operative House Carpenters and Joiners," generally known as the "General Union of Carpenters and Joiners," was formed in London. Postgate says that records prior to 1863 have been lost.(40) A Minute and Letter Book of an Edinburgh branch (1836–37) is, however, now in the Scottish National Library. At a general meeting of the trade attended by a deputation from Glasgow, a branch was formed with fifty-five members on April 1, 1836. Office-bearers were appointed, local rules approved, and monthly meetings arranged; in May affiliation with the English body was accepted. Some Masonic observances were maintained. Delegates were sent on propaganda tours in Fife and the Lothians, through which branches were formed in Dundee, Dunfermline, Kirkcaldy, and Leith. A Quarterly Report a year later shows 218 members in Edinburgh, with a total of nearly 400 in the other four eastern branches. Glasgow joiners had to surrender unconditionally in March 1838 after an eighteen weeks' strike against a winter wage of 18s. for a ten-hour day.(41)

Our next information comes with the foundation in Glasgow in 1856 of the United Joiners by Alexander Campbell, on his return after a chequered career as an Owenite missionary;(42) representatives took part in the Social Science Congress of 1860.(43) In 1861 this organization was absorbed in he new Associated Carpenters' and Joiners' Society, in origin mainly Scottish; there was a fifty years' rivalry between it and the larger Amalgamated Society formed in London the previous year by Robert Applegarth,(44) who in 1867 claimed for it a membership in Scotland of about 5,000 (45). It formed a branch in Glasgow in 1870,(46) but in 1892 could record only 170 members in Edinburgh and 1,200 on the Clyde.(47)

The Associated Society remained the stronger organization in Scotland. Its first secretary was John Proudfoot, who since 1854 had organized a small local society; he became Secretary of Glasgow Trades Council and an outstanding figure in the Trade Union world as Secretary of the National Conference of March 1867.(48) A Society for insurance of tools (*c.* 1854–55) appears to have been the nucleus of the Edinburgh branch (1861) formed after a strike. William Paterson was Scottish Secretary from 1867; he led an agitation against Duncan McLaren because of his unsatisfactory response to Trade Union demands as M.P., and formed an Advanced Liberal Association in Edinburgh.(49) Benefits included insurance of tools; levies were 3d. a week for the trade section, and 3d. for the benefit section, which was optional but included two-thirds of the membership.(50) In 1894 the Society had nearly 7,000 members, in 132 branches, of which twenty-six were outwith Scotland.(51)

Of the other building trades there is little to be said. In the middle of the century some plumbers were organized in an English union, painters, if at all, in small trade clubs.(52) The Scottish Slaters formed a Society in Glasgow in 1866, at a conference of delegates from the principal centres, but it remained small and ineffective; according to Postgate, they constituted less a skilled trade than an indefinite body of "general repairers." (53) The United Operative Plumbers were reconstituted in 1865 as a national body with Edinburgh and Glasgow branches; in 1872 and 1891 breakaways occurred in Scotland, where employment was more regular and habits more conservative.(54) The Plasterers, who had established a remarkably high position, were ruined by a lengthy strike following the collapse of 1878, and Unionism was almost extinct for a decade. In 1888 the Scottish National Operative Plasterers' Federal Union was formed by local clubs, remained very decentralized, and in a few years had about 1,000 members. By agreement with employers, it paid an inspector as a safeguard against scamped work, which had provoked a lock-out. It maintained a five years' apprenticeship, and had strike benefit of 12s.(55) A Scottish National Federation of House and Ship Painters was formed in Glasgow in 1887.(56) At this date the building trades in Glasgow appeared to the Webbs to be contented; despite the large number of non-unionists, who enjoyed the same remuneration and privileges, they maintained their rates and conditions; the renewed growth of the city was doubtless chiefly responsible.(57)

3. MINING

The miners' unions had a particularly chequered career, attributable to the extreme localization of the industry, the segregation of the collier, and the peculiar character of his work, perhaps also to the late condition of serfdom. The evidence submitted to various commissions in the 'forties reveals the prevalence of degrading and barbarous conditions in the mining communities.(58) Unions sprang up sporadically in different localities, had a brief and hectic existence and disappeared without achieving permanence or unity.

Relations between employers and employed are said to have been more amicable in the Lothians than elsewhere. The first reference to a union is to one in Lanarkshire and district, which is said to have raised wages in 1824; "to shield the men from the injurious consequences of regulation," a "company union" was formed by the manager of Govan Colliery in 1826.(59) According to Bremner, "the first union of the Scottish miners was established" in 1835, presumably the initial attempt at national organization. It waged a seventeen weeks' strike in the West of Scotland in 1837, whose ill-success led to its collapse.(60) Sheriff Alison suspected collusion with the employers, who doubled their profits in the shortage of coal.(61) A union or branch centring in Dalkeith at the same date conducted a four months' strike of several hundred men for higher wages, and paid a benefit of 1s. 6d. per week until its funds were exhausted; it appears to have survived as a benefit society.(62)

In August 1842 there was again a general strike of Western

coal and iron miners, involving some 20,000 men; it was directed by a temporarily revived union. It lasted till March 1843, and was attended with rioting and violence; Sheriff Alison, as portrayed in his memoir, was much preoccupied with the suppression of disorder.(63)

Abortive attempts at national organization were made in March 1844, when English delegates were present, including W. P. Roberts, their legal adviser; the Scots declined to contribute to his salary, and rejected a general strike proposal;(64) and in July 1845, when "the miners joined the new consolidated Union of Trades for common industrial action." (65) Effective effort, however, began in the next decade, thanks to Alexander Macdonald, an ex-collier and schoolmaster, who had acquired a modicum of independent means and was able to devote himself entirely to the cause. Himself a native of Lanarkshire, he agitated throughout the country.(66)

In 1852 the Scottish Miners' Association was formed "for the protection of miners' rights and privileges, by providing funds for the support of members out of work." It was a federation of local societies with Macdonald as Secretary, and waged unsuccessful strife in 1853, 1856 and 1858.(67) A Midlothian county union was also formed in 1853; it advocated timerates.(68)

Wages having suffered an average reduction of about 20 per cent, Macdonald apparently despaired of the strike method, and revived the idea of draining off surplus labour through co-operative emigration societies (1865). He extended his activities beyond the Border, and ultimately secured the formation of a National Union of Miners (1863), with which the Scottish Union amalgamated; he remained President until his death in 1881. He sought to improve miners' conditions by legislative action, both before and after his election to Parliament as Liberal member for Stafford (1874). His main achievements were the Checkweighman's Act of 1860, and the comprehensive "Miners' Charter" of 1872. He was also active in the revision of the Master and Servant Act, and in the abolition of truck and of arrestment of wages. He promoted wider activities of the Union in the financing of a co-operative colliery venture

—apparently abortive (1865), and the running of a weekly Trade Union organ, the *Glasgow Sentinel* (started by Robert Buchanan, ex-Owenite missionary and father of the poet), edited in the 'sixties by the versatile Alexander Campbell. This was substituted in 1877 by the *Miners' Watchman*, published in London.(69)

Delegate conferences were held, e.g. in October 1856, when complaints were made of bad ventilation and inadequate inspection; there were only two inspectors to 1,640 pits.(70) In 1866 a Coal and Ironstone Mines Mutual Protection Association of Scotland was formed, and rules were prepared for submission to a conference in Glasgow in April.(71)

The Great Depression affected coal mining like other industries, and Macdonald's last years witnessed the crumbling away of much of his structure, as well as the repudiation of his advice to abstain from hopeless strikes. National Conferences were indeed held in 1879, at one of which James Keir Hardie, already a local agent in Lanarkshire at the age of 23, was appointed "National Secretary," but the organization existed only on paper, until its reconstitution in 1886.(72)

In the 'eighties, several local unions rose and fell in Lanarkshire and Ayrshire. One at Larkhall numbered about 1,500 members in 1887, and there were about a thousand organized at Blantyre. In Lanarkshire, where Robert Smillie was becoming the leading figure, a County Union of sorts existed from 1886, with William Small, an ex-draper, as Secretary. A method adopted in that area at this period was "putting on the block"—i.e. balloting as to which colliery should strike, those rendered idle being supported by those who continued at work in the other pits.(73)

Ayrshire, to which Hardie had transferred his efforts, was rather stronger. After a year's organizing as Secretary of the County Union (1880–81), he led a strike which ended the Union for some five years. It was revived in 1886 with about a thousand members, and aimed with some success at restriction of output. As Scottish Secretary, Hardie with other Scottish leaders lobbied in favour of the Truck Act and of improvements in the Government's Mines Bill (1887); he also founded and for two years edited the *Miner*, a monthly organ (1887–88) (74). At a conference in October 1887, a paying membership of 23,570 was claimed.(75)

The most efficient organizations were those of the Fife and Kinross Miners—over 80 per cent strong—and the Mid- and West-Lothian Miners. John Weir, Secretary (1881–1908) of the former, which was founded by Macdonald in 1869, was one of the most capable leaders of the time, and is highly commended by the rather critical Beatrice Webb as "tall, good-looking, charmingly refined." It had latterly no strikes, and settled disputes by sending deputations to the management; it soon (1870) obtained by agreement an eight-hour day.(76)

Organization in the Lothians had taken the form of a labour protection and sick benefit society, with John Nicholson of Niddrie as "Grand Master" (1863); this was soon dissolved. A Mid- and East-Lothian Miners' Association of even shorter duration followed (1872–73); it was revived sporadically till 1887, "recognized" next year, and represented on a Conciliation Board from 1892. Robert Brown, afterwards Provost of Dalkeith, was latterly Secretary.(77) R. B. Cunninghame-Graham was their Parliamentary champion about 1890, when agitation for a legislative eight-hour day became active. The project seems to have been generally advocated by Scottish mining representatives, but failed to reach the statute book, partly through opposition from the North of England leaders, such as Burt and Fenwick.(78)

The shale miners of the Lothians formed a union (1886) which carried on bitter and protracted conflicts in 1887 and 1889; it secured affiliation with and support from Edinburgh Trades Council. Its Secretary, John Wilson of Broxburn, was arrested for picketing during the latter dispute; he was one of the early "Labour" candidates for Parliament, contesting Central Edinburgh in 1892.(79)

According to the Webbs, there was no effective Miners' Union in Scotland in the early 'nineties. Hardie soon relinquished Trade Union for political activities; Chisholm Robertson of Slamannan, President of the "National Federation of Scottish Miners," was most prominent in the rather shadowy organization. From 1894, however, under the leadership of Smillie, an effective national organization was built up,(80) though the conspicuous rôle recently played in industry and politics by the organized miners is largely a twentieth-century phenomenon.

4. THE HEAVY INDUSTRIES

The gradual substitution of iron and steel, engineering and ship-building for textiles as the staples of Scottish industry involved a corresponding shift in the balance of Trade Unionism. It was, however, a slow and obscure growth.

The woodworkers generally sought to organize shipyard as well as building workers. The Shipwrights were able to enforce the closed shop from 1839 to 1856, but had to abandon it after a strike. For some time thereafter the employers insisted on men "signing the line," i.e. taking a pledge of non-unionism. Alexander Denny, of the Dumbarton shipbuilding firm, was prominent in breaking resistance by importing blacklegs. In the 'eighties, the Associated Shipwrights' Society had 3,000 members in the Glasgow area, all skilled workers; their Secretary, Alexander Wilkie, became a noted figure in the movement and was among the first Scottish Labour M.P.s.(81)

The Associated Blacksmiths' Society—afterwards the Operative Blacksmiths' Protective and Friendly Society—was formed in 1857 as an outcome of a strike at Greenock for the 51-hour week. Starting with a membership of 367 in its West of Scotland branches, it rose to a peak of 1,800 in 1881–82, and then declined somewhat. Branches in Arbroath, Ardrossan, Edinburgh and Renfrew reported to the Commission on Trade Depression in 1886, and an Aberdeen branch to the Royal Commission on Labour in 1892.(82)

The Amalgamated Society of Engineers (A.S.E.), the first great "new model union" (1857), absorbed six or seven Scottish branches of the Steam Engine and Machine-makers started two years before; it had been preceded by a short-lived and obscure Scottish union. There was recurrent friction regarding local autonomy. In 1867 it claimed over 3,000 Scottish members in fully thirty branches; in 1870, seven branches in Glasgow

N

alone. It was in the 'seventies mainly concerned with the struggle for the 51-hour week. This was generally conceded, but the railway shops soon enforced an extension to fifty-four (c. 1877–78); this was the rule in Edinburgh about 1890.

At that date Scotland had about 10 per cent of a national membership of 6,500. The Webbs considered it then really a benefit society; its activities, like those of many other unions, were largely of the "social" order, e.g. annual soirées, often addressed by clerical and political dignitaries. The general strike of 1897, when the issue of "workshop control" was raised, heralds a new era. In general, the A.S.E. gave Scotland the first great example, not merely of a highly organized union, but of one with an efficient central control outwith Scottish soil.(83)

An Associated Patternmakers' Society, extant in Glasgow about 1870, became defunct. The United Kingdom Pattern-makers' Association, formed in 1872, established branches in Dundee (1874) and in Glasgow (1877). In Glasgow about 1890 only 250 out of 800 were in the Union, and bad trade had reduced their pay about one-third during the decade. The Union was to some extent competitive with the A.S.E.; William Mosses, its Secretary (1884), was also prominent in national Trade Unionism.(84)

There was a Boilermakers' and Shipbuilders' Society in existence in 1857 on the Clyde. Despite a local secession in 1886, this was still flourishing in 1892. It comprised branches of the United Society of Boilermakers and Iron Ship-builders, established in 1832, which the Webbs describe as "incomparably the strongest" of this group, "having no rival for the allegiance of its trade, and including practically the whole body of skilled workmen engaged" in it throughout the country.(85) At a conference of their union with the A.S.E. and the Ironfounders, a reserve fund for use against the employers was instituted; this was followed by a lockout (May to August 1877), which ended in a stalemate. The Boilermakers remained out till February 1879; this sectional action left hostility between them and the A.S.E. They had to undergo some reconstruction, but in 1892 were reported to be "recognized" and to have an agreement regulating maximum and

minimum wages for twelve months, details being settled in
conference; the working week was fifty-four hours.(86)

The Associated Society of Ironmoulders of Scotland dated
from 1831 and was thus the doyen of the iron trade; its members
were reckoned as skilled workers. Its Secretary, Colin Steele,
who had for twenty years been a working moulder, gave
evidence to the Select Committee on Master and Servant
(1865) regarding the general change in the trade from weekly
to "minute" contracts. The moulders rigidly asserted rules as
to overtime and apprenticeship, until the employers combined
and locked them out in 1868; after nine weeks they were forced
to surrender their position. The Union survived and was able
a few years later to recover some lost ground and advance
wages.(87) In 1889 the Central Ironmoulders' Association was
founded, mainly to cater for unskilled workers.(88)

Iron and steel manufacture presented almost a caste distinction among employees. The more highly skilled and
responsible jobs obtained relatively high remuneration at the
cost of long hours. They were first organized by the Associated
Society of Iron and Steel Workers, formed in 1862 with headquarters at Darlington; under the direction of John Kane it
adhered to the sliding-scale principle;(89) the father of Rt. Hon.
John Hodge was a branch president and was victimized for his
part in a strike about 1865.(90) Thereafter non-unionism
seems to have prevailed for some time in Scotland. A union of
Iron Puddlers is mentioned at Coatbridge in 1864.(91) The
Association, reconstituted in 1887, was merged in the Iron and
Steel Trades Confederation in 1916.(92)

The two principal grades were organized in the West of
Scotland in the 'eighties. The British Steel Smelters' Amalgamated Association was established in January 1886 as the
result of a strike against worsened conditions at Motherwell,
but under the guidance of John Hodge sought regular and
peaceful relations with the employers. It soon extended its
activities to Yorkshire and South Wales, and in 1892 transferred its head office to Manchester.(93)

The Associated Society of Millmen (April 1888), also of
strike origin, soon evolved into the Amalgamated Society of

Steel and Iron Workers. Although at first organized by Hodge as Honorary Secretary, it declined to amalgamate with the Smelters. It co-operated with the employers in setting up a Board of Conciliation for the Manufactured Steel Trade of the West of Scotland (1890). Its moving spirit was John Cronin, appointed Secretary in April 1889, whom his rival, Hodge, describes as "erratic and impulsive." (94)

The National Association of Blastfurnacemen was an English body, with branches in the West of Scotland, and a Scottish District Secretary, Charles Vickers. They were on strike for twenty-three weeks in 1890, and with the support of the miners and other unions paid 10s. a week aliment, plus 1s. 6d. for each child, but had eventually to accept a 20 per cent reduction. They worked a two-shift system, and had guaranteed day rates, with a tonnage rate in addition; two-thirds of those eligible were said to be in the Union.(95)

Summing up Trade Unionism in the heavy industries of the Clyde in 1892, the Webbs computed that three-fourths of the operatives were "non-society." There were numerous small societies, and an absence of demarcation disputes. The shipwrights and ironmoulders were well organized but inert; the steel smelters and millmen were powerful, but had failed to reduce long hours or abolish Sunday labour.(96) The "new unionism" of the period seems to have affected Scotland little. Of some 150,000 Scottish unionists at this date, 45,000 belonged to the engineering and metal industries.(97)

Finally, a few words may be said of the railwaymen. Among them organization was slow. A Locomotive Engine Drivers' and Firemen's Amalgamated Benefit Society is said to have secured concessions from the Scottish Companies about 1867, but is not mentioned subsequently. The employees of the Caledonian and of the Glasgow and South-Western also had Friendly Societies dating from the 'fifties.(98)

The first permanent Union was the Amalgamated Society of Railway Servants, founded in 1871, which for twenty years remained under philanthropic patronage; it opened a branch in Edinburgh in 1876.(99) Of contemporary origin was the Scottish Society of Railway Servants (1872), whose Secretary,

Henry Tait, was prominent in Glasgow municipal politics. They frequently collaborated in relations with the Companies, though Edinburgh Trades Council was the scene of much friction between their delegates. A strike of Caledonian employees in January 1883 extracted a few disappointing concessions. The Scottish Society increased a 100 per cent within the decade, numbering 4,500 in 1889.(100) After much agitation and negotiation a general strike was launched, against the advice of the Executives of both Unions, just before Christmas 1890. The chief issues were "recognition" of the unions and reduction of hours. About 9,000 participated, and traffic was paralysed for six weeks, but the men had to return with only slight concessions; a civil suit was raised by the Companies, but withdrawn.(101) The Scottish union was so weakened that in June 1891 it had to accept absorption in the English union of its surviving membership of about a thousand. A fraction retained an independent "Scottish Railwaymen's Union" until July 1895; it was dissolved owing to indebtedness, and the English General Railway Workers' Union (formed 1889, chiefly for unskilled workers) agreed to accept its members.(102)

CHAPTER II

TRADES COUNCILS

A PERMANENT nation-wide organization of Scottish Trade Unionism did not come into being until the Scottish Trade Union Congress was inaugurated in 1897, but Scottish unions were affiliated to the British Trade Union Congress from its commencement in the 'sixties, and indeed had an active part in its creation.

Joint local organization is of much earlier origin. In the early 'thirties there was in Glasgow a General Union of Trades, with a Committee of Delegates, of which, e.g., thirty-three were represented at a meeting in December 1833, called to intervene in a builders' strike; its proceedings were marked by "good feeling, general propriety, and tolerable order." (1) A lively account of its doings is given in his *Autobiography of a Beggar Boy*, by James Burn, who represented the hatters. In this period of political excitement there were constant meetings of the General Committee and of its sub-committees, which were "entirely composed of working men, and many of them would have done honour to the highest rank in society." The Chairman was Daniel Macaulay (*d.* September 1835), "a small man with a large mind, fluent in speech and quick in debate." (2) The Committee was much preoccupied with demonstrations for Parliamentary Reform; it ran as its organ successively the *Herald to the Trades' Advocate* (1831–32), whose circulation rose to 4,500 (a complete file is preserved in the Mitchell Library, Glasgow), and the *Trades' Advocate*;(3) the latter was edited by John Tait, brother-in-law of the Chairman, who is credited with great journalistic ability; he died prematurely in 1836.(4)

In April 1834 a conference of trades was held in Glasgow, at which two delegates from London were present, and it was resolved to "correspond and co-operate" with the organization there.(5) After the collapse of this and similar projects of the Owenite epoch, some more or less permanent structure seems to have survived or to have been periodically revivified. A United Trades Association was formed in September 1837, to assist the imprisoned leaders of the Cotton Spinners' trial;(6) the Secretary was Alexander Campbell (1796–1870), whose long and somewhat mysterious career embraced nearly half a century of public life. He had first come into prominence at the Orbiston colony, and was associated with the *Trades' Advocate*; after this he became an Owenite missionary and was evidently away from Glasgow for about fifteen years.(7)

In 1854 a delegate meeting of trades was held in support of a strike in Preston.(8) In 1855 the Operative Masons were associated with the "Central Trade Union of Glasgow." (9)

The actual transformation of this somewhat intermittently functioning body into a permanent Council is assigned to a meeting held on May 13, 1858. Owing to the destruction by a fire in 1909 of the early records, the circumstances are obscure. The veteran Owenite, Alexander Campbell, is usually described as the prime mover, but the Council's own account of its beginnings refers to him only as reporting its proceedings for the *Sentinel*. Only eight unions were at first represented; the first office-bearers were Daniel McLaren of the Masons (President) and Andrew Cumming of the Carters (Secretary). It met weekly and soon adopted as official title "the Council of the United Trades of Glasgow"; it discussed such questions as shorter hours and unemployment.(10) Reports in the local Press indicate that the same autumn the new Council was preoccupied with the emigration question. It arranged a public meeting in support of a scheme by John Crawford (1802–74), known chiefly as a currency reformer, for a settlement in British Columbia.(11)

A surviving Annual Report, issued in July 1860, shows that thirty-three trades were affiliated, including Masons, Joiners, Plasterers, Painters, Bricklayers, Slaters, Shipwrights, Iron-moulders, Iron Dressers, Miners, Hand-loom Weavers, Cotton Spinners, Bleachers, and one branch of the Amalgamated Engineers. A very full account of their activities indicates their participation in the Bleachers' Short Time, Builders' Nine Hour and Drapers' Early Closing movements. They also supported a proposed Free Library and civic Museum. They assisted in a strike of the painters, precipitated by the employers' refusal to renew an annual agreement dating from 1853, and in the arbitration of a dispute between some weavers of Lesmahagow and the "agent" for whom they worked. Matthew Lawrence was now Secretary at a salary of £12 a year.(12)

At the meeting in Glasgow (1860) of the Social Science Association, Archibald Jeffrey Hunter, on behalf of the "Glasgow Council of United Trades," read a paper on "Trade Unions"; he was then Secretary of the Operative Bakers' Friendly Society, and became later Secretary of the Trades Council, a post which he held for the latter years of the century.(13) Further evidence of the respectability of the Council is afforded by the lectures given under its auspices to large audiences by Sir Archibald Alison, the Tory historian (December 1860, March 1861). (14)

Some of its other contemporary doings suggest a rather different standpoint. In April 1860 they communicated with the newly formed Edinburgh Council in support of some vague scheme for a national union which was abortive. A further proposal for a federal union was put forward next year, and considered at a joint meeting with Edinburgh, which subsequently rejected it.(15)

In December 1861 the "Council of Trades Delegates" issued a manifesto favouring political action, and held a demonstration demanding Parliamentary Reform.(16) In 1863 the Council embarked on an agitation against the Master and Workmen Acts; a repeal committee was set up, which in May 1864 was constituted a national executive to co-ordinate the campaign. George Newton, a potter (apparently a small master or independent craftsman), formerly Chairman and now Secretary of the Council, acted as Secretary of this Committee; the Chairman was Alexander Campbell, now editing the *Sentinel*.(17)

The Council thus took the initiative in convening a national Trade Union conference (May 1864), which, according to the Webbs, "marks an epoch in Trade Union history." (18)

In 1866–67 the Council took an active part in the renewed agitation for Parliamentary Reform; e.g. in the demonstration on October 16, 1866, addressed by John Bright;(19) it also demonstrated in support of the London tailors on strike (July 1867)(20). In 1874 a Commission on legislation affecting Trade Unions took evidence from Andrew Boa, a foreman stonemason, who had succeeded Campbell as President of the "Glasgow Repeal Association." The Council then claimed to represent sixty-two trades and 140,000 operatives.(21)

The Council had a Parliamentary Bills Committee, but did not now intervene in trade disputes. In 1873 it co-operated with the Scottish National Education League in running candidates (including Professor Edward Caird and the manager of the Co-operative Wholesale) at the first School Board Election.(22) In 1878 it organized a successful appeal to the Court of Session against the award of damages to a local firm from Trade Unionists who had seduced blacklegs in their employment, and thus secured an important interpretation of the 1871 Act.(23)

In 1887 it supported the municipalization of the tramway system, and in 1890 the nationalization of minerals.(24) In 1892 it organized the local meeting of the Trade Union Congress, at which according to custom its own Chairman, John Hodge, of the Steel Smelters, presided. It had then about 160 members, representing eighty to ninety trades.(25)

Edinburgh Trades Council (26) officially reckons 1867 as the date of its foundation, but it was preceded by a small body termed the "United Trades Delegates' Association," meeting fortnightly in Burden's Coffee House in High Street. (The use of temperance restaurants and hotels is an interesting feature of Scottish Trade Unionism, possibly originating in the association of some of their founders such as Bailie Cranston and James Grant with the Chartist movement which had a marked teetotal bias in Scotland. In Glasgow, Bell's and Neilson's Temperance Hotels were latterly favoured meeting-places; this contrasts with the "everlasting adjournment to the taverns" and consequent inebriety deplored by Burn and others as characteristic of workers' organizations in the 'thirties.(27))

Minutes going back to 1859 have been preserved, from which it appears that the Association had existed continuously from 1849, and was an outcome of the Saturday half-holiday movement; in October 1853 a meeting to further this cause was organized by the "Trades Delegates"—Alexander B. Henry, President, and James G. Bald, Secretary.(28)

When its records commence, the Association included representatives of the Brassfounders, Blacksmiths, Joiners, French Polishers, Masons, and Tailors; William Troup, of the last-mentioned Union, was among the leading spirits; he was President from 1859 to 1866. One of its conspicuous activities was the running of an annual trip; it arranged public meetings, e.g. to protest against Adam Black's anti-Trade Union utterances, and to support the Nine Hours agitation; it discussed legislation affecting Trade Unionism, and sometimes acted in concert with the recently founded Glasgow Council.

The name was changed in April 1860 to "the Council of United Trades Delegates" and new rules were adopted. In 1861–62 a course of public lectures on varied subjects was organized, speakers including Professors Miller, MacAdam, and Archer. The Council possessed a small lending library, the exchange of books among members being a regular feature of its proceedings; and subscribed for the *Sentinel*, the Glasgow Labour organ, because of its "able advocacy of the rights of the working classes." It sponsored abortive projects for the establishment of a paper of its own, *The Scottish Workman and Social Reformer*, and for the acquisition of a Trades Hall.

In 1866 it frequently had to adjourn for lack of a quorum, only representatives of the Tailors, Slaters, and Cabinetmakers being in regular attendance; and in 1867 it was reconstructed as the "Trades Council of Edinburgh" (July 2nd), starting with a balance of £4 8s. 6½d. One of its first acts was to refuse a contribution to the expenses of the London Conference which initiated the annual Trade Union Congress. It sent deputations and questionnaires to M.P.s regarding pending Trade Union legislation; with two dissentients, it approved Free Trade, and it memorialized the Town Council to enforce the Factory Acts.

The Council took a persistent interest in such local concerns as the administration of the Royal Infirmary, and the activities of the "Association for the Improvement of the Condition of the Poor," which it suspected of undercutting wages. It was in touch with the International Working Men's Association (the first "Internationale" of Karl Marx), and after the extension of the franchise in 1867 resolved to take part in municipal elections, but complicated negotiations with other factions broke down.

From 1871 the Council was regularly represented at the Trade Union Congress, though usually against some opposition on the ground of expense. It frequently received deputations from Trade Unionists on strike, and expressed sympathy and commended their cause to the more active help of affiliated bodies. In 1873 it appointed delegates to a Peace Congress in Glasgow, and subsequently petitioned Parliament in favour of International Arbitration. In 1875 two standing committees, on local and on Parliamentary affairs, were appointed.

There is a gap in the records from 1876 to 1881, but from the Press we learn that in 1879 it ran working-men candidates for the School Board; all were defeated.(29)

In the 'eighties, the Council was much dominated still by the Tailors;(30) one of their representatives, Neil McLean, who issued a pamphlet denouncing Sweating Shops (1880)(31), acted for some years as Secretary with great acceptance, and was afterwards Chairman of a Committee set up to organize non-unionist trades. The Council was still preoccupied with local interests. It was critical of the changes effected by the Educational Endowments Commission (1882–89), supported agitation for the reduction of house rents, provision of public baths, libraries, etc., and schemes for "recreative" evening classes, ultimately involving co-operation with the University Extension Courses.

The Council extended its activities with the revival in the late 'eighties. It inaugurated a union recruiting campaign (1889) and assisted in the formation of new unions among carters, dockers, tramwaymen, etc. It also accepted affiliation from unions outwith the city, notably the Lothians shale-miners, whom it supported in protracted disputes (1887, 1889).

The municipalization of gas, water, and land was supported, but while Radical political reforms and working-men candidatures for local bodies were approved, socialistic measures, e.g. the legal enforcement of the Eight Hour Day, were still rejected, and affiliation with the newly formed Scottish Labour Party refused.

On the whole, the Trade Union movement in Edinburgh, whether because or in spite of the lesser industrialization of the capital, seems to show a steadier growth and more consistent strength than the more spectacular and notorious movement on the Clyde. The relatively greater proportion of skilled labour and greater homogeneity of the native population have been suggested as contributory factors.

In Aberdeen a "Delegated Committee of Sympathy" with a regular constitution, subscriptions, etc., was established in 1846 through a joiners' strike and lasted about three years.(32) A more enduring Council dates from 1868. It met fortnightly, and unlike most of the others, gave support in trade disputes.(33) In 1870 it took up the repeal of the Game Laws,(34) and in 1888 the Shorter Hours movement. In 1877 Thomas Gill, its President, took part in the usual working-men's meeting of the Social Science Association.(35)

A "United Trades Council" existed in Dundee in 1869, with George Yule as Secretary, and corresponded with Edinburgh regarding Trade Union legislation.(36) The existing Council was established in 1885. It was from an early date represented on other public bodies, and favoured a legislative Eight Hour Day. It claimed to be comprehensive in its composition.(37) In 1890 its President and Secretary were elected to the Town Council, the former without opposition.(38)

Trades Councils were also set up in Paisley and Greenock by the middle 'seventies, and later at Motherwell (1889) and Govan (1890).(39)

CHAPTER III

BENEFIT SOCIETIES

ANOTHER important and kindred form of organization is the Friendly or Benefit Society, a method of providing financial assistance in ill-health, unemployment, old age, etc., by voluntary co-operation. The method of Mutual Insurance was affirmed by the Webbs in their classical exposition to be a main function of Trade Unionism;(1) it was most conspicuously so during the period of the Combination Laws, and again among the "Model" unions of mid-Victorian days. Most durable unions, in Scotland as elsewhere, have maintained some "benevolent" fund; some were originally friendly societies and developed trade activities. "The Glasgow coopers have had a local trade friendly society, confined to journeymen coopers, ever since 1752." (2) There were occasional charges of diverting funds to use in industrial disputes, e.g. Lothian miners (1837); they survived to pay in the 'forties 2s. 6d. to 5s. per week sick benefit, and 1s. 6d. superannuation.(3) Organization among tailors commenced with "the Glasgow Union Journeymen Tailors' Friendly Society" (1824), amalgamated in 1834 with similar societies in Greenock and Paisley;(4) and on the railways with the Locomotive Engine Drivers' and Firemen's Amalgamated Benefit Society, for sick and accident payments (ante 1867) (5).

Some societies were purely local, associated with a particular mine or factory—e.g. Redding Provident United Society, Polmont; the Friendly Society of Alloa Colliery, and those connected with pits in East Lothian. These were commonly of the rather unsatisfactory or temporary type (sometimes called *menages*), as in the mines of Ayrshire and East Lothian (where initial payments of four or five shillings were made, dwindling to extinction by the end of the year), Coatbridge Ironworks, Hawick mills, and some Edinburgh trades.(6) These were occasionally supervised and subsidized by the employers, as at New Lanark, where the Company contributed £50 a year

to a "Friendly Sick Society," which gave benefits of 5s. to
7s. 6d., and also paid 3s. superannuation allowance;(7) and at
Gartsherrie, where the Company gave 4 per cent on deposits.(8)

In other cases, some continuity may be traced between the
medieval corporations in their mutual aid provisions and the
modern Friendly Societies. As the old organizations became
divorced from craft activities and even personnel, they became
largely administrators of charitable trusts—e.g. Glasgow Incorporated Trades, Paisley and Pollokshaws Weavers. They were
imitated in the late eighteenth and early nineteenth centuries
by newly founded associations. According to Forsyth, "of late
years in all parts of Scotland the common people have adopted
the salutary plan of creating institutions for their own relief, in
case of incapacity for labour in consequence of sickness or old
age. These consist of clubs or societies, the members of which
contribute weekly or monthly a certain sum, which is thrown
into a common fund, and laid out at interest by certain office-
bearers appointed by the society." (9) Alexander Mitchell
illustrates the transition in Dalkeith, in the cases of the Shoemakers and Hammermen;(10) Gavin Burns gives similar evidence for Hamilton, distinguishing the newer type, where
benefit was of right from the older where it was of grace.(11)

In 1830 there were at least six Friendly Societies in the
semi-industrial parish of Neilston (Renfrewshire).(12) In the
parish of Eastwood (suburban Glasgow) there were three
Friendly Societies of Weavers, all of eighteenth-century origin,
giving approximately the same benefits—"bedfast aliment" 3s.
a week, "walking aliment" 2s. 1d., superannuation 1s. 3d. or
2s. 1d.(13) The Societies among the hand-loom weavers, however, almost disappeared during their long-drawn depression,
though among them as among operatives generally funeral clubs
were generally maintained as a last resort against a pauper
grave.(14) The longest-lived of Scottish societies was the Old
Wrights Society of Brechin, founded in 1625 and still extant in
1883. Bo'ness had two societies dating from the seventeenth
century, both primarily for seafarers. Over a dozen local
societies of more than a century's standing were recorded by
the Registrar in 1883.(15)

The mortality rate of some of the later societies was high, partly owing to imperfect acquaintance with actuarial principles, e.g. at Dunfermline (16) and at Hawick and Galashiels, where societies were voluntarily dissolved when their deficiencies in this respect were realized.(17) At Campsie some hostility to them is attributed to theological prejudice against forecasting the dispensations of Providence.(18)

The Highland and Agricultural Society investigated the problem (1820), and as a result of its pioneer attempt "to apply the laws of probability to the insurance of health" an improved financial security was attained.(19) Some such societies were primarily charitable in character. The movement found a champion in Dr. Ralph Wardlaw, the Congregationalist divine, who read a paper on the subject to the Literary and Commercial Society of Glasgow (1817).(20) A well-known and interesting society is that formed in connection with the Edinburgh School of Arts, but subsequently dissociated from it. This is mentioned by William Fraser, the insurance expert, together with Leith Mechanics' Society, Aberdeen Mutual Insurance Friendly Society, the Edinburgh Societies of Compositors, Cabinetmakers and Shoemakers, and the Paisley Equitable Friendly Society, as an example of a society instituted on the principles recommended by the Highland Society.(21)

A House of Commons Select Committee investigated Friendly Societies in 1825 and again in 1827; hence the passing of an Act to regulate them (1829).(22) The Poor Law Commission (1844) ranked Friendly Societies with Savings Banks as deserving institutions, counteracting the necessity of legal provision;(23) R. P. Lamond, reviewing the development of the Poor Law a generation later (1870), commented on the growth of voluntary thrift, through Friendly Societies and otherwise.(24) *Tait's Magazine* affirmed the desirability of compiling statistics of sickness, with a view to the formation of companies to provide sick and superannuation benefits (1860).(25)

In 1870–74 a Royal Commission investigated Friendly Societies and kindred bodies. Considerable mismanagement through incompetence or fraud was disclosed, partly through the mutual recriminations of rival societies—e.g. Scottish Legal, United Reform, etc.(26) Friendly Societies registered in Scotland were proportionately less than in England, which was attributed to the annual contract of service in agriculture; a type of insurance apparently peculiar to the Borders was the "Cow Club." In towns there were many "yearly" or "dividing" clubs, and an absence of the "convivial element"; sometimes a "central society" was instituted as insurance against the instability of the separate clubs.(27) The ordinary Friendly Society was small and diminishing; there was being substituted either the dividing society or the permanent society with limited liability.(28)

In the latter part of the century the great national Orders and the profit-making "industrial" companies, with their local canvassers and collectors, tended to overshadow if not to displace the small local societies and Trade Union Friendly sections. Of the former, two large English institutions had a firm footing in Scotland. The Oddfellows, whose headquarters were in Manchester, was introduced into Edinburgh in 1840; the Royal Liver of Liverpool claimed to have enrolled over 100,000 members in about twenty years. The leading native Society, the Scottish Legal Burial, claimed 191,000 (1874). Among the latter, the "Prudential" commenced its familiar "industrial" activities in 1854; in 1874 it had about 70,000 policy-holders; its chief Scottish rival was the British Legal Assurance of Glasgow with 20,500.(29) In 1892 the Friendly Society Registrar's Report credits Scotland with 1,350 societies, 280,000 members, and one and a quarter million pounds accumulated funds.(30)

CHAPTER IV

HOUSING REFORM

THE provision of shelter is one of the elementary necessities of life, particularly in a country with such a climate as Scotland usually suffers, and the establishment of a home has been a precondition of civilization. Scottish housing standards have, however, always been backward. In earlier times this might be attributed to defence being preferred to comfort; chronic civil and international war encouraged the erection of light and easily restored dwellings in the countryside, of strong and congested structures in the fortified centres. Industrialism promoted a new concentration, alike in the ancient and solid tenements of Edinburgh and Glasgow and in the jerry-built hovels of the miners and other labourers. The attempt to make provision by paternalist methods has already been described; for the rest, private speculative building by such entrepreneurs as Sir James Steel in Edinburgh was mainly relied upon throughout the century.(1) The notorious inadequacy of both methods impressed the need of social action even in the heyday of *laissez-faire*; and public and private effort, charitable, co-operative and municipal, both in investigation and in supply, was recurrently initiated. These experiments, culminating in the Royal Commission of 1912–17 and the post-war Housing Acts, have left the problem still unsolved; the slums still furnish material to journalists for jeremiads and to politicians for perorations.

Here we have to consider some Victorian essays and achievements, especially in the two great capital cities. The building of the "New Town" in the 'sixties and 'seventies of the eighteenth century may be regarded as the first Edinburgh City Improvement Scheme;(2) and in 1827 an Act set up a Commission for that specific purpose which effected drastic alterations in the layout of the Old Town.(3) These, however, were not motived by projects of social welfare, and the latter seems rather to have intensified the problem, by reducing the area available for housing, especially in the West Bow and Grass-market; further encroachment was made by the construction of railways and other industrial establishments, such as the breweries at the Holyrood end of the Canongate.(4)

Public interest seems to have first been definitely aroused in the 'forties; perhaps the Disruption relieved the prolonged concentration on matters ecclesiastical, and enabled thoughts to be turned into more secular channels. At a public meeting on March 20, 1845, it was resolved to form an association to promote the sanitary improvement of Edinburgh, and the amelioration of the condition of the working classes; one of its purposes was defined as the encouragement of "the formation of joint-stock companies for building more commodious, airy and convenient houses for the accommodation of the working classes." (5) The collection of Reports on the Sanitary Con-dition of the Labouring Population of Scotland (1842), em-bodying the results of investigation under the Poor Law Commissioners' auspices, and largely inspired by Dr. W. P. Alison, provided sufficient data. They include a short note on "the Residence of the Poorer Classes in the Old Town of Edinburgh" by William Chambers, the publisher, an early indication of the zeal which found fruition during his Lord Provostship a generation later.(6)

The emphasis on the moral evils of bad housing conditions indicated by Dr. Alison was renewed by representatives of the Church, notably Rev. Dr. James Begg, who during the next two decades was the most active champion of reform. Begg had found fame during the "Ten Years' Conflict" as a stalwart of the Non-Intrusionists; in later life he was equally notorious as the diehard opponent of the Higher Criticism and of unin-spired hymns and instrumental music; his middle years were more serviceably devoted to the challenge of social evils.(7) A similar attitude was taken in Glasgow by Rev. John Smith, a Congregationalist, then editing the *Glasgow Examiner*; in his *Grievances of the Working Classes* (1846) he put forward plans for "improving dwellings" and cited the example of Liver-pool.(8) Inquiries into slum conditions were periodically carried out by the Press—e.g. in 1850 by the *Scotsman* and the

Edinburgh News, and in 1867 by William Anderson, of the *Edinburgh Courant* staff. The results of the latter were published as *The Poor of Edinburgh and their Homes,* with a preface by Rev. Dr. Thomas Guthrie.(9) John Heiton, the laird of Darnick, devoted a chapter of his curious and rather laboured satire on *The Castes of Edinburgh* to the "Conglomerates," as he designated the denizens of the slums.(10)

Begg's first line of approach was through the promotion of credit societies to finance purchase of their own homes by manual workers. Among these elementary forms of the building society were the Scottish Property Investment Company, the first regular Scottish society (*c.* 1849) and the Provident Property Investment Company (1851). The former had £25 shares and 1s. entry money; they petitioned the Corporation without avail to "facilitate building for the working classes" (1850). On its model were framed Building Societies in most Scottish towns. Shares in the Provident Company could be obtained by fortnightly payments of 1s. These institutions were, however, more successful in stimulating the purchase of old houses than the building of new ones and under the existing scarcity tended to force up prices.(11) An "Edinburgh Building Association" issued a prospectus early in 1848; it aimed at 10,000 members paying 2d. a week; the impossibility of "good and cheap" houses was pointed out by critics.(12)

The device of reconditioning old tenements in the heart of the city was adopted by Dr. Robert Foulis in the private philanthropic venture described in his *Old Houses in Edinburgh* (1852). He purchased a block at Warden's (or Burt's) Close in the Grassmarket for £540, expended £247 on reconstruction, and let the accommodation at a total rental of £35 (varying from £8 10s. to £3 per unit) as against £31 10s. formerly; he cleared a return of 11 per cent. The renovated structure included nine dwellings, an unlicensed grocery, a coffee-house, a reading-room and a model lodging-house.(13)

A "meeting of leading citizens" suggested the development of this solution; at a subsequent meeting Dr. Begg asserted the practicability of erecting forty-eight houses of a good class per acre, and letting them at an average of £5 per annum.(14) D. M. Makgill Crichton of Rankeillour, a Fife laird and Free Church leader, and Councillor John Hope, w.s., an aristocratic Evangelical, also took part in agitation on the subject at this period.(15)

Several small-scale ventures in the building of working-class houses were launched in the 'forties and 'fifties. They usually sought to combine philanthropy with commercial success, a conjunction which William Chambers criticized as uneconomic.(16) Among the pioneers was Rev. William Mackenzie of North Leith Free Church, who was responsible for the erection of some model dwellings.(17) Inspired by his example, Rev. William Garden Blaikie, recently called to be first minister of a new Free Kirk at Pilrig, then an industrial hamlet between Edinburgh and Leith, devised a more ambitious project. Along with his brother-in-law, Robert Balfour, an insurance manager, William Chambers the publisher, and other prominent citizens, he formed the "Pilrig Model Dwellings Company" (1849). His chief difficulty was to obtain land, owing to the unwillingness of the Heriot Trust to give feus for such a purpose. A site was found on Leith Walk, and in thirteen years sixty-two cottage dwellings were built at a total cost of some £7,000. These were let at rents varying from £5 to £18, paid quarterly in advance. The Company earned regular dividends of 5 per cent, and was finally wound up in 1892.(18)

An Association for "Improving the Dwellings of the Industrious Classes" erected a tenement at John Knox's Corner, Canongate, to accommodate sixty families (c. 1852). In February 1853 it paid a dividend of 2½ per cent for the half-year.(19) Thirty-nine two-roomed houses at Ashley Buildings, Canongate, with rentals of £8, and some at Rosemount Buildings, let at £6 10s. to £8 10s., were also built by this or some similar association.(20)

Another notable scheme was a block of tenements at Abbeyhill; these still stand facing the King's Park, bearing conspicuously on the façade the title "Dr. Begg Buildings," in commemoration of that divine who laid the foundation-stone. They are described as an "adaptation of the French system"; they are five storeys high and comprise sixty two-apartment dwellings. The proprietor, Robert Cranston, an ex-Chartist and Temperance Hotel owner, enacted by-laws for his tenants and provided a washing-house and what Begg dignifies with the name of 'an infirmary and a library,' but the establishment was criticized as 'defective in conveniences.' (21)

A later enterprise was that of J. R. Findlay of the *Scotsman*, who in 1884 built on the Water of Leith at Dean, in the antique style but with modern equipment, a tenement of superior workmen's houses known as Well Court. Fifty in number, they were let at from £7 to £11 9s. and yielded £3 6s. per cent.(22)

Another line of approach was through voluntary co-operative effort by the working class. Of this Begg became a strong advocate, notably expressing his sympathy in a lecture delivered to the Scottish Social Reform Association on March 6, 1851, and afterwards published. He was impressed by the example given by Birmingham operatives, and with the aid of Chambers and McLaren he organized a series of tours through Scotland by James Taylor of that city, to promote similar schemes. He also prevailed on the Free Church Assembly (1858) to appoint a committee under his Convenership which issued five Reports on the subject. He claimed to have secured the insertion in the 1861 Census of a section relative to housing.(23)

On July 15, 1858, a "public meeting of the working classes" was held to discuss overcrowding. A committee was appointed and a report drawn up by its secretary, A. Macpherson, was issued two years later. The schemes already mentioned were deemed unsatisfactory, because of their cost and their situation too far from the centre. The increase of rentals, which had doubled within forty years, was demonstrated. A growing population was met with a shrinking acreage, owing to the clearance of condemned buildings, especially by the Commission of 1829, and encroachment by factories and railways (1832–41), e.g. by the "Railway Access Company" in the construction of Cockburn Street. "Building Societies," as already noted, had become mere savings agencies. Tenancy was preferred to freehold ownership, and the formation of a joint-stock company was proposed.(24) In November 1860 *Tait's*

Magazine published an article on "Working Men's Houses," by One Who Lives in Them, which advocated a Building Society of Workers, financed by Government loans.(25)

These projects perhaps foreshadowed the most important and enduring experiment in co-operative house-building in Edinburgh. This was an outcome of the three months' strike for the eight-hour day in the spring of 1861. Some of the operatives thus rendered idle formed an Association with the active support of George Lorimer, a master builder, George Troup, then editing the *Witness*, and Hugh Gilzean Reid of the *Weekly News* (afterwards a well-known newspaper proprietor and Liberal M.P. in North-Eastern England). An example cited by Reid was that of a French Association of Masons, who had erected buildings at Mulhouse in 1848.(26)

The "Edinburgh Co-operative Building Co. Ltd." was registered under the Limited Liability Act just passed (1861); the Articles of Association are dated June 28, 1861. Seven masons were the original subscribers and the rules provided for a majority of building operatives among the ordinary directors. (This provision was not repealed until 1920.) It was also stipulated that the first year's profits should be turned into shares, but thereafter they were to be distributed. The duration of the Company was fixed at fifteen years. The capital was to be £10,000 in £1 shares.(27)

Shares at first went slowly, and a crowded public meeting was held on November 25th to promote their sale. William Chambers presided, and Revs. Dr. Begg and Nisbet spoke in support, while Rev. William Graham described a house-building experiment by Newhaven fishermen (as he had done the previous year to the Social Science Association). The object was achieved; while the original shareholders (some seventy) were chiefly workers, sympathizers, such as those mentioned, and Duncan McLaren were among the subscribers.(28)

Meantime the foundation-stone of the first building had been laid at Water Lane, Canonmills, with great ceremony by Dr. Begg (October 23rd).(29) The usual difficulty about land was partly obviated by Chambers's influence with the Heriot Trust, and a large number of dwellings were erected in different parts of the city, chiefly on the outskirts—e.g. Abbeyhill, Restalrig, and Stockbridge. The usual type was a "double-flatted" two-storey erection, the upper and lower storeys forming separate houses, entered from opposite sides; a block, prominently inscribed with the name of the Company (1869), was till 1934 a conspicuous sight at Norton Park opposite the Abbey Church. The object being occupying ownership, houses were usually sold on completion; the original prices were £130 to £250 for houses of from three to six apartments. Loans were at first obtained from the Property Investment Societies, but in 1871 a "partial payment" or instalment purchase scheme was inaugurated, which enabled obligations to be discharged normally in twenty-one years, interest being charged at 5 per cent. Deposits were also received, withdrawable at a month's notice, and yielding 3½ per cent.(30)

Much interest was taken in the venture, which was described to the Social Science Association at its Edinburgh meeting in 1863 by Dr. Begg and Gilzean Reid; a paper was also read by James Gowans of Edinburgh on "Recent Improvements in the Construction of Dwelling Houses." (31) Mr. Johnston quotes references from the contemporary Press, but professes ignorance of its subsequent history; he speaks of Lorimer as a Chartist, but the only builder of that name traceable was a Conservative Councillor, who as Dean of Guild perished at the destruction by fire of the Theatre Royal in January 1865.(32)

The Company continued to prosper, but soon lost its co-operative character. Shares became "safe and lucrative invest-ments," and dividends usually ranging between 7½ and 12½ per cent were paid. The Company undertook all sorts of jobbing work, and owing to difficulties about woodwork did all its own joinery. In 1870 it was put on a permanent basis by an amend-ment of its Constitution, and in 1880 a reserve fund was insti-tuted. Despite the scarcity of suitable sites and the restrictions imposed in feus, it made steady progress in building houses to sell or let.(33)

James Colville, formerly President of the Masons' Union, was manager from the beginning till 1889; his death in January 1892 evoked a note in the *Scotsman* on the history of the

Company. He gave evidence to the Royal Commission on Housing (1884–85). Some 1,400 houses had by that time been built, with rentals assessed at £11 to £25. In the depression of that period the Company was less active than hitherto, employing some sixty to seventy men against a maximum of 250, and paying 7d. an hour to masons as compared with 10d. in 1877–78, though the former figure was still a halfpenny above the usual rate. Colville again complained of the excessive cost of land, owing to feu duties and legal expenses.(34) The Scottish Housing Commission of 1912–17 made reference to the Company when considering the possibilities of co-operative enterprise in house-building; but passed from it with the comment that it had "for many years ceased to provide houses within the means even of better-paid artisans." (35) The Edinburgh scheme was taken as a model by Copenhagen workmen, and was investigated by the Danish Government; the co-operative building society method seems to have flourished more in the land of its adoption than at home.(36)

Similar societies were formed in Edinburgh; one soon failed, but a "City of Edinburgh Association" had at least initial success.(37) Later, a "Blackfriars Building Association," consisting of twenty-four working-men, built two tenements off the Canongate to rehouse members of the "industrious classes" displaced by the 1867 Clearance Scheme.(38)

Glasgow and Dundee followed later.(39) In the lesser burghs, small co-operative housing societies emerged from time to time. One is said to have commenced in Kilmarnock so early as 1824 "to erect houses on a uniform plan" for its eighty-one shareholders; the earliest in Galashiels was founded in 1846 by William Sanderson, a prominent co-operator and Radical.(40) There was a society in Falkirk consisting almost entirely of operatives; it formed three new streets of semi-detached cottages with gardens which became the individual properties of its members.(41) Associations were started in the 'sixties and 'seventies in Dumbarton, Grangemouth, and Hawick; the first had about two hundred members, its chief achievement being Knoxland Square in 1882.(42) These were still in existence at the end of the century; together with

Falkirk they had erected a total of over 1,500 houses, chiefly of two storeys with internal stairs.(43) In Dalkeith a Co-operative Building Society existed from 1863 to 1876; it was of the temporary type, being wound up as soon as it had completed and paid off its allotted quota of fifty houses; a second on a more extensive scale was formed in 1879. The first was organized by a shoemaker, and got on favourable terms land forming part of the glebe.(44)

In some colliery areas, small co-operative societies were formed by the miners themselves. At Larkhall, according to Mr. Smillie, they dated back to the era of Waterloo, the first being founded by ex-soldiers of the Napoleonic Wars, or according to another version in preparation for their demobilization. The societies were of a temporary character, and were dissolved when they had provided for all their members; priority depended on the luck of the ballot. The money was found locally, sometimes from a single lender, and 3½ per cent was usually paid.(45) At Shotts they originated about 1842; the ordinary payment was 2s. 6d. a week.(46) Another notable case was that of the secluded lead-mining village of Leadhills, where three-fourths of the employees owned their houses.(47)

At Chapel Hill Ironworks, near Airdrie, many houses were built by the operatives; ground was feued from the proprietor, who advanced half the cost; the accommodation comprised room and kitchen, with a garden.(48) About 1876 shipyard workers in the rapidly rising Clydebank, "by the aid of a building society erected two rows of neat cottages. . . . The foundation and memorial stones of the edifices were laid with masonic honours." (49)

Inverness joiners on strike established a Trade Building Company. The Associated Carpenters and Joiners of Scotland lent it £200 at 5 per cent on their bond, their main object being to absorb labour and so to avoid paying strike benefit. It was registered as a joint-stock company and was not profit-sharing nor confined to operatives.(50)

One further effort at producers' co-operation in the building trades was the West of Scotland Painting Company, established by the Operative Painters in Glasgow in 1860, also during a strike, at the instigation of the veteran Owenite Alexander Campbell. Two hundred pounds was subscribed in share capital by the Union, and business was carried on for a time with fair success, but owing to a boycott of its members by employers, the Company was wound up.(51)

St. Cuthbert's Co-operative Association, Edinburgh, and a few other retail societies in the smaller burghs also built and let a few houses, but only incidentally to shop accommodation, and not as a regular policy. Their main contribution took the form of loans to their members for house purchase.(52)

A further method of dealing with the problem was by municipal enterprise. An Act of 1855, sponsored by Alexander Murray Dunlop, Liberal M.P. for Greenock, an advocate and leading Free Churchman, and designed to "facilitate the Erection of Dwelling Houses for the Working Classes in Scotland" by giving powers to acquire and demolish dilapidated properties, remained inoperative.(53) The 'sixties saw a growth of the civic conscience in this respect, startled and stimulated by the crash of an Edinburgh tenement in the High Street in November 1861,(54) and by such investigations as those of William Anderson of the *Courant* (1867).(55) The precedent of the rather negative Improvements Scheme of 1827 was followed on a larger scale and with more satisfactory results in the Act of 1867 by which William Chambers signalized his Lord Provostship. Under its provisions the Town Council as Trustees were empowered to acquire property compulsorily, to form new streets, to erect or lease houses to the value of £10,000 for evicted tenants, and to levy an assessment up to 4d. in the pound. Some "2,800 unwholesome houses" were demolished in the Old Town, and over half a million pounds expended. The cleared areas were in practice sold or feued, and rebuilding was left to private enterprise.(56) The first improved tenements built in St. Mary Street, Canongate, still bear witness to the achievement. Municipal housing was opposed by the President of Edinburgh Trades Council before the Housing Commission (1884–85); he advocated cheap loans by the State and compulsory acquisition of land.(57)

Dundee also carried out slum clearance under an Improvement Act (1871), but left building entirely to individual effort.(58) Greenock Corporation bought land under the "Cross" Housing Act of 1875 (1876–77), but failed to rehouse evicted occupants.(59) Leith conducted a survey in 1870, but two successive schemes were rejected on the ground of cost, and it was only after nine years' delay that a "more modest" project was adopted. The expenditure was estimated at £100,000, of which half was borrowed from the Public Works Commissioners (1881). Proceedings were at first dilatory; the local historian, however, asserts that the Improvement Scheme "swept away the greater part of the slums." (60)

In Glasgow also progress was chiefly due to the public authority, by a coincidence led again by a publisher, Lord Provost John Blackie (1805–73). The Glasgow Improvements Act of 1866 constituted the City Council as a Trust for the clearance of congested areas (about ninety acres) and the rehousing of the dispossessed. Loans of one and a quarter million pounds were authorized for the purpose. The Trust had powers to acquire property compulsorily, but preferred to act by private negotiation; it did not at first exercise its option to engage in rebuilding.(61) On the first imposition of a 6d. rate in furtherance of its activities, Blackie for his pains was rejected at the poll by the incensed ratepayers after a bitter contest, though only by a majority of two (154–156), (November 1866).(62)

Areas were dealt with piecemeal and as units to preclude speculation. Incidentally, most of Glasgow's remaining historic buildings were demolished. Thirty thousand inhabitants were displaced. The progress of the scheme was described in articles in the *Glasgow Herald* in June 1870.(63)

After the initial enthusiasm effort stagnated (*c.* 1877–89), and the optimism of Robert Gillespie of the *Evening Star*, who in 1876 affirmed "slums we have none," was distinctly premature.(64) Only about sixty houses were built by the Corporation, and many of the old properties acquired were left standing. The commercial crisis of 1878 and its consequences furnished a pretext for inaction. "At the end of this period of *laissez-faire*, the properties still in the hands of the Trustees

were probably the worst and most insanitary in the city." (65)
One effect of the depression was that property owners were
without a profitable market for their land; like them, the
Improvements Trust "held for a rise." (66) At the same time
the encroachment of railways, docks, and shipyards on inhabited
areas and the conversion of some better-class dwellings into
business offices increased the congestion, while speculative
building at inflated values had merely intensified the crash
precipitated by the City of Glasgow Bank failure.(67)

In 1888, thanks to such reformers as Bailie Samuel Chisholm
and Dr. J. B. Russell, City Medical Officer of Health (1872–
98), activities were resumed, and most of the scheduled areas
were reconstructed by the end of the century. By 1890 a net
cost of nearly a million pounds had been incurred, three-fourths
of which fell on the ratepayers; about half of the gross expenditure had been recovered by the sale of properties acquired.
Further powers were obtained by an Act of 1897.(68) By 1909
the Corporation had built well over 2,000 houses, "all in blocks
and centrally situated, occupied chiefly by artisans; only 28
per cent have been reserved for the poorest class of
tenants." (69)

The Glasgow Landlords' Association and Association of
House Factors in Glasgow, the "oldest and largest of its class
in Scotland," wrote to the Housing Commission (1884–85)
regarding demolition by the Improvements Trust and by
Railway Companies. They stated that the yearly average of
unoccupied houses had in recent years been nearly 10,000, and
considered that the supply was adequate; hence there was no
necessity for public or other building.(70) Their sanguine outlook was not universally shared by more disinterested citizens.
Dr. Donald Macleod, brother of the better-known Norman,
sought to awaken concern in the Church. In the Assembly of
1888 he moved an Overture from Glasgow Presbytery in a
speech which was republished under the title of "Non-Churchgoing and the Housing of the Poor." He demonstrated that
30 per cent of the houses still consisted of one room, and were
occupied by one-fourth of the population; the mortality
rate was thirty-eight.(71) In consequence, a Committee

on the Housing of the Poor was set up, which existed till 1891.(72)

The Kyrle Society (1877) and the Glasgow Social Union (1890) also interested themselves in the question; the former organized hygiene classes and relief work, and experimented in the then fashionable "slumming" expedient of appointing supervisory rent collectors.(73) Among the more practical efforts of private philanthropy were the Suburban Dwellings Company (1870), the creation of Lord Provost Sir James Watson, and of Thomas Corbett, an Australian merchant, whose establishment of "Cooking Depots" to provide cheap meals also won him renown as a social reformer.(74) In April 1890 the "Glasgow Workmen's Dwellings Company" was established, "for the purpose of providing healthy and comfortable dwellings for the working classes." It had a capital of £50,000 and dividends were limited to 5 per cent. Among the Directors were the industrial magnates Sir James King, Bart., (Chairman) and Sir Charles Tennant, Professors Gilbert Murray and James Mavor, and J. G. A. Baird, M.P. (of the Gartsherrie family), with Daniel M. Stevenson, afterwards Lord Provost, as Secretary. It constructed two hundred houses and was deemed to be of "real importance." (75)

These efforts were, however, infinitesimal in proportion to the problem, and neither by charitable intention nor by the socio-political revival of the 'eighties was any effective motive force engendered.

SCOTLAND AT THE END OF THE
NINETEENTH CENTURY

SCOTLAND in the 'nineties had sustained many material changes from the Scotland of sixty years before. The relative quiescence of the late Victorian period makes effective comparison easier; the Great Depression had apparently been surmounted, the renewed rumblings of class strife had softened, and international rivalry had not reached the acute phase which precipitated havoc early in the next century. Perhaps the most fundamental transformation lay in the gradual and imperceptible development by which Scotland was converted from a virtually self-sustaining unit to an essential component of Great Britain; its distinctive features from the economic standpoint thus became regional rather than national.

The constitutional structure had been modified, in relation to the United Kingdom, only by the restoration of the Secretaryship for Scotland (1885), and in general only by the successive extensions of the franchise (1867, 1884). A half-century's devotion to Liberalism had been somewhat shaken by the Irish Home Rule controversy.

In local administration, however, vital changes had been accomplished. The Poor Law Act of 1845 had set the model for the establishment of a series of elective bodies, predominantly *ad hoc* in character, constituting a complexity of areas and of functions. Of these the School Boards (1872) and the County Councils (1889) were the most important. The creation of burghs had also been carried to an excessive degree, over a hundred small communities being thus dignified within the latter half of the century, most flagrantly in the suburbs of Glasgow; extension of boundaries was the natural retort of the larger towns. A dyarchy of Town Council and Police Commissioners survived at least nominally in some Royal Burghs until a Consolidating Act of 1900.(1)

The population of Scotland in 1891 was a little over four millions, of whom almost exactly two-thirds were town dwellers. Lanarkshire was the most populous area, numbering over one million inhabitants, of whom some 600,000 may be reckoned as citizens of Glasgow; the complex and varied boundaries of local government preclude an exact figure. About a quarter of a million were still engaged in agriculture; about 180,000 were included in the rather widely defined "commercial group" (which embraced 26,284 on the railways); "industry" claimed rather over one million, of whom nearly three-fourths were males.(2) We have nothing comparable to the Statistical Accounts for this period, but the Reports of the Royal Commissions on Depression of Trade (1886) and on Labour (1892–94) incidentally provide considerable information illustrative of industrial conditions.

The cotton industry had long since become relatively negligible; the American Civil War dealt a final blow to its hopes. The famous mills at Deanston and a few factories in the East End of Glasgow represented the once dominant trade. Printing and dyeing, though coming under the control of English combines, still flourished, and thread-making, in the hands of the now amalgamated firms of Coats and Clark, had become one of the most gigantic and profitable of British enterprises. Three thousand two hundred and forty-five men and 13,188 women were employed in the manufacture of cotton, which had thus fallen to the lowest rank among textiles.(3)

In the textiles generally, in strong contrast with the rising heavy industries, there was a marked preponderance of female labour. Wool, linen, and jute were running a fairly even race for supremacy, at least as regards the provision of employment. The first still led, and was most equally divided between the sexes—13,300 men to 17,200 women; in linen 19,200 women and in jute 21,500 outbalanced a male contingent of some seven to eight thousand in either case.(3)

The heavy industries had definitely displaced the textiles as the "secret of Scotland's greatness." This was indeed but one example of a world trend, in which capital goods rather than consumptional goods become the characteristic basis of industry; this is sometimes regarded as indicating a new phase of capitalist development.

Iron manufacture gave employment to 35,000; steel as yet to little over 4,000. Among kindred industries may be noted 13,000 engine and machine-makers, 17,000 fitters and turners, 10,000 boiler-makers, and 13,000 iron shipwrights; in all these groups women constituted but a handful. The mining group numbered 74,000 engaged in the extraction of coal, 5,000 in shale, and now under 3,000 in ironstone—a considerable fall during the decade.(4) (Of 7,360 foreigners domiciled in Scotland, about five hundred were Poles, chiefly connected with Lanarkshire coalfields.) (5)

The concentration of these industries on the Clyde had made much more emphatic the economic dominance of Glasgow, around which a network of towns and villages—some an expansion of ancient foundations, e.g. Paisley, Hamilton, Dumbarton; others mushroom growths, e.g. Motherwell, Clydebank—had grown up as exclusively economic units, designed to provide a maximum of production and a minimum of livelihood in anything but the most material sense.

Marine engineering, the peculiar glory of the Clyde, evolved from the pioneer efforts of the Napier cousins and the Elders, father and son; a large proportion of the firms so engaged were the creation of men trained in their yards.(6) The final triumph of the Clyde, the transfer of Yarrows from the Thames, was delayed till next century (1906).(7) The tonnage annually launched on the Clyde had risen to over 400,000 in the 'eighties.(8)

Among minor industries a relative newcomer was the manufacture of linoleum, commenced in 1847 at Kirkcaldy by the firm of Nairn, which thus gave a fresh economic repute to the birthplace of Adam Smith.(9) A late application of machinery to textiles initiated the lace manufacture of the Irvine Valley (Ayrshire), introduced about 1870 by Alexander Morton of Darvel and Joseph Hood of Newmilns.(10)

The "romance of modern science" in its industrial aspect was signally illustrated by the rise of the shale oil manufacture and its by-products, largely the creation of James Young, the "Sir Paraffin" of his fellow-student and lifelong friend David Livingstone.(11) The gradual transition from the age of iron to

P

the age of steel, especially in shipbuilding, which commenced in the 'seventies, was also a triumph of scientific investigation; the introduction of the Bessemer process is associated with the disputed claims of Robert Mushet, son of the discoverer of the blackband ore.(12) Lord Kelvin, long doyen of the Glasgow Professorate, is identified with the adaptation of research in physics to commercial uses.(13)

Railway expansion, after the hectic phase of the 'forties, proceeded somewhat fitfully, but by the end of the century all Scotland was linked up, most dramatically, by the contruction of the Forth and Tay Bridges; by successive amalgamations a measure of order had been imposed on the primitive chaos. The North British, Caledonian, Glasgow and South-Western, Highland, and Great North of Scotland virtually shared internal transport; canal traffic had become of little account, and the competition of road motors was not yet imagined.(14)

The shipping of the East Coast ports, notably Leith, Dundee, and Aberdeen, had continued to grow, and more purely industrial outlets such as Grangemouth and the new-born Methil also flourished; but for world commerce the Clyde was again paramount. To the Cunard had been added such lines as the City (1840), the Allan (1852), the Anchor (1856), and the Clan (1878).(15) The Clyde Trust, established in 1858, did much to make a river not favoured by nature a suitable resort for ocean traffic; its revenue rose to £350,000 a year.(16) The organization of a lighthouse service, with which as well as with romantic literature is associated the family of Stevenson, had ensured greater safety of navigation. The tonnage cleared in Scottish ports had quadrupled in the thirty years 1850 to 1880, rising from 5 to 20 millions. Imports in the same period rose from 9 to 38 millions, exports from 5 to 21 million pounds.(17) Inter-imperial trade was furthered, and the bounds of empire sometimes extended, as in the part played in the settlement and annexation of Nyasaland by the African Lakes Corporation and the activities of Sir William Mackinnon in Zanzibar. Scots were also to the fore in the older centres of trade in the Orient, and the newer of South America; Arthur

Anderson and Donald Currie are among the promoters of British maritime supremacy.

The Scottish banks, now reconciled to Peel's restrictive Acts of 1844–45, obeyed the world-wide tendency to concentration, a process perhaps accelerated by successive crises, especially the collapse of the Western Bank in 1857 and that of the City of Glasgow in 1878. Bonds with England were strengthened by the opening of branches across the Border (c. 1870), an "invasion" at first much resented,(18) and by the acceptance from 1863 of the Bank of England rate as a general guide to Scottish charges.(19) Small-scale local and private banking disappeared; the banks surviving in 1900 were the Bank of Scotland, the Royal, Commercial, National, Union, Clydesdale, Caledonian, Town and County, and North of Scotland.(20)

A growth of retail distribution is manifest. The "universal provider" had its early Scottish exemplar in John Anderson (c. 1845), founder of the Polytechnic emporium in Glasgow, followed towards the close of the century by Walter Wilson and his Colosseum. Sir Thomas Lipton also began in Glasgow his career as creator of the multiple store. The small individual enterprise, however, retained its vitality and supremacy in the consumptive trades.

In manufacturing industry the enactment of limited liability (1862) had fostered the growth of the joint-stock company, and the trend of economic development had been towards the larger unit, with the elimination or absorption of competitors. The combined firm of Coats and Clark in Paisley (1896) carried this process to the verge of monopoly. Not far behind were the Distillers Company Ltd. (1877), the United Alkali Company (1890), the United Turkey Red Company (1898), and the Calico Printers Association (1899); the Imperial Tobacco Company was an early offspring of the new century, swallowing the chief Glasgow firms.(21) The large-scale unit without a monopoly is illustrated chiefly by heavy industry, in firms like the Bairds of Gartsherrie, the Beardmores of Parkhead, and the Dennys of Dumbarton.

Transformation into joint-stock form is most noteworthy in the case of coal-mining, which had in most cases been carried on by small contractors, or in the East by the ground landlord. Other well-known enterprises like the Cunard Company (1878), the Fairfield Shipbuilding Company (1886), and Sir William Arrol & Co. (1893) were nominally converted, but effective control and to a large degree shareholding seem to have remained in the same hands. The establishment of Stock Exchanges in the cities, preoccupied at first with railway speculation, had latterly facilitated soberer investment, while investment trusts and kindred organizations offered better outlets for small savings; thus Scotland contributed perceptibly to the export of capital.

Agriculture had undergone much technical change. Primitive institutions—runrig, triple rotation, self-contained economy— were just disappearing in the remoter areas. Drainage became common; the use of artificial fertilizers and ensilage became known; reaping and mowing machines had become general by the middle of the century. Cattle and sheep rearing displaced much arable; wheat production declined by one-fourth between 1863 and 1893. Dairy and fruit farming, especially in Ayrshire and the Clyde Valley, were encouraged by the growing demand of the industrial population. Rents tended to rise between 1850 and 1880, until large-scale importation from the New World provoked general depression.(22)

Some minor modifications in the peculiarly complicated Scots land law had been effected by legislation; the Rutherford Act of 1848 and the Dunlop Act of 1860 relaxed the stringency of entail,(23) and the Conveyancing Act of 1874, though ostensibly intended only to simplify the forms of titles, altered the "substantial rights of parties" in effect, and so occasioned much litigation.(24) The Ground Game Act (1880), the abolition of Hypothec—i.e. the landlord's prior claim for rent against other creditors—and the Agricultural Holdings Act (1883) were designed in the interest of the tenant farmer.(25) William McCombie in Aberdeenshire and George Hope in East Lothian were noted representatives of the best type of agriculturist, distinguished in public as well as in business life.

The Highlands remained, perhaps to an increasing degree, an area apart. By persistent emigration, congestion was relieved to the pitch of depopulation, but economic life stagnated. Belatedly legislative action, stimulated by a renewal of agrarian disturbance in the early 'eighties, had endeavoured after exhaustive inquiry by a Royal Commission to safeguard the position of the crofter by the Act of 1886 which gave him security of tenure, fair rents and compensation for improvements.(26) While material standards were improved, the drift from the countryside was not appreciably checked, and the imposition on the Highlands of an administrative system designed for Lowland requirements handicapped recovery.(27)

Laissez-faire and individual enterprise remained the accepted bases of economic activity, and the long surviving patriarchalism had become obsolescent. Minor encroachments had been made by factory and other social legislation, but these present no specifically Scottish features, and are indeed an indication of the growing absorption in "Great Britain" of Scottish economic life.

Scottish Trade Unionism, affected by the general trend of economic development, now found its chief sphere in the heavy rather than in the textile industries, but it had received no marked impetus from the ferment of the 'eighties. Sporadically active for two generations in mining, in the constructional industries it was better organized but quiescent in policy. Trades Councils in the larger centres had won a recognized place in local life.

The co-operative movement was reborn in Scotland in the 'sixties, and had gone from strength to strength by concentration on limited practical schemes of retail distribution and subsequent wholesale manufacture (1868). Occasional experiments in co-operative production had little more success than in the days of Owen. The hardheaded and God-fearing men who now guided its destinies had little in common with the secularist visions of its prophet, whose pristine idealism was reflected only in an enduring concern for education fostered by the Co-operative Union (1828).(28)

Friendly Societies were widespread, and in the absence of State provision shared the field of "mutual insurance" against the risks of working life with the Trade Unions and "industrial" insurance companies (chiefly English); large national societies, some also located in England, were to some extent displacing the small local group.

Public Health, after its initial setback by the spread of the congested urban slum, had improved considerably in later decades through the development of municipal government and the enlightened zeal of officials like Dr. J. B. Russell of Glasgow and Sir Henry Littlejohn of Edinburgh.(29) Glasgow's "Epic of Municipalization," the Loch Katrine Water Scheme (1859), is the most spectacular instance of a reviving municipal patriotism.(30) Housing conditions, despite the recurrent agitation and effort, chiefly on philanthropic lines, remained deplorable. Even the City Improvement Schemes of Glasgow and Edinburgh in the 'sixties had only grazed the problem, and in the provision of this elementary need of civilized life private enterprise scored its worst failure.

Culturally, despite the undoubted improvement in material conditions of life, Scotland had marked time. The effects of the educational revolution of the 'seventies had hardly had time to reveal themselves; the reform of the Universities, especially under the Act of 1858,(31) had doubtless raised the general level of instruction, but inspired no outburst of genius. The Mechanics' Institutes had ceased to be an effective force, and the new University Extension courses were limited in their appeal.(32) The political organization of the working class, revived by Keir Hardie with Socialist aims, was at the stage of a novel heresy.(33)

Scottish men of letters, like Macaulay and Carlyle, were Scottish in origin rather than in product, in mannerism rather than in substance; the purely Scottish output in literature all but degenerated into parochialism. The vigorous if ephemeral crop of journals that had flourished in the early part of the century had almost disappeared by its close; the newspaper Press was also becoming centralized and stereotyped. Perhaps the Scottish intellect was finding its best expression in the sciences, notably geology and surgery.

The disruption had been the culmination of schismatic tendencies in the Scottish Church, and the movement for consolidation was advancing. It is perhaps significant of its lessened vitality that the acute controversies, intellectual and social, of the later period excited little but a few personal "heresy hunts" directed against the more indiscreet innovators. The secularization of the education of the young and of the care of the poor had deprived the Church of much of its direct influence on social life, though Chalmers had impressed its civic duties on a whole generation, and many of the clergy were active in local administration.(34)

Scotland thus lacked the intellectual and moral leadership which the Church had given in the past, and which statesmen and publicists provided in other lands; consequently its industrial development during the Victorian Age suggests the successful elaboration of means towards an end unknown and unconsidered.

REFERENCES

SCOTLAND AT THE COMMENCEMENT OF THE VICTORIAN AGE

1. A. URE, *Philosophy of Manufactures*, 80.
2. BAINES, *Cotton Manufacture*, 390; *Manufactures of West of Scotland* (British Assoc., 1876), 198.
3. R. BROWN, *Flax*, 2nd Edn. (1851).
4. Ibid., 38.
5. A. J. WARDEN, *Linen Industry*, 592–94.
6. Ibid., 607.
7. Ibid., 564; W. NORRIE, *Dundee Celebrities*, 231–33; cf. *Factory Inquiry*, 1st Report, 11.
8. JEANS, *Iron Trade*, 22; cf. SCRIVENER, *Iron Industry*, 295–97.
9. PAGAN, *History of Glasgow*, 91–92; SCRIVENER, *Iron Trade*, 134; cf. STRANG, a. *Proc. Brit. Assocn.* (1855), 193–94; MUSHET, *Iron and Steel*, 424.
10. G. MACINTOSH, *Life of C. Macintosh*, 37, 102; *Manufactures W. of Scotland*, ut sup., 222–23.
11. *Report from Asst. Commrs. on Hand-loom Weavers* (1839).
12. J. FRANCIS, *English Railways*, II, 18–29; H. G. LEWIN, *Early British Railways*, passim.
13. A. W. KERR, *Banking in Scotland*, 223.
14. IRVING, *Eminent Scotsmen*, 538.
15. W. NORRIE, *Dundee Celebrities*, 152.
16. *Comparative Account of Population*, 1801–31, 367–406.
17. *Scottish Educational Journal*, Sept. 12, 1930; "P. Colquhoun."
18. Ibid., Feb. 26, 1932, "A. Campbell."
19. Ibid., Oct. 3, 1930, "H. Duncan"; cf. R. CAMPBELL, "Provident Institutions," 212–14; S. HALL, H. Duncan, 56–75.
20. *Scottish Educational Journal*, Jan. 29, 1932, "W. P. Alison"; cf. J. GLASSE, Pauperism in Scotland, 17–27.
21. J. W. HARPER, *Social Ideal and Dr. Chalmers' Contribution*; G. C. WOOD, *Chalmers and the Poor Law*.
22. W. P. ALISON, *Observations on Management of Poor* (1840), Preface.
23. *Poor Law Commn. Local Reports on Sanitary Condition* (1842).
24. E.g. JESSOP, *Education in Angus*.
25. *Journal of Adult Education*, VI, 3 (Oct. 1933), 292–309.

I. LANDOWNERSHIP

I. MINERAL VALUES

1. J. U. NEF, *Rise of British Coal Industry*, II, 6–8.
2. A. CUNNINGHAM, *Mining in Mid- and East-Lothian*, ch. viii; CARRICK, *Abbey of Newbottle*, 87–94.
3. A. CUNNINGHAM, *Mining in Fife*, 45–9; id., *Culross*, 95–7.
4. *Old Country Houses of Glasgow Gentry*, 41; *Glasgow Past and Present*, 56–64.
5. *New Statistical Account*, VI, 376–8.
6. A. GEIKIE, *Scottish Reminiscences*, 185–6.
7. *Scottish Notes and Queries*, 3rd ser., III (1925), 132.
8. GEIKIE, op. cit., 190–3.
9. CUNNINGHAM, *Mining in Lothian*, ch. xvii, xxi.
10. CUNNINGHAM, *Mining in Fife*, 45–7; *Memoir of R. G. E. Wemyss*, 50–4, 150.
11. CUNNINGHAM, *Mining in Lothian*, 112–13; *Stock Exchange Intelligencer* (1933), 1503.
12. *Royal Comm. on Mining Royalties* (1890–91), 2nd Report, 98–106.
13. Ibid., 73–81.
14. Ibid., 94–6; *Scotsman*, June 11, 1934.
15. Ibid., 97–8.
16. Ibid., 68–73.
17. Ibid., 1st Report, 192–3.
18. MILNE, *Lothian Coalfields*, 144.
19. H. KEDDIE, *Three Generations*, 127–9, 142–4, 147.
20. *Hundred Glasgow Men*, 13–20; MACGEORGE, *Bairds of Gartsherrie*, 29–33, 45–51.
21. MACARTHUR, *New Monkland*, 281; 360–3.
22. CHALMERS, *Dunfermline*, I, 49.
23. Ibid., I, 42; II, 92; CUNNINGHAM, *Mining in Fife*, 49; *Return of Owners of Land* (1874), Fife.
24. "SENEX," *Old Glasgow*, 61–3.
25. *Scotsman*, Nov. 15, 1933.
26. MACLEOD, *Dumbarton*, 134; IRVING, *Dumbartonshire*, III, 357.
27. RAIT, *Union Bank*, 43–4; G. STEWART, *Curiosities of Glasgow Citizenship*, ch. i; J. O. MITCHELL, *Old Glasgow Essays*, 164–75.
28. *Land Return*, ut sup., *Lanarkshire*; MILLER, *Coatbridge*, 95–7; MACARTHUR, *New Monkland*, 202–4.
29. *Land Return*, ut sup.; MILLER, op. cit., 30–4; MACARTHUR, op. cit., 188–91; MACGEORGE, *Bairds of Gartsherrie*, 77; IRVING, *Dumbartonshire*, III, 346–7.
30. Ibid.; NIMMO, *Stirlingshire* (1880), I, 395–6; II, 259–60; GILLESPIE, *Falkirk*, 263–4.

31. Ibid.; NIMMO, op. cit., II, 260–1; 279.
32. Ibid., MILLER, *Coatbridge*, 109–15.
33. NIMMO, *Stirlingshire*, II, 272; MACGEORGE, *Bairds of Gartsherrie*, 55, 78–9.
34. *Land Return*, passim; cf. *New Statistical Account*, V, 328.
35. *Commn. on Coal* (1871), C. 47 and seq.
36. *Royal Commn. on Mining Royalties*, 1st Report, 192–3; cf. *Scottish Land Report* (1914), 339–40.
37. *Royal Commn. on Trade Depression*, Final Report, Appendix A; 2nd Report, Appendix D.
38. *Royal Commn. on Mining Royalties*, 2nd Report, 107–12, 124–9, 323–8.
39. FORSYTH, *Beauties of Scotland*, I, 269.
40. GALLOWAY, *Annals of Coalmining*, 2nd ser., 230.
41. J. URQUHART, *Memoir of W. H. Gillespie*, 67, 97–105; H. M. CADELL, *The Forth*, 199–202; R. GILLESPIE, *Falkirk*, 343–6; CROAL, *Recollections*, 108–10; "James Young" (*Scotsman*, May 31, 1933); *Scottish News*, May 11, 1886.
42. *Scotsman*, ut sup., and May 31, 1894; BREMNER, *Industries of Scotland*, 484–5; LEARMONTH, *West Calder*, 66–7; 137–41; *Scottish Bankers' Magazine*, IV, 281–8.
43. MILLER, *Coatbridge*, 104–8; MURPHY, *Captains of Industry*, 145–9.
44. NIMMO, *Stirlingshire*, II, 261–2.
45. PATERSON, *Counties of Ayrshire and Wigton* (art. "St. Quivox"), I, pt. ii, 671.
46. *New Statistical Account*, VI, 617–19; *Hundred Glasgow Men*, 166.

II. SITE VALUES

1. W. CHAMBERS, *Improved Dwelling Houses* (1855), 7; cf. *Scottish Land Report*, 288–320.
2. I. F. GRANT, *Economic Development of Scotland*, 265.
3. Ibid., 285; cf.; FORSYTH, *Beauties of Scotland*, III, 540–3.
4. *Scottish Land Report*, liii, 330.
5. *Municipal Glasgow* (1914), 21.
6. GORDON, *Glasghu Facies*, 1128; cf. *British Association (Glasgow) Proceedings* (1840), 174–5; GALLOWAY, *William Harley*, 21–8, 60.
7. JOHNSTON, *Our Noble Families*, 12–18; "SENEX," *Old Glasgow*, 111–16; GORDON, ut sup., 468–74; *Glasgow Past and Present*, 316–25.
8. GORDON, ut sup., 1128.
9. *Old Country Houses of Glasgow Gentry*, 246; W. SIMPSON, *Glasgow in 1840*, xxxv; *Glasgow Past and Present*, 132.
10. C. TAYLOR, *Partick*, 116–17.
11. *Old Country Houses*, 24.

12. SIMPSON, *Glasgow in 1850*, xii; GORDON, *Glasghu Facies*, 1137.

13. J. O. MITCHELL, *Old Glasgow Essays*, 346.

14. *Glasghu Facies*, 1137.

15. *Memoirs of Hundred Glasgow Men*, 33–5; *Memoir of Thomas Binnie*, 79; but cf. J. ORD, *Gorbals*, 57–8; *Glasgow Past and Present*, 146–7.

16. *Hundred Glasgow Men*, 277–8.

17. Ibid., 99–101; *Old Country Houses*, 65; GORDON, *Glasghu Facies*, 771–6; *Glasgow Past and Present*, 39; *Glasgow Herald*, May 17, 1930.

18. ACWORTH, *Scottish Railways*, 104.

19. J. B. FLEMING, *John Park Fleming*, 34–8; *Hundred Glasgow Men*, 139–40; *Glasgow Past and Present*, 79.

20. *Old Country Houses*, 122; COUTTS, *University of Glasgow*, 443–4.

21. *Landowners' Return* (1874), sub *Glasgow*.

22. GROOME, *Ordnance Gazetteer*, I, 412.

23. *Scotsman*, Sept. 5, 1904; *Edinburgh and the Lothians* (Pike's New Century Series), 326.

24. CHAMBERS, *Improved Dwelling Houses*, 7.

25. B. BALFOUR-MELVILLE, *The Balfours of Pilrig*, 245–6; *Scotsman*, June 14, 1901; *Proceedings Old Edinburgh Club*, X, 32–5.

26. *Landowners' Return* (1874), sub *Edinburgh and Midlothian*; RUSSELL, *Story of Leith*, 67–9; *Men of the Reign*, 627.

27. *Landowners' Return* (1874), passim.

28. NICOL, *Vital Statistics of Glasgow* (1885), 5.

29. *Landowners' Return, Midlothian*; *Heriot Trust Report on Unfeued Land* (1894); STEVEN, *History of Heriot's Hospital*, 33, 58–65, 115–21, 230–1; A. HERON, *Rise of Merchant Company*, 228–31, 367–99.

30. *Hundred Glasgow Men*, 33–5.

31. CRAWFORD, *Trades House*, 186; "SENEX," *Old Glasgow*, 51–2; *Glasgow Past and Present*, 18.

32. CRAWFORD, op. cit., 207; "SENEX," op.cit., 44–5; *Old Country Houses*, 143; *Lord Provosts of Glasgow* (1883), Appendix, 26–7.

33. *Lord Provosts*, ut sup, 34, 38.

34. NIMMO, *Stirlingshire*, I, 266.

35. T. SMITH, *Memoir of Begg*, ch. xlviii; BLAIKIE, *Recollections*, ch. x; cf. *Scottish Land Report*, 325–9, 390–5.

36. *Royal Commission on Housing* (1884–85), 2nd Report, 35–7, 38–42.

37. A. ALISON, *Life*, I, 344–50.

38. *Hundred Glasgow Men*, 81–6; cf. Burke's *Landed Gentry*.

39. MACGEORGE, *Bairds of Gartsherrie*, passim.

40. BOASE, *Modern Biography*, II, 790; DAY, *Public Administration*, 183–4.

41. MACKIE, *Life of D. McLaren*, I, 54; *Edinburgh Courant*, 1879, passim.
42. C. COWAN, *Reminiscences*, 380.
43. RANKIN, *History of Our Firm*, 23–25, 34–40, 47; ALISON, *History of Europe*, 1815–51, VIII, 780.
44. C. HOPE, *George Hope*, 234, 305–6, 367.
45. MCCONNACHIE, *Deer and Deer Forests*, 40–6; *Scottish Notes and Queries*, 3rd, ser., II, 124.
46. D. MURRAY, *Early Burgh Organization*, I, ch. xv; cf. J. J. BELL, *I Remember*, 54–71.
47. D. NAPIER, *Autobiographical Sketch*, 114–16; cf. GILLESPIE, *Glasgow*, 61.
48. M. MACKAY, *Memoir of James Ewing*, 94–96.
49. H. G. LEWIN, *Early British Railways*, 5, 16–17.
50. IRVING, *Eminent Scotsmen*, 125; *Dictionary of National Biography*, XXXVIII, 303, 307; MACGEORGE, *Bairds of Gartsherrie*, 79–82; MCILWRAITH, *Glasgow and S.-W. Railway*, 24.
51. MCILWRAITH, op. cit., 25, 49.
52. *Tait's Magazine* (1839), 695–6.
53. G. HAY, *History of Arbroath*, 391; J. M. MCBAIN, *Arbroath*, 198–9; ibid., *Bibliography of Arbroath*, 116–18.
54. A. H. MILLAR, *Fife*, 43–9.
55. J. H. ANDERSON, *An Inverness Lawyer*, 215.
56. "Making of Berwickshire Railway" (*Edinburgh Evening News*, Oct. 8, 1932).
57. ANDERSON, op. cit., 211; cf. SCRIVENER, *Railways of U.K.*, 566, 684.
58. A. S. CUNNINGHAM, *Mining in Lothian*, 132–6.
59. CUNNINGHAM, *R. G. E. Wemyss*, 117–19, 127–8.
60. NIMMO, *Stirlingshire*, I, 283–4; FORSYTH, *Beauties of Scotland*, III, 431–2.
61. H. KEDDIE, *Three Generations*, 242–4.
62. R. WILSON, *History of Hawick*, 289–90, 309–10.
63. BREMNER, *Industries of Scotland*, 335–6; MACKINNON, *Social History*, II, 253; MCCALLUM, *Midlothian*, 15; J. ADAMS, *Professor Penny*, 16–18; HALL, *Galashiels*, 369–72.
64. FORSYTH, *Beauties of Scotland*, I, 304–5.
65. CRAIG, *A Century of Papermaking*, 14; *Scotsman*, April 25 and 26, 1890.

II. ORGANIZATION OF INDUSTRY

1. N. S. B. GRAS, *Business History*, *Econ. Hist. Rev.*, IV, 4 (April 1934), 385–98.
2. L. H. JENKS, *Migration of British Capital*, 233.

I. OWNERSHIP AND CONTROL

1. H. L. WEAVERS, *Report* (1841), 42–43.
2. CLELAND, *Annals of Glasgow*, I, 46, 176–80; *Curiosities of Glasgow Citizenship*, 113–16, cf. *Glasgow Past and Present*, 64–77.
3. P. F. ANSON, *Fishing Boats on East Coast*, ch. i.
4. *Scotsman*, June 29, 1933, Supplement; cf. C. COWAN, *Reminiscences*; CRAIG, *Century of Papermaking*, passim.
5. CARRAGHER, *Arbroath*, 39–41.
6. *Curiosities of Glasgow Citizenship* (*Stirlings*); *Hundred Glasgow Men*, 222; MACLEOD, *Lennox*, 12–14.
7. GILLESPIE, *Falkirk*, 38.
8. MITCHELL, *History of Montrose*, ch. xi.
9. A. MILLER, *Coatbridge*, 126.
10. cf. SHANNON, *Coming of Limited Liability*, "Economic History," Jan. 1931, 267–91.
11. J. R. CHRISTIE, *Juridical Review*, XXI (1909–10), 128–47; cf. *Scottish Bankers' Magazine*, II, 162.
12. SHANNON, ut sup., 267, 290.
13. A. MITCHELL, in *Transactions Soc. Science Assn.* (1874), 254–6.
14. ANDERSON, *History of Edinburgh*, 377.
15. REID, Manual of Scottish Shares (1842), 172–7; *Glasgow Herald*, Nov. 11, 1931.
16. FENN'S *Compendium* (1869), 524–37.
17. *Scotsman*, Feb. 16, 1872.
18. REID, op. cit., 159–61; CLAPHAM, *Econ. History of Modern Britain*, II, 135; CUNNINGHAM, *Mining in Lothians*, 121–3; *New Statistical Account*, VI, 947; *Manufactures of W. of Scotland* (1876), 41; *Stock Exchange Year Book* (1933), 1944; *Edin. Courant*, July 21, 1871.
19. H. M. CADELL, *The Forth*, 143–94; GILLESPIE, *Falkirk*, 101–16; POLLOCK, *Dictionary of Forth*, 76–8.
20. cf. RAIT, *Union Bank*, 276–9; 317–23; GRAHAM, *One Pound Note*, 257–62.
21. CLAPHAM, op. cit., II, 139.
22. *Memoir of C. Macintosh*, 53, 102; LEWIS, *Topographical Dictionary*, II, 342; *Manufactures W. of Scotland*, 225.
23. *One Hundred Glasgow Men*, 165–6; *Manufactures of W. of Scotland*, 42; *Stock Exchange Year Book* (1933), 1877.
24. HODDER, *Life of G. Burns*, 197–203; W. S. LINDSAY, *Merchant Shipping*, IV, 178–84; CLAPHAM, op. cit., II, 139; *Life of R. Napier*, 141–3; J. P. Fleming, 29–32.
25. MILLER, *Coatbridge*, 120–1; BOASE, *Modern Biography*, II, 1099; HARVEY, *Engineering in Glasgow*, 19; ABERCONWAY, *Basic Industries*, 216; MCLEAN, *Industries of Glasgow*, 22, 27; *Scotsman*, Oct. 7, 1903.

26. *W. of Scotland Manufs.*, ut sup., 41, 49–50; MCLEAN, op. cit., 26.

27. CUNNINGHAM, *Mining in Fife*, 47.

28. *Manufactures W. of Scotland*, 228–9; MCLEAN, op. cit., 29.

29. ABERCONWAY, *Basic Industries*, 207–8; CUNNINGHAM, *Culross*, 115–16, 123; Id., *Fife Coal Company, 1872–1922.*

30. *Manufactures W. of Scotland*, 57; MCLEAN, op. cit., 26; cf. J. HODGE, *Workman's Cottage to Windsor*, chs. iv, v.

31. MCLEAN, op. cit., 26.

32. GILLESPIE, *Falkirk*, 341–6; BREMNER, *Industries*, 483–5; JEANS, *Western Worthies*, 66; CADELL, *The Forth*, 199–202; LEARMONTH, *West Calder*, 137–40.

33. *Scotsman*, June 29, 1933, Supplement.

34. NORRIE, *Edinburgh Press*, 10–15.

35. MURPHY, *Captains of Industry*, 83–9; MACROSTY, *Trust Movement*, 45; cf. *Hundred Glasgow Men*, 115–22, 267–8.

36. J. O. MITCHELL, *Two Old Glasgow Firms* (*Glasgow Herald*, Oct. 11, 1893).

37. *The Post-Victorians*, 334–9; BRIDGES and TILTMAN, *Kings of Commerce*, 152–6; cf. *Scotsman*, March 9 and 12, 1898.

38. STEWART, *Curiosities of Glasgow Citizenship*, ch. i; MITCHELL, *Old Glasgow Essays*, 338–42.

39. Cf. EVANS, *Facts, Failures, and Frauds.*

40. CAMERON, *Campsie*, Appx., 8–12.

41. *Scotsman*, June 29, 1933, Supplement.

42. MACLEOD, *Clyde District*, 21–4, 148–53, 171–3; IRVING, *Dumbartonshire*, III, 463–4.

43. JEANS, *Western Worthies*, 153–4; *Life of G. Troup*, 45–7; *Edin. Courant*, Jan. 8 and 29, May 4, July 15, 1848; CROAL, *Recollections*, 26–7; MACGEORGE, *Bairds of Gartsherrie*, 88–9.

44. NIDDRIE AND BENHAR Coal Co., *Fifty Years' Retrospect*; BAIRD, *Duddingston*, 90; CUNNINGHAM, *Mining in Lothians*, 118–19; *Edin. Courant*, Jan. 8 and Feb. 6, 1879, Aug. 9, 1882, etc.; *Scotsman*, Sept. 5, 1904, Jan. 20, 1872.

45. MILLER, *Coatbridge*, 39–40, 107–8; MACARTHUR, *New Monkland*, 184; KNOX, *Airdrie*, 84–5; *Land Return* (1874), *Lanarkshire*; RAIT, *Union Bank*, 293; *Witness*, July 20, 1861; *Scotsman*, March 11 and 19, 1879; May 19, 1888.

46. MACGEORGE, *Bairds of Gartsherrie*, 126–8; *Royal Commn. on Labour*, 2nd Report (1892), 235; *Stock Exchange Year Book* (1933), 1972.

47. *Life of R. Napier*, 190, 201, 214–15; HARVEY, *Engineering*, 13–15; MURPHY, *Captains of Industry*, 133–8; *Eminent Arbroathians*, 407–14.

48. *Hundred Glasgow Men*, 115–22, 267–8; MURPHY, op. cit., 83–9; HARVEY, op. cit., 22–3; *Manufactures W. of Scotland*, 154; RANKINE, *J. Elder*, 6–7.

49. MURPHY, op. cit., 103–6; *Glasgow Herald*, July 3, 1931; *Shipbuilding on the Clyde* (Barclay, Curle), passim.

50. D. NAPIER, *Autobiography*, 120–1; C. TAYLOR, *Partick*, 116; *Glasgow Evening News*, Sept. 21, 1929.

51. HARVEY, op. cit., 23–4; MACLEOD, *Clyde District*, 128–9; 169–70, 197–206; CORMACK, *Shipbuilding*, 383–7; IRVING, *Dumbartonshire*, III, 470–1; *Scotsman*, April 24, 1890.

52. HARVEY, op. cit., 25–6; BLAIR, *Technical College*, 14–15; *Manufactures W. of Scotland*, 105–6; MCLEAN, *Industries*, 37, 66–7.

53. *Hundred Glasgow Men*, 81–6.

54. BAIRD, Duddingston, 450–2.

55. CAMERON, *Campsie*, Appx., 12–20; JEANS, *Western Worthies*, 36; *New Statistical Account*, VIII, 254.

56. *Hundred Glasgow Men*, 323–6.

57. Ibid., 103–5.

58. MILLER, *Coatbridge*, 118.

59. *Hundred Glasgow Men*, 313–15.

60. Ibid., 85.

61. J. NAPIER, *Life of R. Napier*, 49–54, 58–9, 96–9; MACGEORGE, *Bairds of Gartsherrie*, 89–90.

62. *Hundred Glasgow Men*, 127–8; cf. Broomhall, *Arch. Orr-Ewing*, 3–5, 10.

63. Ibid., 267–8.

64. ABERCONWAY, *Basic Industries*, 208; *Who's Who in Glasgow* (1909).

65. ROBBIE, *Aberdeen*, 496–7.

66. CRAIG-BROWN, *Selkirkshire*, 177–82.

67. MCILWRAITH, *Glasgow and S.-W. Railway*, 61, 131; *Hundred Glasgow Men*, 13–20, 11–12, 127–8, 169–70, 173–6, 183–4; C. COWAN, *Memoir*, 217, 225; *Edin. Courant*, May 13, 1867 (*re* Dunlop).

68. *Hundred Glasgow Men*, 11–12, 129–31, 169–70, 183–4; RAIT, *Union Bank*, Appendix.

69. ANDERSON, *Commercial Bank*, Appendix.

70. ROBBIE, *Aberdeen*, 360–6; WARDEN, *Linen*, 540–1; BOASE, *Banking in Dundee*, 374.

71. MACLEOD, *Clyde District*, 106–8, 159–63; WATSON, *Kirkintilloch*, 330–5, *Tait's Magazine*, April 1849, 270; cf. *Factory Commissioners*, 1st Report (1833), A., 73–6.

72. *Memoir of C. Macintosh*, passim; *Dictionary of National Biography*, XXXV, 112; *Manufactures W. of Scotland*, 225–7; cf. R. BAIN, *A Highland Industrial Pioneer* (in *The Active Gael*, ed. P. MacDougall).

73. ABERCONWAY, *Basic Industries*, 226.

74. *Life of R. Napier*, 187–90.

75. NORRIE, *Men of Dundee*, 144–7.

76. ABERCONWAY, op. cit., 217; KNOX, *Airdrie*, 73–4; *New Statistical*

Account, VI, 617–19; *Hundred Glasgow Men*, 165–6; MITCHELL, *Old Glasgow Essays*, 294–5; CUNNINGHAM, *Culross*, 105, *Mining in Fife*, 55; *Manufactures West of Scotland*, 42–3.

77. CADELL, *Forth*, 143–94; GILLESPIE, *Falkirk*, 101–16; NIMMO, *Stirlingshire*, II, 293–306.

78. *Manufactures W. of Scotland*, 37–8.

79. MILLER, *Coatbridge*, 104–7; *Hundred Glasgow Men*, 103–5; MURPHY, *Captains of Industry*, 145–9; *Manufactures W. of Scotland*, 36–7.

80. MILLER, op. cit., 116–20; *Manufactures*, op. cit., 45; MCLEAN, *Industries*, 21; MACGEORGE, *Bairds of Gartsherrie*, 90.

81. MILLER, *Coatbridge*, 122–7; MCLEAN, op. cit., 21; MACARTHUR, *New Monkland*, 382; *Manufactures*, op. cit., 40.

82. DENNYS, *Dumbarton*, passim; cf. MACLEOD, *Dumbarton, Castle and Town*, 194–203; IRVING, *Dumbartonshire*, III, 362–70.

83. Cf., pp. 58–9.

84. *Book of Anchor Line*, 7–26.

85. MACLEOD, *Dumbarton*, 125–6.

86. ACWORTH, *Railways of Scotland*, 3, 39; MURPHY, *Captains of Industry*, 9.

87. BREMNER, *Industries*, 92–6.

88. ACWORTH, op. cit., 77; MCILWRAITH, *Glasgow and S.W. Railway*, 120; D. CAMPBELL, *Railway Amalgamation* (1873).

89. BLAIR, *Paisley Thread*, 62–7; cf. *Scotsman*, June 4, 1896.

90. MACKINNON, *Social History*, II, 85; *Scotsman*, Feb. 1, 1893; *Stock Exchange Year Book* (1933), 2198.

91. MCLEAN, *Industries*, 165; FITZGERALD, *Industrial Combination*, 221.

92. MACROSTY, *Trust Movement*, 241.

93. IRVING, *Dumbartonshire* (1924), v. III, 424.

94. FITZGERALD, *Industrial Combination*, 216–7.

95. MACROSTY, op. cit., 230; FITZGERALD, op. cit., 224.

PATENTS

96. *Encyclopaedia Britannica*, 11th edn., Vol. 20, p. 903; cf. *North British Review*, No. XLVIII, pp. 231–67.

97. DUNDONALD, *Autobiography of Seaman*, XXXII–XXXIII; I, 5–10, 535–40, etc.; cf. MACLEOD, *Clyde District*, 117; CADELL, *The Forth*, 200; BEVERIDGE, *Culross*, II, 232–7.

98. MACINTOSH, *Memoir*, 83.

99. *North British Review*, VII, 139–42; SMILES, *Industrial Biography*, 158–9; MACINTOSH, *Memoir*, 106–10: MACKENZIE, *J. B. Neilson*, 31–32; *Report of Trial*, Neilson v. Househill Co. (1842).

100. C. COWAN, *Reminiscences*, 246–8.

101. *Edin. Evening News*, May 19, 1934.

102. JEANS, *Western Worthies*, 66; J. ADAMS, *Professor Penny*, 11.

Q

103. *Scotsman,* March 6 and 17, 1879.
104. MURPHY, *Captains of Industry,* 257–63; S. P. THOMSON, *Kelvin,* 717, 1155; CASSON, *Kelvin,* 36.
105. J. D. NAPIER, *D. Napier,* 59–65; J. NAPIER, *R. Napier,* 89–93, 246.
106. RANKINE, *John Elder,* 31–7.

II. FINANCIAL ASPECTS

(1) STOCKS AND SHARES

1. A. W. KERR, *Banking in Scotland,* 55–7; N. MUNRO, *Royal Bank,* 69–70; W. BAIRD, *One Pound Note,* 31–2; H. M. ROBERTSON, *Economic Individualism,* 100.
2. *Royal Comm. on Trade Depression,* 1st Report, 81, Final Report, 218–22; WARDEN, *Linen,* 632; *Brit. Assocn. Handbook Dundee* (1912), 118, 347–56.
3. ABERCONWAY, *Basic Industries,* 232.
4. *Stock Exchange Year Book* (1933), passim.
5. CARR-SAUNDERS, and WILSON, *The Professions,* 209–10.
6. *Hundred Glasgow Men,* 187–8, *Lord Provosts of Glasgow,* 295–99; JEANS, *Western Worthies,* 152–3; *Scotsman,* Aug. 15, 1889.
7. REID, *Scottish Stocks* (1842), 178; cf. J. ANDERSON, *History of Edinburgh,* 377–8.
8. L. H. JENKS, *Migration of British Capital,* 131–2; cf. REID, *Scottish Stocks,* Pt. 2, 48–9.
9. W. MCILWRAITH, *Glasgow and S.W. Railway,* 11–29; cf. *Hundred Glasgow Men,* 25–8.
10. *Ibid.,* 50, 61; *Hundred Glasgow Men,* 173–6.
11. I. H. ANDERSON, *Inverness Lawyer and His Sons,* 207–21.
12. *Tait's Magazine* (1837), p. 336, (1842), p. 138.
13. MACKIE, *D. McLaren,* 54; cf. *Dict. National Biography,* XXVIII, 145; *Tait's Magazine* (1849), 402.
14. MCILWRAITH, op. cit., 72.
15. BRIDGES, *Sir A. Agnew,* passim; MCCRIE, *Agnew,* 374, 382–9, 394–5, 403–7.
16. *Tait's Magazine* (1837), 405; (1841) 810; (1850) 159–61; *Witness,* March 21, 1840, Aug. 15, 1840, Jan. 9, 1841.
17. J. R. FLEMING, *Church in Scotland,* 5, 213.
18. *Edinburgh Corporation MSS. Minutes,* passim, e.g., Vol. 206, 8; Vol. 221, 163; Vol. 241, 232; Vol. 277, 359.
19. J. FRANCIS, *History of English Railways,* 66–7.
20. BREMNER, *Industries of Scotland,* 86–9; *Scottish Educational Journal,* June 29, 1928.
21. DISRAELI, *Lord George Bentinck,* 375–6.
22. BREMNER, op. cit., 90.
23. *Ibid.,* 91; cf. FRANCIS, op. cit., 256.

24. BREMNER, op. cit., 91–92; cf. MARTIN, *W. E. Aytoun*, 104–17; FAY, *Great Britain from Adam Smith*, 194.

25. COCKBURN, *Journal*, II, 129–31.

26. T. MARTIN, *W. E. Aytoun*, 106; cf. W. E. AYTOUN, *Norman Sinclair*.

27. *Tait's Magazine*, June 1869, pp. 402–5.

28. BREMNER, *Industries*, 92–8; *Edin. Courant*, Jan. 1868; SCRIVENER, *Railways of United Kingdom*, 559–691.

29. *Ordnance Gazetteer* (1886), II, 87–90; ACWORTH, *Railways of Scotland*, passim.

30. *Encyclopædia Britannica*, XXVII, 164–5.

31. *Edinburgh Courant*, Sept. 30 and Dec. 28, 1871.

32. *Scotsman*, May 25, 1871; *Sentinel*, Jan. 6, 1872.

33. MACKINNON, *Social History*, II, 250–1; *Edinburgh in Nineteenth Century*, 173.

34. BELL AND PATON, *Glasgow*, 292–303.

35. ANDERSON, *History of Edinburgh*, 414–15.

36. *Edinburgh Almanac* (1836), 414; cf. *Edinburgh Corporation MSS. Minutes*, e.g., Vol. 206, 99; Vol. 224, 376; Vol. 233, 123.

37. *Corporation Minutes*, Vol. 300, 192, 204; Vol. 305, 356; COCHRANE, *Pentland Walks*, 71; *Edinburgh in 19th Century*, 144–5; J. COLSTON, *Edinburgh Water Supply*; D. LEWIS, *Edinburgh Water Supply*.

38. *Municipal Glasgow* (1914), 270–4; J. S. CLARKE, *Epic of Municipalization*; MURPHY, *Captains of Industry*, 43–9; GALLOWAY, *William Harley*.

39. REID, *Scottish Stocks* (1842), 174.

40. FENN'S *Compendium* (1869), 544–54.

41. MURPHY, *Captains of Industry*, 50–3; *Municipal Glasgow*, 121–2.

42. ANDERSON. *Edinburgh*, 328, 374, 467; *Edinburgh in 19th Century*, 64, 77, 166.

43. *Edinburgh in 19th Century*, 175; *Municipal Glasgow*, 127; MURPHY, op. cit., 53–7.

(2) THE BANKS AND INDUSTRY

44. J. L. ANDERSON, *Commercial Bank*, 3–4; COCKBURN, *Memorials*, 238–40.

45. KERR, *Banking in Scotland* (1902), 224–5, 251–2, 258–62; BOASE, *Banking in Dundee*, 374; GRAHAM, *One Pound Note*, 200–3, 238–40; RAIT, *Union Bank*, 289–91.

46. TAIT'S *Magazine*, May 1858, 300–6; *Scottish Bankers' Magazine*, I, 94; SOMERS, *Scotch Banks*, 124–9; *Edin. Courant*, Nov. 10–14, 1857.

47. WALLACE, *City of Glasgow Bank Trial* (1908), passim, esp. 1–11; CLAPHAM, *Economic History*, II, 384; KERR, *Banking in Scotland*,

228, 294–9; RAIT, *Union Bank*, 310–11; GRAHAM, *One Pound Note*, 252–4; BOASE, *Banking in Dundee*, 409; CRAIG, *Century of Papermaking*, 20; *Scottish Bankers' Magazine*, I, 97–101; CAIRNCROSS, *Glasgow Building Industry* (*Review of Economic Studies*, II, 1, 1–17); *Royal Comm. on Trade Depression*, 2nd Report, Appx. D.

48. G. KINNEAR, *Rise of Exchange Companies in Scotland, Banks and Exchange Companies* (1847); cf. FAY, *Great Britain from Adam Smith*, 194.

49. BOASE, *Banking in Dundee*, 437.

50. KERR, op. cit., 247–8.

51. Ibid., 245–7; GRAHAM, op. cit., 234; KINNEAR, op. cit.; MACKIE, D. McLaren, I, 56; *Edinburgh Courant*, Jan. 17 and Feb. 12, 1848; *Scotsman*, Oct. 25, 1845.

52. *Courant*, April 3, 1848.

53. KINNEAR, op. cit.; KERR, op. cit., 248.

54. D. M. EVANS, *Facts, Failures, and Frauds*, 268–390; *Trail of Royal British Bank Directors* (Lea's edition, 1857); MACLEOD, *Theory and Practice of Banking* (1856), II, 511–14; *Dictionary of National Biography*, 2nd Supplement, II, 540; TAIT'S *Magazine*, April 1849, 267–8; May 1857, 318–9; *Courant*, October 6 and 22, 1856, etc.

55. MUNRO, *Royal Bank*, 207–8.

56. BOASE, *Banking in Dundee*, 363, 560.

57. Ibid., 430–1.

58. RAIT, op. cit., 303.

59. GRAHAM, *One Pound Note*, 263.

60. BOASE, op. cit., 473; cf. KERR, op. cit., 255–6, 324; J. S. FLEMING, *Scottish Banking*.

61. FEAVERYEAR, *Pound Sterling*, 272–3; POSTGATE, *Builders' History*, 324–5, 326–7; GRAHAM, op. cit., 256.

62. S. HALL, *Dr. Duncan*, 56–73; R. CAMPBELL, *Provident Institutions*, 212–14; *Tait's Magazine*, May 1850, 275–84.

63. *Tait's* Magazine, September 1844, 605–6.

64. *Scottish Guardian*, January 6, 1854.

65. KERR, op. cit., 226–7, 268–9; GRAHAM, *One Pound Note*, 243; REID, *Scottish Stocks*, Pt. 2, 26–7, 31; MUNRO, *Royal Bank*, 225–6.

66. "Dunedin Bank," Prospectus (1844).

67. KERR, op. cit., 327; *Scotsman*, May 20, 1881; *Edin. Courant*, Jan. 29 and Feb. 13, 1883.

68. Ibid., 324–5; "People's Bank" Prospectus.

69. *Scotsman*. July 27 and Dec. 29, 1887.

70. *Scots Magazine*, Vol. X (1892), 17–22, 297–302; KERR, op. cit., 325–6.

(3) MIGRATION OF CAPITAL

71. G. P. INSH, *The Company of Scotland*, esp. pp. 27–8.

72. D. MURRAY, *York Buildings Company*.

73. *Manufactures of W. of Scotland* (1876), 121–2; MACLEOD, *Clyde District*, 164–6, 180–95.

74. *Manufactures*, ut sup., 123–4.

75. BREMNER, *Industries*, 363; *Edin. Courant*, Jan. 14, 1861; *Scotsman* (prospectus), May 5, 1906; *Edin. Evening News*, May 19, 1934; *Stock Exchange Year Book* (1933), 2979.

76. *Manufactures*, ut sup., 231; MCLEAN, *Industries*, 178–80; SCHUCK and SOHLMANN, *Life of Nobel*, 118–22.

77. MACKINNON, *Social History*, II, 121; MCLEAN, *Industries*, 178–80; MAVOR, *My Windows*, I, 144; MIALL, *British Chemical Industry*, 24–6; A. JAMES, *Cyanide Practice*, 1–5; *Scottish News*, Dec. 9, 1886.

78. PATON and MILLAR, *Dundee*, 118–20.

79. Ibid., 351–3.

80. REID, *Scottish Stocks*, 161–3.

81. *Blackwood's Magazine*, Oct. 1884, 468–80; Feb. 1885, 269–84; W. R. LAWSON, *Scottish Investor's Manual* (1884), 62–72; cf. SHANNON, *Limited Companies* (*Economic History Review*, IV, 3, Oct. 1933), 305.

82. LAWSON, ut sup.; *Scottish Banking Magazine*, Feb. 1879, and seq.

83. *Edin. Courant*, Sept. 2, 1856; FENN, *Compendium* (1869), 532, 560.

84. *Edin. Courant*, April, 20, 1877.

85. WALLACE, *City of Glasgow Bank Trial*, Appx., 465; Reports of Assets Co. (*Scotsman*, 1882, and seq.).

86. GRAHAM, *One Pound Note in Scotland*, 267.

87. T. J. GRAYSON, *Investment Trusts*, 11, 14, 34.

88. G. GLASGOW, *Scottish Investment Trust Companies*, VIII, 48, 62, 68; *Scotsman*, Oct. 24, 1933; cf. CLAPHAM, *Economic History*, II, 358.

89. GRAYSON, op. cit., 191; GLASGOW, op. cit., 48.

90. GRAYSON, op. cit., 5, 52; *Memoir of W. B. Blaikie*, 4; *Scotsman*, Oct. 16, 1905; *Edin. Courant*, March 29, 1870.

91. GLASGOW, op. cit., 5–6.

(4) SPECIAL TYPES OF INVESTMENT MECHANISM
(a) The Building Society

92. BRABROOK, *Building Societies* (*Encyclopaedia Britannica*, 11th edn., IV, 766–78).

93. Ibid.; BEGG, *Happy Homes*, 115–16; W. CHAMBERS, *Social Science Tracts*, V, 5–8; BLAIKIE, *Better Days*, 188–9; SCRATCHLEY, *Industrial Investment*, vii–viii, 1, 4.

94. *Royal Comm. on Friendly Societies*, 2nd Report, 291–3.
95. *Encyclopaedia Britannica*, ut sup.; BRABROOK, *Building Societies*.
96. BEGG, op. cit., 115–16.
97. CHAMBERS, op. cit., V, 20; J. SMITH, *Grievances of Working Classes*, 112.
98. BEGG. *House Buying* (1851); reprinted, *Happy Homes*, ch. iii, 107–52.
99. BEGG, *Happy Homes*, 24–5; SMITH, *Memoir of Begg*, II, 399–403.
100. *Report of Comm. of Working Classes* (1860).
101. BLAIKIE, *Better Days*, 188–9; cf. CHAMBERS, op. cit., V, 20–21.
102. LAWSON, *Scottish Investors' Manual*, 16–26; *Scotsman*, Mar. 24, 1877.
103. *Scottish Banking Magazine*, 1879–89, passim, esp. Jan. 1879; cf. *Edin. Courant*, 1879–86, passim.
104. *Royal Commn. on Labour*, 4th Report, Pt. I, LII, 75.
105. *Building Societies' Year Book* (1933).
106. *Scotsman*, January 4, 1896.
107. BEGG, *Happy Homes*, 220–1; *Edinburgh Courant*, March 22, 1861; RAIT, *Union Bank*, Appx.
108. *Scotsman*, April 14, 1934.

(b) *Insurance Societies*

109. REID, *Scottish Stocks* (1842), 80–81.
110. FRANCIS, *Life Insurance*, 317–21.
111. FRASER, *Life Assurance*, 2–4, 19.
112. FRANCIS, op. cit., 323–6; FENN, *Compendium of Funds*, 533–7; REID, op. cit., 87–94; *Scotsman*, March 22, 1934, Dec. 7, 1932; J. W. GUILD, *Plea for Life Assurance* (1850).
113. FRANCIS, op. cit., 234–42; REID, op. cit., XXIX-XXX; P. MACKENZIE, *Reminiscences of Glasgow*, II, 596–631.
114. W. FRASER, "Remarks on . . . Associations for Life Assurance"; cf. *Edinburgh Advertiser*, June 8, 1838.
115. *One Hundred Glasgow Men*, 289–90.
116. *Dictionary of National Biography*, XXXVIII, 69; *Scottish Notes and Queries*, III (Oct. 1889), 72–4.
117. *Tait's Magazine*, Feb. 1839, p. 134.
118. Ibid., May 1849, pp. 325–32.
119. FRANCIS, op. cit., 327.
120. *Edinburgh Courant*, Nov. 1, 1860.
121. C. COWAN, *Reminiscences*, 243–4.

III. INTERNAL ADMINISTRATION

1. *New Statistical Account*, IV, 18, 34, 269, 285.
2. Ibid., V, 371; VI, 559; VIII, 101.

3. *Glasgow Trades Council, Annual Report* (1860).
4. BLAIR, *Paisley Shawl*, 2, 3, 47; *Comm. on Children's Employment* (1842), 3rd Report, Pt. I, 31; Pt. II, Appx.
5. GILMOUR, *Paisley Weavers*, ch. ii and iii.
6. *Handloom Weavers Comm.*, Report (1841), I, 6–9.
7. BLAIR, *Paisley Shawl*, 23–4; METCALFE, *Paisley*, 465; *Information from Mr. C. Wigham*; cf. *Edinburgh Directory* (1844–57).
8. A. SMITH, *Alfred Hagart's Household* (1866).
9. *Handloom Weavers Comm.*, *Report* (1841), 90–91; cf. *Asst. Commissioner's Report* (1839), 9, 22, 60, 90–4; *Report on Crime in Glasgow* (1841), 7.
10. WARDEN, *Linen Trade*, 554–8; *Comm. on Employment of Children*, 2nd Report (1864), 224–6; cf. CHALMERS, *Dunfermline*, I, 358–62. POLLOCK, *Dictionary of Forth*, 106; J. M. MCBAIN, *Arbroath*, 120–1.
11. J. MYLES, *Dundee Factory Boy* (1850).
12. WARDEN, op. cit., 598; PATON and MILLAR, *Dundee*, 272–3.
13. STRANG, *Journal Statistical Society*, Dec. 1861; *Century Dictionary*, VI, 6175; *Old Statistical Account*, XII, 22; cf. *Scottish Historical Review*, Vol. XXI, No. 83, April 1924, 214.
14. *Royal Comm. on Trade Unionism*, 7th Report (1868), 38–59; *Royal Comm. on Labour*, 2nd Report, 41–66; 182–225.
15. *Comm. on Employment of Children*, 2nd Report. Appx. K, 29; *North British Review*, XV, 58–68.
16. *Royal Comm. on Labour*, 2nd Report, 366–88; HODGE, *Workman's Cottage*, ch. iii, v, ix.
17. *Comm. on Children's Employment*, 1st Report (1842), 197–98.
18. JENKS, *Migration of British Capital*, 135.
19. MACARTHUR, *New Monkland*, 388; *Scotsman*, Jan. 19, 1888.
20. J. TAYLOR, *Poems* (Edinburgh, 1876): *Autobiographical Sketch*, pp. 1–48.
21. *North British Review*, XXV, 73–5.
22. ACWORTH, *Railways of Scotland*, 23.
23. NIMMO, *Stirlingshire*, II, 33–4; cf. PRATT, *Scottish Canals*, 126, 163.
24. *Royal Commn. on Labour* (1892), 2nd Report, Pt. II, 108–25.
25. BREMNER, *Industries of Scotland*, 123.
26. *Children's Employment Commn.*, 4th Report (1865), H, 81–6.
27. *New Statistical Account*, VII, 303; BURN, *Commercial Enterprise*, 135–9.
28. CHALMERS, *Dunfermline*, I, 373.
29. NORRIE, *Dundee Celebrities*, 368.
30. MAVOR, *My Windows*, I, 46–7.
31. *Royal Commn. on Trade Depression*, 2nd Report, cf. HALL, *Galashiels*, 342–50.
32. WARDEN, *Linen Industry*, 629.
33. J. G. SMITH, *Organized Produce Markets* (1922), 151–2.

34. *Edinburgh Courant*, May 17, 1881.
35. ABERCONWAY, *Basic Industries*, 214; G. C. ALLEN, *British Industries*, 124.
36. *Glasgow Herald*, Aug. 7, 1893, Dec. 11, 1929 (Wm. Connal & Co.); cf. ACWORTH, *Railways of Scotland*, 127–8.
37. IRONS, *Leith*, II, 496–9; *Encyclopaedia Britannica*, 13th ed., Supp. II, 671.
38. *Comm. on Payment of Wages*, 163–6; *Social Science Assocn.* (1860), 746.
39. HEITON, *Castes of Edinburgh*, 300.
40. *Hundred Glasgow Men*, 81–86; cf. HAMILTON, *Industrial Revolution*, 149; sub., ch. iv.
41. *Factory Comm. Inquiry*, 1st Report (1833), 64–7; *New Statistical Account*, X, 1233; *Dictionary of Eminent Scotsmen*, 482; cf. THOMSON, *History of Scottish People*, VI, 592–3, 597.
42. *Proceedings of Inst. of Civil Engineers*, Vol. 87 (1886), 374–5, 381; FORSYTH, *Beauties of Scotland*, III, 412–14; POLLOCK, *Dictionary of Forth*, 76–8.
43. WARDEN, *Linen Industry*, 572–4; *Brit. Assocn.* (Dundee, 1867), 15; THOMSON, *Dundee* (1874), 337–40; *Scottish Bankers' Magazine*, II, 122.
44. CARRAGHER, *Arbroath*, 41.
45. RANKIN, *History of Our Firm*, 19–20; HODDER, *Sir G. Burns*, 122; *Hundred Glasgow Men*, 60–68, 281–4.
46. *Book of Anchor Line*, 7–26; LINDSAY, *Shipping*, IV, 287–90.
47. Information from Mr. J. McKenna (Messrs. Collins); cf. *Scottish Educational Journal*, Feb. 19, 1932.
48. *Hundred Glasgow Men*, Appx.; cf. *Social Science Assocn.* Meeting, (1863), 811–13.
49. J. D. BURN, *Commercial Enterprise*, 144.
50. JEANS, *Western Worthies*, 58–69; *Lord Provosts of Glasgow*, 69–70; *Hundred Glasgow Men*, 69–78; J. D. BURN, *Commercial Enterprise*, 104–7; KOHL, *Travels in Scotland*, ch. ii; *Glasgow Herald*, Sept. 5, 1932.
51. MACKIE, D. McLaren, I, 34–35.
52. *Stock Exchange Intelligencer* (1933), 610; *Scotsman*, Nov. 25, 1922; cf. *Hundred Glasgow Men*, 295–6.
53. MURPHY, *Captains of Industry*, 279–84.
54. *Niddrie & B. Coal Company Retrospect*, 6.
55. *Glasgow Evening News*, Sept. 21, 1929; J. ORD, *Gorbals*, 30.
56. WILSON, *Walter Wilson*, passim.
57. BURN, *Commercial Enterprise*, 108–13.

IV. COMMERCIAL DEVELOPMENT

1. "Scottish Colonial Schemes" (1922), "The Company of Scotland" (1932).
2. "Iatros," PATRICK COLQUHOUN; *Scottish Educational Journal*, Sept. 12, 1930.
3. *Encyclopaedia Britannica*, 11th edn., XXVIII, 611; FAY, *Great Britain from Adam Smith*, 291.
4. H. DUNLOP, *The Cotton Trade* (lecture, 36 pp.), Glasgow, 1862.

(1) SCOTTISH "SPHERES OF INFLUENCE"

5. MACKAY, J. *Ewing*, 38–40; *Tait's Magazine*, Nov. 1833, 257; "Kirkman Finlay" (*Scottish Educational Journal*, Sept. 5, 1930).
6. *Journal*, ut sup.; J. O. MITCHELL, *Old Glasgow Essays*, 26–40.
7. *Hundred Glasgow Men*, 79–86.
8. *New Statistical Account*, VI, 148; HAMILTON, *Industrial Revolution*, 149; *Stock Exchange Year Book* (1933), 2793; *Stock Exchange Intelligencer*, 714.
9. *Lanarkshire Leaders; Who Was Who* (1897–1916); *Scotsman*, Aug. 7, 1903; *Lord Provosts of Glasgow*, 461–6.
10. RUSSELL, *Leith*, 424–5.
11. MACKAY, J., *Ewing*, 101; GILLESPIE, *Glasgow*, 50–2; *New Statistical Account*, VI, 170.
12. LUBBOCK, *China Clippers*, 36–7, 106.
13. *Select Comm. on Commercial Relations with China*, 117–21.
14. *Hundred Glasgow Men*, 87–90; J. O. MITCHELL, "Two Old Glasgow Firms" (*Glasgow Herald*, Aug. 7, 1893); "Wm. Connal & Co." (*Glasgow Herald*, Dec. 11, 1929).
15. IRVING, *Eminent Scotsmen*, 206; BOASE, *Biography*, I, 1371.
16. *Hundred Glasgow Men*, 57–8; *Comm. on China*, ut sup., 54–7.
17. Ibid., 153–4; JEANS, *Western Worthies*, 43–44; *Scotsman*, May 27, 1926; BURKE'S *Baronetage*, 1678–9; *Stock Exchange Year Book*, 2677; cf. "Jubilee of Merchiston Castle" (1883).
18. WALLACE, *City of Glasgow Bank Trial*, 201–8, 235.
19. RUSSELL, *Leith*, 419; IRONS, *Leith*, II, 491.
20. CONOLLY, *Men of Fife*, 473.
21. LINDSAY, *Shipping*, IV, 455–61; *Dictionary of National Biography*, Suppt., III, 127–8; *Scotsman*, Jan. 23 and 29, 1893.
22. *Scottish Notes and Queries* (1904–5), 34, 149–50.
23. BRIDGES and TILTMAN, *Kings of Commerce*, 138–40; *Scotsman*, May 24, 1932.
24. LANNING and COULING, *Shanghai*, 467–70; *Select Comm. on China Trade* (1840), 89–120, 133–54, 187; *Select Comm. on Commercial Relations with China* (1847), 158–81, 236–9, 340–3.
25. *Men of the Reign*, 611; cf. Part I, pp. 41–2, supra.

26. LUBBOCK, *China Clippers*, 4–7, 22–3, 33–5, 108, 196–7; Appx. II, III.

27. IRVING, *Eminent Scotsmen*, 339; BOASE, *English Biography*, II, 790.

28. *S. C. China Trade* (1840), ut sup., 100; *The Times*, Feb. 20, 1901.

29. Ibid., 90–1.

30. BURKE'S *Baronetage, Landed Gentry*; *The Times*, Feb. 18, 1905; *Scotsman*, Feb. 18, 1905.

31. *The Times*, March 11, 1912; *Who's Who*.

32. *Hundred Glasgow Men*, 273–6.

33. *Lord Provosts of Glasgow* (1883), 191–2.

34. *Tait's Magazine*, Nov. 1833, 257; *Edin. Courant*, June 10, 1861.

35. NORRIE, *Dundee Celebrities*, 222–4.

36. RUSSELL, *Leith*, 423–8; IRONS, *Leith*, II, 390–93; *Edinburgh Almanac* (1836), 288–93.

37. IRONS, *Leith*, II, 484–7; *Scotsman*, Oct. 11, 1887.

38. *Hundred Glasgow Men*, 5–8; LINDSAY, *Shipping*, IV, 261; *Lanarkshire Leaders; Scotsman*, Nov. 17, 1919.

39. HODDER, *Geo. Burns*, 197–203; JEANS, *Western Worthies*, 74–5.

40. *Hundred Glasgow Men*, 141–4; LINDSAY, op. cit., IV, 461–5; LUBBOCK, *Colonial Clippers*, 354–5.

41. BRUCE, *Life of W. Denny*, 55.

42. Ibid., 389–401.

43. J. RANKIN, *A History of Our Firm* (Liverpool, 1908).

44. PAGAN, *Glasgow*, 83; cf. *Brit. Assocn.* (1840), 175.

45. CORNFORD, *Sea Carriers*, 24–40, 52–68; LUBBOCK, *Colonial Clippers*, 29–30.

46. J. NICOLSON, *A. Anderson* (1914), passim; LINDSAY, *Merchant Shipping*, IV, 378–406; BOASE, op. cit., I, 60; *Eminent Scotsmen*, 9.

47. *Men of Reign*, 611; *Eminent Scotsmen*, 339; *Who's Who*; *Scotsman*, Jan. 3, 1922, and May 24, 1932.

48. *Encyclopaedia Britannica*, 11th edn., IV, 604–5.

49. In Memoriam, A. L. Bruce (1894); *Scotsman*, Nov. 28, 1893; F. L. M. MOIR, *After Livingstone*, 177–8.

50. H. DRUMMOND, *Tropical Africa*, esp. 81–2, 220–1; M. FOTHERINGHAM, *Adventures in Nyassaland*, 4–7; N. MACLEAN, *Africa in Transformation*, 32–47, 87–91; J. WELLS, *Stewart of Lovedale*, 126–7, 139; J. STEVENSON, *Arab in Central Africa*, 14–16; LUGARD, *Rise of East African Empire*, I, passim; H. L. DUFF, *Nyasaland under Foreign Office*, passim; W. P. LIVINGSTONE, *Laws of Livingstonia*, passim; *Encyclopaedia Britannica*, 11th edn., IV, 597–8; F. L. M. MOIR, *After Livingstone*, esp. chs. ii, xxvii; A. HETHERWICK, *Romance of Blantyre*, passim.

51. *Report World Missionary Conference* (1910), III, 271–2.

52. J. S. DENNIS, *Christian Missions and Social Progress*, III, 481.

53. *Free Church Year Book* (1888), 57.

54. MACLEAN, op. cit., 59, 91; cf. DUFF, op. cit., 380.
55. MOIR, op. cit., 179.
56. LUGARD, op. cit., I, 72; cf. DUFF, op. cit., 377.
57. LIVINGSTONE, op. cit., 255.
58. E.g. W. MARWICK, *William and Louisa Anderson* (1897), W. P. LIVINGSTONE, *Mary Slessor*.
59. *Encyclopaedia Britannica*, 11th edn., III, 216.
60. Ibid., XVI, 84; cf. *Dictionary of National Biography*, XXXI, 407; C. W. THOMSON, *Scotland's Work*, 726–7.
61. *Who's Who*; *The Times*, July 12, 1916.
62. *Encyclopaedia*, ut sup., 681–2.
63. A. MCPHEE, *Economic Revolution in British West Africa*.

(2) SUPPLIES

64. PAGAN, *Glasgow*, 86.
65. URE, *Cotton Manufacture*, II, 379.
66. Cf. H. DUNLOP, *The Cotton Trade* (1862).
67. THOMSON, *History of Dundee* (1874 edn.), 335; cf. *Social Science Assoc.* (1863), 806–7; PATON and MILLAR, *Dundee*, 277–80.
68. NORRIE, *Dundee Celebrities*, 235–6; BOASE, *English Biography*, II, 1099–1100; PATON and MILLAR, op. cit., 277.
69. BOASE, op. cit., IV, 783; THOMSON, op. cit., 333–4, 338.
70. WARDEN, *Linen* (1867), Suppt. 18.
71. *Scotsman*, Oct. 31, 1861.
72. *British Assocn.* (1867), 29–38; ACWORTH, *Scottish Railways*, 123–6; *Soc. Science Assocn.* (1863), 808.
73. R. BROWN, *Flax, its Culture* . . . (2nd edn., 1851); cf. PATON and MILLAR, op. cit., 266–8; *Brit. Assocn.* (1867), 6.
74. *Edinburgh Council Records*, Vol. 220, p. 238 (Dec. 1835).
75. BROWN, *Flax*, 15.
76. *Edinburgh Courant*, Jan. 3, 1848; cf. SMEATON, *Alex. Thomson*, 139–40.
77. BROWN, op. cit., 38.
78. WARDEN, *Linen*, Suppt. 3.
79. PATON and MILLAR, op. cit., 275–6.
80. *Soc. Science Assocn.* (1863), 795; PRINGLE, *Peebles and Selkirk*, 61; LUBBOCK, *Colonial Clippers*, 129–30; CRAIG BROWN, *Selkirkshire*, I, 564.
81. PAGAN, *Glasgow*, 86.
82. HAMILTON, *Industrial Revolution*, 179–82; BREMNER, *Industries*, 39–40; MACKENZIE, *J. B. Neilson*, 11–31; SMILES, *Industrial Biography*, 141–8, 154–8.
83. *North British Review*, VII (Nov. 1845), 133–4.
84. BREMNER, op. cit., 35.
85. Ibid., 34.

86. *Manufactures of W. of Scotland* (1876), 5.
87. HAMILTON, op. cit., 189; MACKINNON, *Social History*, 89.
88. ABERCONWAY, *Basic Industries*, 217.
89. *Memoir of C. Macintosh*, Appx. IV
90. MACKINNON, op. cit., 121.
91. WATSON, *Kirkintilloch*, 340–7; MCLEAN, *Industries*, 30.
92. MCLEAN, op. cit., 190.
93. *Memoir of G. Hope*, 108; cf. *Edinburgh Courant*, Jan. 1, 1861.
94. PAGAN, *Glasgow*, 83.
95. GILMOUR, *Story of our Firm*, 213–18.
96. CORMACK, *Shipping*, 139; cf. LUBBOCK, *Colonial Clippers*, 140.
97. ACWORTH, *Railways of Scotland*, 139–42.
98. *Brit. Assocn.* (1856), 153–4.
99. ACWORTH, op. cit., 137.
100. MACLEOD, *Clyde District*, 171.
101. MCCALLUM, *Midlothian*, 68.
102. WATSON, *Statistics of Glasgow* (1865), 94.
103. NICOL, *Statistics of Glasgow* (1881–85), 94.
104. ACWORTH, *Railways of Scotland*, 100–1.
105. NICOL, op. cit., 246–7.
106. NICOL, *Statistics* (1885–91), 322–3; cf. MCLEAN, *Industries*, 186.
    Royal Commn. on Trade Depression, 3rd Report (1886), 248.
107. "Wm. Connal & Co." (*Glasgow Herald*, Dec. 11, 1929).
108. *British Assocn.* (1867), 47–8.

(3) MARKETS

109. CORMACK, *Shipping*, 251.
110. *Life of R. Napier*, 70, 157–63, 208–18; JEANS, *Western Worthies*, 147–9; BREMNER, *Industries*, 70–1; *Manufactures of W. of Scotland*, 173–4.
111. *Manufactures*, op. cit., 161, 174.
112. PATON and MILLAR, *Dundee*, 106; GROOME, *Ordnance Gazeteer*, I, 423; STURROCK, *Linen and Jute Trades* (Soc. Science Assn., 1863), 804.
113. MCLEAN, *Industries*, 39–40.
114. *Manufactures*, op. cit., 87–8.
115. *British Assocn.* (1867), 7; *Royal Commn. on Trade Depression*, 2nd Report, 218.
116. BREMNER, *Industries*, 47; NIMMO, *Stirlingshire*, II, 306–7; GROOME, *Ordnance Gazeteer*, II, 3.
117. BREMNER, op. cit., 70–1.
118. BREMNER, op. cit., 68.
119. Ibid., 251; WARDEN, *Linen*, Suppt. 14.
120. WARDEN, op. cit., Suppt. 3; cf. 618–19.
121. HAY, *Arbroath*, 408.

122. *New Statistical Account*, X, 94.
123. Ibid., VIII, 195.
124. W. M. METCALFE, *Paisley*, 466.
125. NIMMO, *Stirlingshire*, II, 322–4; cf. CAMERON, *Campsie*, Appx., 27–9.
126. BREMNER, op. cit., 288.
127. *Royal Commn. on Trade Depression* (*Aberdeen Chamber of Commerce Report*), 1st Report, 74.
128. LEIGHTON, *Fife* (1840), II, 161–3; cf. BREMNER, op. cit., 242.
129. CUNNINGHAM, *Mining in Lothians*, 136; *Mining in Fife*, 27–29; cf. MACKINNON, *Social History*, 83.
130. NIMMO, *Stirlingshire*, I, 283.
131. *North British Review*, Nov. 1848, 130–1.
132. J. STRANG, *Statistics in Brit. Assocn.* (1855), 193.
133. BREMNER, op. cit., 30–1.
134. STRANG, ut sup., 193–5.
135. BREMNER, op. cit., 33–4.
136. NICOL, *Statistics of Glasgow* (1881–5), 260–1.
137. *Manufactures of W. of Scotland*, 118.
138. MCLEAN, *Industries*, 63–4.
139. BREMNER, op. cit., 48; cf. NIMMO, *Stirlingshire*, II, 306–7; GILLESPIE, *Falkirk*, 38–9.
140. LUBBOCK, *China Clippers*, 144.
141. *Manufactures*, op. cit., 165–6.
142. MCLEAN, op. cit., 98–9.
143. *Royal Commn. on Trade Unions* (1867), I, 145–57.
144. *Scotsman*, Nov. 2, 1898.

V. COMBINATIONS OF CAPITAL

1. HAMILTON, *Industrial Revolution*, ch. ix.
2. CUNNINGHAM, *Mining in Lothian*, 87–9; *Royal Commn. on Mining Royalties*, 1st Report, 194–5.
3. *Tait's Magazine*, Jan. 1837; cf. MILNE, *Lothian Coalfield*, 144.
4. MILNE, op. cit., 148–9; *Comm. on Employment of Children* (1842), 1st Report, passim; *Tait's Magazine*, June 1842, 375–9.
5. *Royal Commn. on Labour* (1892), 2nd Report, 226, 244–5; *Royal Commn. on Royalties*, 193–4; CUNNINGHAM, *Mining in Fife*, 41.
6. MACROSTY, *Trust Movement*, 92; cf. *Royal Commn. on Labour*, 2nd Report, Appx. A, 309; *Scotsman*, Feb. 27, 1935.
7. *Royal Commn. on Labour* (1892), 2nd Report, 226–35, cf. Appx. A, 310.
8. *Select Comm. on Master and Servant* (1865), 106–15.
9. *Royal Commn. on Mining Royalties*, 1st Report, 192.

10. *Scotsman,* June 16, 1873, May 8 and 26, 1888, June 15, 1887, Jan. 10 and Feb. 1, 1893; *Scottish Bankers' Magazine,* IV, 281–8.
11. *Glasgow Electors' Mentor* (1847), No. V, 9, 3; cf. *Representation of Scotland,* 141.
12. MACROSTY, op. cit., 58.
13. *Royal Commn. on Labour,* 2nd Report, Appx. A, 297.
14. MACROSTY, op. cit., 66.
15. *Royal Commn. on Trade Unions* (1868), 9th Report, 42–44; cf. Final Report, Appx., XI, 267–70; CORMACK, *Shipping,* 263.
16. CORMACK, op. cit., 272.
17. *Amalgamated Society of Engineers, Jubilee Souvenir* (1901).
18. *Royal Commn. on Labour,* 2nd Report, II, 52–6, 112–48.
19. BREMNER, *Industries,* 285; *Select Commn. on Trade Unions* (1838), 1–20.
20. *Sanitary Report* (1842), 162.
21. BREMNER, op. cit., 285.
22. *Scottish Guardian,* March 3, 1854.
23. BREMNER, op. cit., 180.
24. *Royal Commn. on Labour,* 2nd Report, Pt. II, 305–10.
25. E.g. *Edinburgh Courant,* March 8 and May 4, 1861.
26. *Royal Commn. on Trade Unions* (1867), 1st Report, 110, 145–7; cf. *Edinburgh Courant,* March 5 and April 12, 1861.
27. *Witness,* Feb. 12, 1853; cf. C. COWAN, *Reminiscences,* 196–211.
28. *Witness,* Jan. 1, 1853; cf. NICHOLSON, *Adam Black,* 147–8.
29. *Royal Commn. on Labour,* 4th Report, Pt. I, 351–64.
30. *Life of G. Troup,* 54–9; *Scottish Educational Journal,* "G. Troup" (March 16, 1934).
31. *Scotsman,* Feb. 9, 1888.
32. "P. Colquhoun" (*Scottish Educational Journal,* Sept. 12, 1930); "Iatros," *Memoir of Colquhoun; Lord Provosts of Glasgow,* Appx., 18–21.
33. "Brief Account of Edinburgh Chamber of Commerce" (1861).
34. *Royal Commn. on Labour* (1892), 1st Report, 96; HALL, *Galashiels,* 297, 542–3.
35. *Report of Conference on Technical Education* (Royal Society of Arts, 1868).
36. *Scottish Guardian,* Jan. 6, 1854.
37. SOMERS, *Currency and Banking* (1862).
38. "Brief Account," ut sup.; cf. *Edin. Courant,* Jan. 14, 1861; *Tait's Magazine,* Jan. 1860, 57–61.

VI. SURVEY OF DEVELOPMENT

1. Cf. *supra,* Part II, ch. i, iii, v.
2. Ibid., ch. iv.

3. A. SMITH, *Wealth of Nations*, e.g. Book I, ch. x.

4. E.g. PIOTROWSKI, *Cartels and Trusts*.

5. Cf., e.g. KEYNES, *The End of Laissez-Faire*.

6. Cf. *supra*, Pt. II, ch. ii.

7. Cf. GRANT, *Economic History of Scotland*, 203–66; HAMILTON, *Industrial Revolution in Scotland*, 1–12.

8. *Tait's Magazine*, March 1832, 126–8.

9. ANDERSON, *History of Edinburgh*, 377, 384.

10. A. ALISON, *England in 1815 and 1845*; cf. RAIT, *Union Bank*, 269–73.

11. H. MILLER, *Words of Warning on Peel's Currency System* (1844).

12. J. CRAWFORD, *Philosophy of Wealth* (1837, 2nd edn., 1846); W. CROSS, *Monetary Reform* (1837).

13. KERR, *Banking in Scotland*, 188–94; *Edin. Courant*, Dec. 12 and 19, 1857.

14. EVANS, *Commercial Crisis*, 35; *Tait's Magazine*, Nov. and Dec. 1857, 641–5, 753–9; cf. HYNDMAN, *Crises in Nineteenth Century*, 78–79.

15. Cf. supra, Pt. II, ch. ii (2).

16. Cf. W. R. LAWSON, *Scottish Investors' Manual*, passim; *Scottish Banking Magazine*, 1879.

17. MAVOR, *My Windows*, I, 52–7, 142–3.

18. *Royal Commission on Trade Depression*, e.g. 1st Report, 74–109.

19. *Tait's Magazine*, 1838, p. 201.

20. URE, *Cotton Manufacture*, II, 314.

21. K. FINLAY, *Letter to Ashley* (1832).

22. MAVOR, op. cit., ch. iv; BREMNER, *Industries*, 288–90; cf. sup., ch. iv.

23. GROOME, *Ordnance Gazeteer* (1885), III, Survey, 81–2.

24. STRANG, *Journal of Statistical Society*, Dec. 1861.

25. *Scottish Educational Journal*, Feb. 12, 1932; cf. sup., Pt. III, ch. iv.

26. R. BROWN, *History of Paisley*, II, 218–23, 443; W. M. METCALFE, *Paisley*, 464–7; *Poor Law Commn. Report on Scotland* (1909), 166; ALISON, *History of Europe* (1815–51), VII, 362.

27. "P. Brewster" (*Scottish Educational Journal*, Oct. 10, 1930).

28. D. GILMOUR, *Paisley Weavers* (1874); M. BLAIR, *Paisley Shawl*, esp. ch. ii, vi; D. MCCALLUM, *Edifying Information* (1889).

29. MILLAR, *Fife*, 43–9; CHALMERS, *Dunfermline*, I, 353–62.

30. GROOME, *Ordnance Gazeteer*, III, Survey, 81.

31. PATON and MILLAR, *Dundee*, 275.

32. BEVERIDGE, *Ochils*, 136–7.

33. HALL, *Galashiels*, 342–58; CROCKETT, *Roxburghshire*, 78.

34. PATON and MILLAR, op. cit., 280; cf. Sup., ch. ii.

35. CORMACK, *Shipping*, 136, 139–40.

36. *Glasgow Herald*, Dec. 30, 1927.

37. *Royal Commn. on Trade Depression*, 1st Report, 85–90.
38. MILNE, *Lothian Coalfields*, 144–6.
39. CHALMERS, *Dunfermline*, II, 87; BEVERIDGE, *Ochils*, 52; CUNNING-HAM, *Fife Coal Co.* (1922), esp. 12–16.
40. *Scots Magazine*, I (1888), 155–6.
41. HENDERSON and WADDELL, *By Bothwell Banks*, 176; cf. *Edinburgh Courant*, June 10, 1872, July 17, 1876.
42. BURN, *Commercial Progress*, 142.
43. *Scotsman*, Oct. 31, 1861.
44. *Witness*, Oct. 7, 1840.
45. Ibid., May 2, 1840.
46. BREMNER, *Industries*, 484; GILLESPIE, *Falkirk*, 340–1.
47. *Scotsman*, May 31, 1933, Feb. 1, 1934, March 19, 1935.
48. *Social Science Assocn.* (1880), 770–2; THOMSON, *History of Scottish People*, VI, 599; CADELL, *Story of Forth*, 214–15; LEARMONTH, *West Calder*, 86, 137–42; *Scottish Bankers' Magazine*, IV, 281–8; *Blackwood's Magazine*, Sept. 1884, 344–5.
49. *Glasgow Herald Supplement*, Dec. 30, 1925; *Scotland*, I, 7 (1935), 11–13, 17; H. R. J. CONACHER, *Oil Shales of Lothians (Geological Survey)*.
50. Cf. sup., ch. v.
51. PRIDE, *Neilston*, 136–7; MURPHY, *Captains of Industry*, 176–80.
52. MURPHY, op. cit., ch. vi, vii.

III. LIFE AND LABOUR

I. LABOUR SUPPLY AND MIGRATION

1. "DAVID DALE" (*Scottish Educational Journal*, July 29, 1930).
2. R. J. CAMPBELL, *Livingstone*, 26, 31, 38; *New Statistical Account*, X, 1234.
3. *Children's Employment Commn.*, I, 25–6.
4. M. BLAIR, *Paisley Thread*, 35.
5. N. MACLEOD, *Reminiscences of a Highland Parish*, 405–8.
6. *Handloom Weavers Report* (1839), 19; cf. MYLES, *Rambles in Forfarshire*, 25–6.
7. GALLOWAY, *Annals of Coal Mining*, 2nd ser., 169; cf. *Sanitary Reports* (1842), 223; MILLER, *Coatbridge*, 187.
8. BLAIR, *Technical College*, 13.
9. ALISON, *History of Europe* (1815–51), VII, 353, *Memoir*, I, 583–4; CROAL, *Recollections of a Journalist*, 38–9.
10. R. COWAN, *Vital Statistics of Glasgow* (1840), 5.
11. STRANG, *Money Rate of Wages* (Brit. Assocn., 1856), 158, cf. *Reports on Census of Glasgow*, 1851, 1861.
12. BURNS, *Commercial Enterprise*, 135–9.

13. F. H. GROOME, *Ordnance Gazeteer*, II, 122; BREMNER, *Industries of Scotland*, 307–10.
14. *Manufactures of W. of Scotland* (1876), 207–8.
15. BREMNER, op. cit., 47; MILLER, *Coatbridge*, 170–4.
16. E.g. "George Woden—"The Great Cornelius," "Mungo."
17. BREMNER, op. cit., 20–1.
18. *Edinburgh Courant*, Jan. 6, 1848.
19. Ibid., July 31, 1848.
20. G. BELL, *Day and Night in the Wynds of Edinburgh* (1849).
21. *Handloom Weavers Report* (1839), 45.
22. *New Statistical Account*, V, 371.
23. *Sanitary Report* (1842), 253.
24. *Sanitary Report, Glasgow* (1839), 185.
25. R. COWAN, *Vital Statistics of Glasgow* (1840), 19.
26. GILLESPIE, *Glasgow*, 22.
27. *Minutes of Edinburgh Trades Council*, Dec. 13, 1887; *Scotsman*, Nov. 24, 1887.
28. *Census of Scotland* (1891), Vol. II, Pt. 2, xvi.
29. *New Statistical Account*, VIII, 148.
30. E.g. BREMNER, op. cit., 484, GALLOWAY, op. cit., 169.
31. J. HODGE, *From Workman's Cottage to Windsor Castle*, ch. iii.
32. W. STEWART, *Keir Hardie*, 4–6.
33. NIMMO, *Stirlingshire*, II, 326–7.
34. *Edinburgh Courant*, Sept. 20, 1861.
35. *New Statistical Account*, VI, 559.
36. Ibid., II, 87; cf. ibid., IV, 186.
37. *Sanitary Reports* (1842), 93.
38. M. M. LEIGH, in *Scottish Journal of Agriculture*, XI, 4 (1928), 5–6. A. J. ROSS, *Life of Bishop Ewing*, 206–10; *North British Review*, No. XXXV, 269–71; cf. CARROTHERS, *Emigration*, 174–6; COCKBURN, *Journal*, 192–3; ANDERSON, *Edinburgh*, 470, 520; *Tait's Magazine*, March 1838, 200; April 1840, 270–2.
39. *Edinburgh Courant*, March 23, 1848.
40. NICOL, *Statistics of Glasgow* (1885–91), 255.
41. LEIGH, op. cit., 6–8; CARROTHERS, op. cit., 233–5; DAY, *Public Administration in Highlands*, 122–4.
42. ALISON, *History of Europe*, 1815–51, VI, 400–4.
43. R. BROWN, *History of Paisley*, II, 443.
44. *Edinburgh Corporation Minutes*, Vol. 238, 217; Vol. 241, 39, etc.
45. CARROTHERS, op. cit., 139–40.
46. W. W. WATSON, *Statistics of Glasgow* (1865), 79–80.
47. NICOL, *Statistics of Glasgow* (1881–5), 254–5.
48. "P. E. DOVE" (*Scottish Educational Journal*, Sept. 8, 1933); cf. *Glasgow Herald*, May 2, 1873; M. DAVIDSON, *Precursors of Henry George*.

R

49. G. E. TROUP, *George Troup*; "G. Troup" (*Scottish Educational Journal*, March 16, 1934).

50. A. SWINTON, *Cotton Spinners' Trial*, Appx. III.

51. *Handloom Weavers' Committee* (1841), 119; CARROTHERS, op. cit., 77.

52. J. CRAWFORD, *Social Science* (1861), cf. ch. viii, sub.

53. "ALEXANDER MACDONALD" (*Scottish Educational Journal*, March 4, 1932).

54. *Scottish News*, June 10, 1886.

II. EMPLOYMENT OF CHILDREN

1. E. S. HALDANE, *Scotland of Our Fathers*, 360.

2. *Factories' Inquiry Commn.*, 2nd Report, 1833, SIR D. BARRY'S *Report*, Introduct.

3. A. URE, *Philosophy of Manufactures*, 299–306.

4. *New Statistical Account*, VII, 332.

5. *Old Statistical Account*, IX, 387–8.

6. J. MYLES, *Dundee Factory Boy*, passim.

7. JOHNSTON, *History of Working Classes*, 318–19; cf. *Factories Inquiry Commn.* (1832–3), passim.

8. K. FINLAY, *Letter to Ashley* (1833); cf. "ALFRED", *Factory Movement*, I, 46, 70

9. CUNNINGHAM, *Mining in Lothians*, 47; *Children's Employment Commn.*, 1st Report, 18–19, 489–92; MACKINNON, *Social History*, 80–2.

10. MACKINNON, op. cit., 82; *Tait's Magazine*, June 1842, 375–9; cf. *North British Review*, XV, 52–81.

11. BREMNER, *Industries of Scotland*, 6; JOHNSTON, op. cit., 332–3; *Children's Employment Commn.*, 18–20, 110–11.

12. *Employment Commn*, ut sup., 459; *Sanitary Reports* (1842), 127–8.

13. *Select Commn. on Trade Unions* (1838), 50–75.

14. *Employment Commn.*, op. cit., 2nd Report, Appx. I, 3–8; HUTCHINS and HARRISON, *Factory Legislation*, 95, 127; JOHNSON, op. cit., 321; COOKE TAYLOR, *Factory System*, 86.

15. WARDEN, *Linen*, 672–3.

16. *Report on Education in Glasgow* (1866), Pt. I, 2, 37; Pt. II, 115; *Children's Employment Commn.*, 2nd Report (1843), Appx. I, 41; *Children's Employment Commn.* (1864–5), passim; e.g. 4th Report, H., 81–6.

17. G. ANDERSON, *Education of Working Classes* (1857); JEANS, *Western Worthies*, 50.

18. *Royal Commn. on Labour*, 2nd Report, Pt. 2, Group C, 35–42, 1st Report, 101–2.

19. *Children's Employment Commn.*, 2nd Report (1843), K, 6–7; cf. 3rd Report (1864), 44–5.

20. *Children's Employment Commn.*, 2nd Report (1843), K, 8–9.
21. MORGAN, *Scottish Education*, 164–8; cf. 2nd Report on *Education in Scotland* (1867).

III. APPRENTICESHIP

1. *New Statistical Account*, VII, 263.
2. *Children's Employment Commn.*, 2nd Report (1843), Appx., 43.
3. Ibid., K, 6–7.
4. *Select Commn. on Master and Servant* (1866), 2.
5. *Report on Education in Glasgow* (1866), I, 54.
6. *Royal Commn. on Trade Depression*, 2nd Report, Pt. II, Appx. D, 29.
7. Ibid., 8–9, 18, 30–1, 40–1.
8. *Royal Commn. on Labour*, 2nd Report, Pt. IV, Appx., 441.
9. Ibid., 2nd Report, Pt. IV, Appx., 607–23; *Royal Commn. on Trade Depression*, 2nd Report, Pt. 2, Appx. D, 90.
10. *R. C. Trade Depression*, 2nd Report, Pt. 2, Appx. D, 97.
11. *Royal Commn. on Labour*, 2nd Report, Pt. 1, 41–2.

IV. WAGES

1. *Handloom Weavers' Commn.* (1841), Vol. I, 6–9.
2. W. M. METCALFE, *History of Paisley*, 467.
3. *Handloom Weavers' Commn.* (1741), I, 18–20.
4. MCCALLUM, *Edifying Information*, 5.
5. R. GIBSON, *Old Berwickshire Town*, ch. xxiii.
6. T. JOHNSTON, *History of Working Classes*, 315–16.
7. "SIR J. MAXWELL" (*Scottish Educational Journal*, Feb. 12, 1932); cf. W. FRASER, *Maxwells of Pollok*, 111–20, esp. 118–19.
8. *Handloom Weavers' Commn.* (1841), I, 6–9.
9. *Sanitary Reports* (1842), 164.
10. A. URE, *Cotton Manufacture*, II, 344.
11. *New Statistical Account*, V, 715.
12. OMOND, *Lord Advocates*, 2nd ser., 37; *Select Commn. on Trade Unions* (1838), 20, 50–75.
13. STRANG, *Money Rate of Wages* (*Brit. Assocn. Report*, 1856, 155).
14. *Report of Factory Inspectors* (1883), ap. HUTCHINS and HARRISON, *Factory Legislation*, 268.
15. *Reports from Asst. Handloom Weavers' Commrs.* (1839), 183–97, but cf. MYLES, *Rambles in Forfarshire*, 80–94.
16. W. THOM, *Rhymes and Recollections of a Handloom Weaver*; ed. 1880 by W. Skinner, *Biographical Sketch*, passim.
17. J. MYLES, *Dundee Factory Boy*, 15–17.

18. G. HAY, *History of Arbroath*, 488–9.
19. *Social Science Assocn.* (1863), *Proceedings*, 804.
20. A. J. WARDEN, *Linen Industry*, Suppt., 25–6.
21. *British Assocn. Report* (1867), *Local Industries*, 12.
22. HUTCHINS and HARRISON, op. cit., 273–4.
23. *Royal Commn. on Labour* (1892), 2nd Report, Pt. 2, Group C, 35–42.
24. Ibid., 1st Report, C, 101–2.
25. *Handloom Weavers' Commn.* (1841), *Harding's Report*, 17.
26. HALL, *Galashiels*, 355.
27. BREMNER, *Industries of Scotland*, 171.
28. *Royal Commission on Labour*, 1st Report, 96.
29. *MSS. Minutes, Friendly Soc. of Carpenters, Edin. Branch* (1836).
30. *Sanitary Reports* (1842), 164.
31. *Commrs. on Scottish Poor Law, Report* (1844), 174–83.
32. WATSON, *Statistics of Glasgow* (1866), 71.
33. *Royal Commn. on Trade Unions*, 1st Report (1867), 145–57.
34. Ibid.
35. Ibid.
36. *Royal Commn. on Labour*, 2nd Report, Pt. 2, C, 278–87; Pt. IV, 429, 440–1, 493.
37. *Royal Commn. on Trade Depression*, 2nd Report (1886), Appx., Pt. 2, 55–6.
38. *Royal Commn. on Labour*, ut sup.
39. ASHTON and SYKES, *Coal Industry of 18th Century*, 82.
40. J. R. PHILIP, "Early Labour Law in Scotland" (*Juridical Review*, June 1934, 129).
41. MILLER, *Coatbridge*, 188; GALLOWAY, *Annals of Coal Mining*, 2nd ser., 16–18.
42. *Select. Commn. on Master and Servant* (1865), 25–6, 55, 93–4; GALLOWAY, op. cit., 168–9.
43. *Royal Commn. on Trade Unions*, 7th Report (1868), 38–59.
44. JOHNSTON, op. cit., 334–49; CUNNINGHAM, *Mining in Lothians*, 47; MILNE, *Lothian Coalfields*, 142; NIMMO, *Stirlingshire*, II, 311–21; ALISON, *History of Europe* (1815–51), VII, 258.
45. *Glasgow Herald*, "Mining in Renfrewshire," Dec. 29, 1927.
46. CHALMERS, *Dunfermline*, I, 24–6.
47. *Royal Commn. on Labour*, 2nd Report (1892), 53–4; SMILLIE, *Life*, 39–40, 57–9; MAVOR, *My Windows*, I, 143; JOHNSTON, op. cit., 348–9.
48. *Royal Commn. on Labour*, ut sup.
49. BREMNER, op. cit., 22.
50. NIMMO, *Stirlingshire*, II, 305, 309–10.
51. *Select Commn. on Master and Servant*, 31–3, 93–4.
52. *Commn. on Children's Employment*, 1st Report (1842), 158.
53. STRANG, *Money Rate of Wages* (*Brit. Assocn. Report*, 1856, 155–9).

54. *Royal Commn. on Labour*, 2nd Report, 389–98; Pt. 3, Appx. 88.
55. BREMNER, op. cit., 51.
56. *Royal Commn. on Labour*, 2nd Report, Appx. 33.
57. STRANG, ut sup.
58. CORMACK, *Shipping*, 258–61.
59. *Royal Commn. on Trade Depression*, 2nd Report, Appx. D, 30–31.
60. NIMMO, *Stirlingshire*, II, 37.
61. BREMNER, op. cit., 104.
62. *New Statistical Account*, VI, 22.
63. Ibid., IV., 186.
64. *Handloom Weavers' Commrs. Report* (1839), 3–7.
65. JOHNSTON, op. cit., 336–7.
66. Ibid., 346.
67. BREMNER, op. cit., 22; MILNE, *Lothian Coalfields*, 139.
68. *Royal Commn. on Labour*, 2nd Report, 43–44, 226–35.
69. *Commn. on Payment of Wages* (1842), 69–73.
70. *Royal Commn. on Labour*, 1st Report, 96, 101–2.
71. BRUCE, *W. Denny*, 79, 90–2.
72. *Encyclopaedia Britannica* (11th edn.), II, 647.
73. *Select Commn. on Trade Unions*, 1st Report, 169–73, 191–226.
74. *Select Commn. on Payment of Wages*, 69–73, 78–80.
75. COWAN, *Vital Statistics of Glasgow* (1840), 36.
76. JEANS, *Western Worthies*, 49; *Social Science Transactions* (1860), 743–8; ALISON, *Life*, II, 245–7.
77. JEANS, op. cit., 53–4; JOHNSTON, op. cit., 260; *Glasgow Herald*, April 23 and 25, 1870; *Encyclopaedia Britannica*, ut sup.

V. HOURS OF LABOUR

1. STRANG, *Statistics of Glasgow* (1857), 32.
2. *New Statistical Account*, IV, 269.
3. Ibid., IV, 285.
4. Ibid., IX, 735.
5. Ibid., V., 715.
6. *Handloom Weavers' Report* (1841), I, 6–9.
7. "ALFRED," *History of the Factory Movement* (1857); cf. R. W. COOKE-TAYLOR, *The Factory System* (1894), HUTCHINS and HARRISON, *History of Factory Legislation* (1903, revd. edn., 1911).
8. STRANG, *Money Rate of Wages in West of Scotland* (*Brit. Assocn. Report*, 1856, 156).
9. MILNE, *Lothian Coalfields*, 139; *Report on Sanitary Conditions* (1842), 98.
10. *Royal Commn. on Labour*, 2nd Report, 244–55.
11. Ibid., 45, 53–4.
12. *Iron and Steel Industry*, 70–1.

13. MACGEORGE, *Bairds of Gartsherrie*, 70; JOHNSTON, *History of Working Classes*, 256–7.

14. *Royal Commn. on Labour*, 2nd Report, Appx., 297; cf. 371, 389–98.

15. *Royal Commn. on Trade Unions*, 1st Report (1867), 145–7.

16. *Royal Commn. on Trade Depression*, 2nd Report (1886), Appx. D.

17. *Royal Commn. on Labour*, 2nd Report, Pt. 4, Appx., passim.

18. WEBB, *Trade Unionism*, 524–5; MAVOR, *Scottish Railway Strike*, 10, 66; JOHNSTON, op. cit., 356–60.

19. *North British Review*, XCI (1868), 17.

20. MAVOR, op. cit., passim; JOHNSTON, op. cit., 360.

21. SMITH, *Memoir of Dr. Begg*, ch. xxix, xxxviii; *Autobiography of T. Guthrie*, II, ch. vii; *Witness*, Sept. 7, 1853.

22. JAMIE, *John Hope*, 163.

23. SMEATON, *Thomson of Banchory*, 314–23; cf. Pt. II, ch. 2, sup.

24. *Witness*, April 11, 1840.

25. *Commn on Employment of Children*, 2nd Report, 1843, K. 8–9.

26. JAMIE, op. cit., 293–4.

27. *Edin. Courant*, Feb. 23, 1861.

28. *Edin. Courant*, July 30, 1861.

29. *Witness*, Oct. 7, 1840; *Scotsman*, Dec. 21, 1842.

30. *Scottish Guardian*, Feb. 17, 1852; *Edin. Courant*, Nov. 3, 1856; *MSS. Minutes Edin. Corporation*, Vol. 261, 407, 263, 85.

31. *Witness*, Aug. 20, 1853; *Soc. Science Assocn. Proceedings* (1863), 689–91.

32. *Scottish Guardian*, Jan. 24, Feb. 17, April 4, May 13, 1854; *Witness*, June 25, 1853.

33. *Tait's Magazine*, Jan. 1856, 90.

34. *Edin. Courant*, Sept. 28 and Oct. 2, 1861.

35. *Soc. Science Assocn. Transactions* (1863), 689–91.

36. *Royal Commn. on Labour*, 3rd Report (1893–4), C, 65–85.

37. *Encyclopaedia Britannica*, 11th edn., XVI, 19; COOKE TAYLOR, op. cit., 135–6.

38. "ALFRED," op. cit., II, 249–50.

39. HUTCHINS and HARRISON, op. cit., 132.

40. Ibid., 137.

41. COOKE TAYLOR, op. cit., 94–101.

42. *Edin. Courant*, Jan. 1 and 10, 1868.

43. COOKE TAYLOR, op. cit., 106–7.

44. HAY, *History of Arbroath*, 408–9.

45. *Witness*, July 9, 1853.

46. *Edin. Courant*, Feb. 21, Mar. 1 and 2, Aug. 19, 1861; *Transactions Soc. Science Assocn.* (1862), 722–6.

47. GILLESPIE, *Labour and Politics*, 136.

48. *Glasgow Herald*, Jan. 8 and 21, Feb. 14, June 22, 1870.

49. *A. S. E. Jubilee Souvenir* (1901), 59–61, 71.

50. *Scotsman*, Mar. 6, 7, 11, 1879; *Royal Commn. on Trade Depression*, 2nd Report (1886), Appx. D., passim.
51. *Tait's Magazine*, Jan. 1856, 3.
52. *Commn. on Trade Depression*, ut sup., Appx. D., 8–9.
53. *Royal Commn. on Labour*, 3rd Report (1893–4), 1–12.
54. D. CARSWELL, *Brother Scots*, 207–9; HUGHES, *Keir Hardie*, 85–93.
55. *Edin. Trades Council Minutes*, March 13, 1888.
56. *Scotsman*, Jan. 9, 1888; JOHNSTON, *op. cit.*, 349.
57. *Scottish Liberal*, 1890 (Feb. 21st, Mar. 28th, etc.).
58. *Royal Commn. on Labour*, 2nd Report, Pt. IV, 442.

VI. SOCIAL PROVISION

1. R. L. HILL, *Toryism and the People*, 113; cf. 178.
2. J. U. NEF, *Rise of British Coal Industry*, II, 162–3.
3. *Sanitary Reports* (1842), 243; *New Statistical Account*, VI, 22.
4. *Tait's Magazine*, June 1838, 405; *New Statistical Account*, VI, 323–4, X, 1234; V. 140; MACDONALD, *Rambles Round Glasgow*, 63–4.
5. *New Statistical Account*, VIII, 254; *Hundred Glasgow Men*, 93–8.
6. *Commn. on Employment of Children* (1842), 489.
7. HUTCHINS and HARRISON, *Factory Legislation*, 91–2.
8. Ibid., 127–8; JOHNSTON, *History of Working Classes*, 321, 326.
9. A. URE, *Philosophy of Manufacture*, 414–15.
10. *Factory Commn.* (1833), 2nd Report, 68.
11. *Scottish Guardian*, Sept. 22, 1854.
12. BREMNER, *Industries of Scotland*, 171.
13. *Factory Commn.* (1832), 2nd Report, 2.
14. WARDEN, *Linen Industry*, 621.
15. THOMSON, *Dundee*, 330.
16. *Royal Commn. on Labour*, 2nd Report, Appx., 441.
17. *Scottish Guardian*, July 25, 1854.
18. Ibid.; MURPHY, *Captains of Industry*, 284; *Century of Papermaking*, 86–8.
19. *North British Review*, No. LXXXII, 276–7.
20. *New Statistical Account*, V, 140.
21. BRUCE, *William Denny*, 78–95; MACLEOD, *Dumbarton* (1884), 62–4.
22. *Royal Commn. on Labour* (1892), 1st Report, 96–100.
23. CLAPHAM, *Economic History*, I, 562; J. R. PHILIP, "Early Labour Law in Scotland" (*Juridical Review*, June 1934, 129).
24. CLAPHAM, op. cit., 410; FRANCIS, *English Railways*, ch. 3, cf. *Scotsman*, Jan. 19, 1888; *Commn. on Truck* (1871), XLI; HALL, *Galashiels*, 124–5.

25. *Select Commn. on Payment of Wages* (1842), 69–73, 78–80, 160–6; cf. ASHTON and SYKES, *Coal Industry*, 145; *Report of Commn. for Mining Areas* (1844), 23–31.

26. *Social Science Assocn. Proceedings* (1860), 738–43.

27. *Comm. on Truck* (1871), XV, 137; cf. JOHNSTON, op. cit., 342.

28. Ibid.; cf. BREMNER, op. cit., 23–4; CLAPHAM, op. cit., II, 457.

29. *Comm. on Truck*, XV, XXXIX–XL, LXXVI, etc., cf. *Tait's Magazine* (1842), 377.

30. Ibid., XXX–XXXI, LXXIV, LXXIX.

31. *Comm. on Payment of Wages* (1842), 160–3.

32. *Sanitary Reports* (1842), 95.

33. JOHNSTON, op. cit., 342–3.

34. *New Statistical Account*, V, 371.

35. *Sanitary Reports* (1842), 243.

36. MRS. CRANSTON LOW, "Langshaws" (1934).

37. *Tait's Magazine*, July 1856, 385–9.

38. JOHNSTON, op. cit., 280.

39. *Commn. on Payment of Wages*, 163–6.

40. *Commn. on Truck*, LXXI–LXXVIII.

41. BREMNER, op. cit., 23.

42. Ibid., 40.

43. *Royal Commn. on Labour*, 2nd Report, Pt. I, 45.

44. JOHNSTON, op. cit., 280; *Commn. on Truck*, 137–8.

45. JOHNSTON, op. cit., 327; CLAPHAM, op. cit., II, 458; *Report by Chief Inspector of Factories* (1887).

46. *Royal Commn. on Labour*, 2nd Report, 275–86.

47. *Commn. on Truck*, LXXIX–XC.

48. MAXWELL, *Co-operation in Scotland*, 147–51; cf. BRUCE, *Wm. Denny*, ch. iv.

49. COOKE TAYLOR, *Factory System*, 74; HUTCHINS and HARRISON, op. cit., 77.

50. *Factory Inspectors' Report on Educational Provisions* (1839), 65–70.

51. ANDERSON, *Education of Working Classes*, 10–14.

52. MILNE, *Lothian Coalfields*, 149.

53. CARRICK, *Newbottle*, 343.

54. *Commn. on Trade Unions*, 7th Report (1868), 1–5.

55. *Social Science Assocn. Proceedings* (1860), 372–9.

56. *Report of Inspector of Mines, West of Scotland* (1864), 145.

57. "Coalmining in Renfrewshire" (*Glasgow Herald*, Dec. 29, 1927).

58. CHALMERS, *Dunfermline*, II, 81, 98.

59. *Commn. on Employment of Children* (1842), 1st Report, Appx. 314.

60. *Commn. on Employment of Children* (1864), 3rd Report, 45.

61. *Scottish News*, Oct. 6, 1887.

62. HODGE, *Workman's Cottage*, 3.

63. *Commn. on Truck*, 171, XLV.

64. *Commn. on Truck*, 245–7.
65. *Commn. on Employment of Children*, 1st Report, Appx. 492.
66. Ibid.
67. BURN, *Commercial Enterprise*, 119.
68. *Commn. on Employment of Children*, 2nd Report, Appx. K, I; *Children's Employment Commn.* (1862–5), 4th Report, H, 81–7.
69. *Commn. on Truck*, 28–9.
70. *Commn. on Employment of Children*, I, 21; *New Statistical Account*, VIII, 254; LEWIS, *Topographical Directory*, II, 166.
71. *New Statistical Account*, X, 449.
72. *New Statistical Account*, X, 1234; *Commn. on Payment of Wages*, 69–73.
73. *Report on Education in Glasgow* (1866), I, 20–1.
74. *New Statistical Account*, VI, 323; LEWIS, op. cit., I, 136; *Commn. on Truck*, II, 245–7.
75. CAMPBELL, *Livingstone*, 43, 50–1.
76. *Commn. on Truck*, II, 224.
77. *Commn. on Employment of Children*, 2nd Report, Appx. K, 8–9; BREMNER, op. cit., 335; COWAN, *Reminiscences*, 70; *Children's Employment Commn.* (1862–5), 4th Report, H, 178.
78. *Commn. on Employment of Children*, ut sup.
79. MACKENZIE, *J. B. Neilson*, 8; *Glasgow Mechanics' Magazine*, Jan. 1825; *Hundred Glasgow Men*, 245–8; SMILES, *Industrial Biography*, 153–4.
80. WATT, *Vital Statistics of Glasgow* (1843–4), 10–11.
81. *Factory Report* (1845), ap. *J. H. Dawson, Statistical Account*, 468.
82. J. C. JESSOP, *Education in Angus*, passim.
83. *Reports of Education Commission* (1864–7).
84. Ibid., *Report on Education in Glasgow* (1866), 126–7.
85. *Comm. on Truck*, 138; *Commn. on Payment of Wages*, 160–3; JOHNSTON, op. cit., 339.
86. HUTCHINS and HARRISON, op. cit., 78.
87. *Commn. on Truck*, 28–9, 116–23; MACGEORGE, *Bairds of Gartsherrie*, 93–4.
88. BREMNER, op. cit., 30, 40.
89. LEARMONTH, *West Calder*, 145–6.
90. *Royal Commn. on Labour*, 1st Report, 101–2.
91. *Factory Inquiry Commission*, 2nd Report (1833), 2, 4–5.
92. URE, *Philosophy of Manufacture*, 412–14; *Sanitary Reports* (1842), 243.
93. *Commn. on Payment of Wages* (1842), 160–3.
94. SMILLIE, *Life*, 36–8.
95. *Commn. on Trade Unions*, 7th Report (1868), 38–59; *Commn. on Truck*, 28–9.
96. CHALMERS, *Dunfermline*, II, 81, 91, 98.
97. *Royal Commn. on Labour*, 2nd Report, 66–97, 182–225; Appx., 190.

98. BREMNER, op. cit., 30.
99. BURN, *Commercial Enterprise*, 119.
100. MUNRO, *Autobiographic Sketch*, 12–17; RANKINE, *John Elder*, 53.
101. *Royal Commn. on Royalties*, 1st Report (1890), 193.
102. *Report of Mines Inspector*, ap. *Commn. on Employment of Children* (1842), 1st Report, Appx.
103. MILLER, *Coatbridge*, 192; *Scottish Land Report*, 410.
104. *Royal Commn. on Labour*, 1st Report, 220–32.
105. *Royal Commn. on Sc. Housing*, 124–45.
106. *Royal Commn. on Labour*, 2nd Report, Pt. I, 50.
107. *Royal Commn. on Sc. Housing*, 148.
108. BREMNER, ut sup., 27–8.
109. *Commn. on Employment of Children* (1842), Appx., 315
110. *North British Review*, XV, 77.
111. MILLER, *Coatbridge*, 16.
112. *Royal Commn. on Sc. Housing*, 145.
113. *Royal Commn. on Labour*, 2nd Report, 235–43.
114. Ibid., 275–86.
115. BREMNER, op. cit., 485; JEANS, *Western Worthies*, 67; LEARMONTH, *West Calder*, 145–6.
116. CRAIG, *Century of Papermaking*, 70.
117. MACLEOD, *Clyde District*, 128–9.
118. *New Statistical Account*, X, 1234.
119. *New Statistical Account*, VI, 322; LEWIS, *Topographical Dictionary*, I, 136.
120. J. O. MITCHELL, "Two Old Glasgow Firms" (*Glasgow Herald*, Oct. 11, 1893).
121. MACLEOD, *Lennox*, 143, 168–9.
122. MACLEOD, *Dumbarton*, 166.
123. WEBER, *Protestant Ethic and Spirit of Capitalism*, passim.
124. E. MUIR, *John Knox* esp. 114–15.
125. H. M. ROBERTSON, *Rise of Economic Individualism*, 88, 95–6.
126. D. CARSWELL, *Brother Scots*, 13–15, 62.
127. J. WILSON HARPER, *Social Ideal and Dr. Chalmers' Contribution*, IX, etc.
128. T. CHALMERS, *Alison on the Poor Law*, etc.
129. CARSWELL, op. cit., 61.
130. J. R. FLEMING, *Church in Scotland* (1843–74), 150.
131. G. A. SMITH, *Henry Drummond*, 57–63.
132. FLEMING, op. cit., 232; JEANS, op. cit., 85–6.

IV. SOCIAL ORGANIZATIONS AND MOVEMENTS

I. TRADE UNIONISM

(1) TEXTILES

1. *Trade Union Congress Souvenir*, Glasgow (1919).
2. *Royal Comm. on Labour*, 4th Report (1894), Appx. LII, 75.
3. A. SWINTON, *Trial of Cotton Spinners* (1838); J. MARSHALL, *Trial of Cotton Spinners* (1838); A. H. MILLAR, *Black Calendar of Scotland*, 98–132; JOHNSTON, *History of Working Classes*, 307–8; COCKBURN, *Journal*, I, 155–9; *Handloom Weavers' Comm.* (1841), 106–8; *Factory Comm.* (1833), 2nd Report, 39; URE, *Philosophy of Manufacture*, 285–7.
4. COCKBURN, op. cit., 164–5.
5. *Select Comm. on Trade Unions* (1838), 1st Report, passim.
6. *Tait's Magazine*, Feb. 1838, 78–81.
7. COCKBURN, op. cit., 155–7, 159–60.
8. J. L. GRAY, "The Law of Combination in Scotland" (*Economica*, Dec. 1928, 332–50); *Select Comm. on Artisans* (1824), 59–64, 363–8, 484–9; *Select Comm. on Combination Laws* (1825), 318–27.
9. BREMNER, *Industries of Scotland*, 286.
10. *Scottish Guardian*, Jan. 17 and 31, 1854.
11. *Glasgow Herald*, Jan. 8 and 13, 1870.
12. *Handloom Weavers' Comm. Rept.* (1839), 16–17, 27, 55; (1841), 105–8.
13. *Children's Employment Comm.* (1864), 2nd Report, 228.
14. *Glasgow Courier*, Feb. 24, 1848.
15. CAMERON, *Campsie*, 27–9.
16. URE, ut sup.; ALISON, *My Life*, I, 394–402.
17. "Scottish Chartist Leaders" (*Glasgow Herald*, Feb. 10, 1934).
18. WEBB, *Methods of Social Study*, 192.
19. THOMSON, *Dundee*, 328.
20. BOASE, *Banking in Dundee*, 382.
21. JOHNSTON, op. cit., 309–10; cf. MYLES, *Rambles in Forfarshire*, 69, 79.
22. *Royal Comm. on Labour*, 1st Report, 102–3; 2nd Report, Pt. 2, C, 35–42; Pt. IV, Ans. 674.
23. BREMNER, op. cit., 172; *Scotsman*, April 12, 1887; information from Mr. R. A. Anderson, Galashiels.

(2) BUILDING

24. CLAPHAM, *Economic History*, I, 71–2; 162–6; cf. POSTGATE, *Builders' History*, 28–31.
25. POSTGATE, op. cit., 117–18.
26. Ibid., 132–3.

27. *Comm. on Trade Unions* (1867), 1st Report, 145–57; 4th Report, 13–17.
28. POSTGATE, op. cit., 140.
29. *Glasgow Argus*, March 21, 1836.
30. H. MILLAR, *My Schools and Schoolmasters* (Collins edn.), 333–49.
31. *Scottish Poor Law Commn. Evidence*, 174–83.
32. BAYNE, *Hugh Miller*, I, 147–52.
33. HOGDEN, *Workers' Education*, 129; MACKINNON, *Social History*, 164.
34. POSTGATE, op. cit., 141.
35. Ibid., 251–3.
36. *Witness*, Sept. 19, 1840.
37. Cf. sup., Pt. 3, ch. v.
38. POSTGATE, op. cit., 256–9, 324–9, 349–50; *Royal Commn. on Labour*, 2nd Report, Pt. 2, C, 278–87.
39. POSTGATE, op. cit., 260.
40. Ibid., 43–4.
41. *MSS. Minute Book, General Union of Carpenters*, Edinburgh Branch, 1836–7.
42. POSTGATE, op. cit., 261.
43. *Soc. Science Assocn.* (1860), 762.
44. POSTGATE, op. cit., 385–8.
45. *Commn. on Trade Unions* (1867), 4th Report, 43.
46. *Glasgow Herald*, Jan. 19, 1870.
47. *Royal Commn. on Labour*, 2nd Report, Pt. IV, C., Ans. 440–1.
48. *Comm. on Trade Unions*, 4th Report (1867), 88; *Report of Trades Conference Comm.* (1867); WEBB, *History of Trade Unionism*, 272–3.
49. POSTGATE, op. cit., 261; MACKIE, *D. McLaren*, II, 53–4; *Commn. on Master and Servant Act*, 2nd Report (1875), 54; *Glasgow Herald*, Jan. 11, 1870; *Proceedings Soc. Science Assocn.* (1862), 723; LEWIS, *Edinburgh Water Supply*, 304; *Edin. Courant*, Dec. 1, 1883.
50. *Comm. on Trade Unions*, 4th Report, 80–8.
51. POSTGATE, op. cit., 348.
52. Ibid., 231–3, 237–8.
53. Ibid., 261–2, 326.
54. Ibid., 319–21, 348.
55. Ibid., 325; *Royal Commn. on Labour*, 2nd Report, Pt. V, 222.
56. *Royal Commn. on Labour*, 2nd Report, Pt. V, 218; *Scotsman*, Nov. 2, 1887.
57. WEBB, *Methods of Social Study*, 191–2.

(3) MINING

58. E.g. *Commn. on Employment of Children* (1842); *Sanitary Reports* (1842).

59. JOHNSTON, *History of Working Classes*, 331; *Report of Commissioner on Mining Districts* (1844), 36.

60. BREMNER, *Industries of Scotland*, 24–5; GALLOWAY, *Annals of Coal Mining*, 2nd ser., 169.

61. *Select Comm. on Trade Unions* (1838), 106–7.

62. MILNE, *Lothian Coalfields*, 144–5, 150; CUNNINGHAM, *Mining in Lothian*, 92–8.

63. BREMNER, op. cit., 25; JOHNSTON, op. cit., 334; ALISON, *My Life*, I, 486–99; *History of Europe* (1815–51), VII, 25–8.

64. GALLOWAY, op. cit., 175–6; JOHNSTON, op. cit., 334.

65. JOHNSTON, op. cit., 335.

66. "A. Macdonald" (*Scottish Educational Journal*, Mar. 4, 1932); WEBB, *Trade Unionism*, 300; JOHNSTON, op. cit., 260–1, 336–48, etc.

67. JOHNSTON, op. cit., 336–8; BREMNER, op. cit., 25–6; ALISON, *My Life*, II, 211–15.

68. *Witness*, Sept. 21, 1853.

69. *Scottish Educational Journal*, ut sup.; cf. *Commn. on Truck*, I, 137–8; *Comm. Trade Unions* (1867), 7th Report, 38–59; *Commn. on Master and Servant* (1865), 24; JOHNSTON, op. cit., 345–8; H. JAY, *Life of R. Buchanan*, 17, 22; *Glasgow Sentinel*, Feb. 19, 1870, Dec. 29, 1877; *Glasgow Herald*, Feb. 15, May 11, 1870, etc.; WEBB, *Industrial Democracy*, 261 n.

70. *Edin. Courant*, Oct. 5, 1856.

71. "Rules of Coal Miners' Assocn." (*Glasgow Sentinel*, 1866).

72. JOHNSTON, op. cit., 347; STEWART, *Keir Hardie*, 10–11.

73. *Royal Commn. on Labour*, 2nd Report, 41–97; Pt. II, 116; SMILLIE, *My Life*, 31–2, 40–57.

74. STEWART, *Keir Hardie*, 12–16; HUGHES, *Keir Hardie*, 4; JOHNSTON, op. cit., 263–4, 347–9; *Royal Commn. on Labour*, 2nd Report, 182–225.

75. *Scottish News*, Oct. 6, 1887.

76. *Royal Commn. on Labour*, 1st Report, 220–32, 2nd, 244–55; CUNNINGHAM, *Mining in Fife*, 16, 24; WEBB, *Social Study*, 178.

77. CUNNINGHAM, *Mining in Lothians*, 92–8; *Scotsman*, Mar. 5, 1888; information from Mr. Andrew Clarke, J.P., Sec. of Union.

78. *Scotsman*, Jan. 29 and Mar. 5, 1888; *Scottish Liberal*, Mar. 28, 1890; STEWART, *Keir Hardie*, 28–31; WEBB, *Trade Unionism*, 391–4.

79. *Scotsman*, Aug. 24, 1887, Jan. 27, 1888; *MSS. Minutes Edinburgh Trades Council*, Aug. 23, Sept. 26, Dec. 13, 1887, Mar. 12, 1889, etc.; *Representation of Scotland*, 112; information from Co. Councillor J. Byrne, J.P., Broxburn, Treasurer of Union.

80. WEBB, *Social Study*, 174–5; 193; STEWART, *Keir Hardie*, 35–57; JOHNSTON, op. cit., 393–4; *Scotsman*, Feb. 18, 1888. *MSS. Minutes, Scottish Miners Federation*, 1894, and seq.

(4) HEAVY INDUSTRIES

81. *Royal Comm. on Trade Depression,* 2nd Report, Appx. D, 30–1; *Comm. on Trade Unions,* 9th Report (1868), 32–42; MACLEOD, *Dumbarton,* 168–70.

82. Ibid., 32; *Royal Comm. on Labour,* 2nd Report, Pt. III, 77; CORMACK, *Shipping,* 263.

83. Ibid., 8–13; *A.S.E. Souvenir* (1901), 59–61, 71, 125; WEBB, *Trade Unionism,* 484–5; *Social Study,* 191; BREMNER, op. cit., 134; CORMACK, op. cit., 262, 274, 276–9; *Glasgow Herald,* May 28, 1870; *Courant,* Mar. 20, 1875.

84. Ibid., 40–1; *Royal Comm. on Labour,* 2nd Report, Pt. III, Ans. 82; CORMACK, op. cit., 265; W. MOSSES, *History of Pattern-makers' Association,* passim.

85. Ibid., 18; WEBB, *Trade Unionism,* 430; *Scottish News,* Sept. 3 and 11, 1886.

86. *Royal Comm. on Labour,* 2nd Report, Pt. II, 125; CORMACK, op. cit., 265–70.

87. WEBB, *Trade Unionism,* 430; *Commn. Trade Depression,* 2nd Report, Appx. D, 29; JOHNSTON, op. cit., 367, 369; BREMNER, op. cit., 135–6; *Edin. Courant,* Jan. 30 and April 8, 1868.

88. JOHNSTON, op. cit., 370.

89. WEBB, *Trade Unionism,* 430–1; JOHNSTON, op. cit., 368.

90. HODGE, *From Workman's Cottage,* ch. i.

91. JOHNSTON, op. cit., 368.

92. *Souvenir Iron and Steel Trades Confederation,* 6.

93. WEBB, *Trade Unionism,* 430; *Souvenir,* ut sup., 11; HODGE, op. cit., ch. v, viii, x, xii; *Royal Comm. on Labour,* 2nd Report, Pt. III, 88, 389–98.

94. "Iron and Steel Industry," 63; HODGE, op. cit., ch. vii and ix; *Royal Commission on Labour,* 2nd Report, Pt. III, 89, 366–88; *Scotsman,* Feb. 9, 1888.

95. *Royal Commission on Labour,* 2nd Report, 275–86, Pt. III, 86; *Scotsman,* Oct. 25, 1890.

96. WEBB, *Social Study,* 191.

97. MACKINNON, *Social History,* 169.

98. JOHNSTON, op. cit., 358; GEMMELL, *Societies of Glasgow,* 58, 65.

99. COLE and ARNOT, *Trade Unionism on Railways,* 16; WEBB, *Trade Unionism,* 365, 439; *Edin. Courant,* Jan. 1, 1887.

100. *Glasgow Sentinel,* Mar. 30, 1872; *MSS. Minutes, Edinburgh Trades Council,* e.g. Nov. 8 and 22, 1881; Dec. 29, 1885, Aug. 20, 1889; *Edin. Courant,* 1881, passim.

101. MAVOR, *Scottish Railway Strike,* passim; HODGE, op. cit., ch. xi; JOHNSTON, op. cit., 360; *Scotsman,* Aug. 1890 to Jan. 1891, passim.

102. COLE and ARNOT, op. cit., 16; *Report of Annual General Meeting, A.S.R.S. for Scotland,* June 1891; *Reports of General Railway Workers' Union,* 1895.

II. TRADES COUNCILS

1. *Edinburgh Courant*, Dec. 28, 1833 (Quoting *Glasgow Courier*); POSTGATE, *Builders' History*, 117–18.
2. BURN, *Beggar Boy*, 123–5; *Glasgow Argus*, Sept. 10, 1835.
3. POSTGATE, op. cit., 117; *Hundred Glasgow Men*, 199; *Herald to Trades Advocate*, passim.
4. *Tait's Magazine*, Mar. and Nov. 1836; *Scottish Notes and Queries*, VI (1892–3), 26; *Glasgow Argus*, Oct. 20, 1836.
5. *Tait's Magazine*, May 1834, 285.
6. *Select Comm. on Trade Unions* (1838), 99, 210.
7. "Alexander Campbell" (*Scottish Educational Journal*, Feb. 26, 1932); *Glasgow Courant*, Feb. 19, 1870.
8. *Scottish Guardian*, April 21, 1854.
9. POSTGATE, op. cit., 253.
10. *Trade Union Congress Souvenir* (1919), 5–7, 11–13; WEBB, *History of Trade Unionism*, 243.
11. *North British Daily Mail*, Aug. 5 and 12, Sept. 17, 1858; GILLESPIE, *Labour and Politics*, 134–5; CRAWFORD, "Social Science" (1861).
12. *Glasgow Trades Council Report* (1860), passim.
13. *Social Science Assocn.* (1860), 875; HODGE, *From Workman's Cottage*, ch. viii; *Royal Commn. on Trade Depression*, Appx. D, 94–5.
14. ALISON, *My Life*, II, 297–301; *Courant*, Mar. 2, 1861.
15. *MSS. Minutes Edinburgh Trades Council*, April 24, 1860, May 7, July 10, Sept. 10, 1861.
16. *North British Daily Mail*, Dec. 10, 1861; GILLESPIE, op. cit., 207.
17. *Edin. Trades Council*, Aug. 26, 1863; WEBB, op. cit., 251–3; JOHNSTON, op. cit., 267, 282–3; *Commn. on Master and Servant* (1866), 1–23.
18. WEBB, op. cit., 252, 280–1; HOWELL, *Labour Legislation*, 151.
19. GILLESPIE, op. cit., 271–3; JOHNSTON, op. cit., 260; *Courant*, Oct. 17, 1866; *N. B. Daily Mail*, Oct. 17, 1866.
20. JOHNSTON, op. cit., 380; *N. B. Daily Mail*, July 5, 1867.
21. *Commn. on Master and Servant Act*, 1st Report (1874), 159.
22. JOHNSTON, op. cit., 261–2; *Glasgow Herald*, Mar. 20, 1873.
23. *Report of Appeal: Macfarlane v. Couper* (1879).
24. *Royal Commn. on Labour*, 2nd Report, Pt. V, 460.
25. J. HODGE, *From Workman's Cottage*, ch. x.
26. *MSS. Minutes Edin. Trades Council*, passim; *Edin. Courant*, passim.
27. "Scottish Chartist Leaders" (*Glasgow Herald*, Feb. 10, 1934); BURN, *Beggar Boy*, 125.
28. JAMIE, *John Hope*, 293–4; cf. sup., Pt. III, ch. v.

29. *Edin. Evening Courant,* April 2 and 7, 1879.
30. *Social Science Assocn.* (1880), Introduction.
31. "The Sweating System in the Tailoring Trade" (*Operative Tailors,* 8 pp., 1880).
32. POSTGATE, *Builders' History,* 252.
33. *Royal Commn. on Labour,* 2nd Report, Pt. V, 448.
34. *Edin. Trades Council MSS. Minutes,* Feb. 15, 1870.
35. *Soc. Science Assocn.* (1877), XXXIII.
36. *Edin. Trades Council, MSS. Minutes,* April 26, June 22, 1869.
37. *Royal Commn. on Labour,* 2nd Report, Pt. V, 459; PATON and MILLAR, *Dundee,* 343–7.
38. *Scotsman,* Nov. 5, 1890.
39. *Royal Commn. on Labour,* 2nd Report, Pt. V, 461, 472; *Edin. Trades Council MSS. Minutes,* Jan. 25, 1876; *Scotsman,* Jan. 11, 1873; *Report of Appeal, Macfarlane* v. *Couper* (1879).

III. BENEFIT SOCIETIES

1. WEBB, *Industrial Democracy,* Pt. II, ch. i.
2. WEBB, *Trade Unionism,* 24.
3. *Commn. on Children's Employment,* 1st Report (1842), 403–5; CUNNINGHAM, *Mining in Lothians,* 48–51.
4. JOHNSTON, *History of Working Classes,* 379.
5. Ibid., 358; BREMNER, *Industries of Scotland,* 105; *Report of Asst. Comm. on Friendly Societies* (1874), 141.
6. *Sanitary Reports* (1842), 102; *Commn. on Employment of Children* (1842), 402, 405; *Sc. Poor Law Commn.* (1844). MILLER, *Coatbridge,* 85; WILSON, *Hawick,* 138–9.
7. *Sanitary Reports* (1842), 243.
8. *Report Asst. Comm. Friendly Societies* (1874), 137.
9. R. FORSYTH, *Beauties of Scotland,* I, 388–9.
10. A. MITCHELL, *Political Movements in Dalkeith,* 31.
11. G. BURNS, *Principles of Friendly Societies* (1821), 8–9.
12. PRIDE, *Neilston,* 248–51.
13. *New Statistical Account,* VII, 44; MCCALLUM, *Pollokshaws,* ch. ix.
14. *Asst. Handloom Weavers' Commrs. Report* (1839), 23; JOHNSTON, op. cit., 382–3.
15. *Report of Asst. Commr. Friendly Socs.* (1874), 174–7; JOHNSTON, op. cit., 381–2.
16. CHALMERS, *Dunfermline,* I, 455.
17. WILSON, *Hawick,* 138; HALL, *Galashiels,* 123.
18. CAMERON, *Campsie,* Appx., 36–7.
19. FRASER, *Life Assurance,* 3–4.
20. WARDLAW, *Essay on Benevolent Associations* (1818).

21. FRASER, op. cit., 4; *Royal Commn. on FriendlySocieties*, 2nd Report, 203–7; "History of Friendly Societies" (*Edin. New Philosophical Journal*, 1827); *Sc. Poor Law Commn.*, 174–83, 236–42.

22. FRASER, op. cit., 5.

23. *Sc. Poor Law Commn. Report*, Appx., Pt. III.

24. R. P. LAMOND, *Scottish Poor Laws*, revised edn., 1890.

25. *Tait's Magazine*, Oct. 1860, 537–49.

26. *Royal Commn. on Friendly Societies* (1871–4), 2nd Report, 183–6, 239–50.

27. Ibid., *Asst. Commr. for Scotland*, Report 1–2, 13.

28. Ibid., 15.

29. Ibid., 16–17; 2nd Report, 180–3, 207–16; JOHNSTON, op. cit., 383.

30. *Royal Commn. on Labour*, 4th Report, Appx. LII.

IV. HOUSING REFORM

1. CHAMBERS, *Improved Dwelling Houses* (1855), 7; cf. sup., Pt. I, ch. ii; Pt. III, ch. vi (4).

2. ANDERSON, *History of Edinburgh*, 231–4, 237, 241.

3. Ibid., 393–4; *Edinburgh in 19th Century*, 88–89; cf. *Edinburgh Courant*, Sept. 18, 1858.

4. *Courant*, ut sup.

5. ANDERSON, op. cit., 508–9.

6. *Local Reports on Sanitary Condition of Labouring Population*, 153–9.

7. "Dr. James Begg" (*Scottish Educational Journal*, May 15, 1931); T. SMITH, *Memoir of Begg*, passim.

8. J. SMITH, *Grievances of Working Classes* (1846), chs. ii, iv, vi, ix.

9. W. ANDERSON, *Poor of Edinburgh* (1867).

10. J. HEITON, *Castes of Edinburgh* (1859).

11. SMITH, *Memoir of Begg*, ch. xl; *Soc. Science Assocn.* (1857), II, 264, 309–10; (1862), 807–8; *Royal Commn. on Friendly Societies*, 2nd Report (1872), 198–200; BEGG, *Happy Homes*, 24–5; *Edin. Corporation Minutes*, Vol. 253, p. 269 (1850); cf. Pt. II, ch. ii, sup., *Scotsman*, April 7 and 13, 1887.

12. *Tait's Magazine*, Feb. 1848, 144.

13. FOULIS, *Old Houses* (1852), passim; ANDERSON, *Poor of Edinburgh*, 54–6.

14. ANDERSON, *History of Edinburgh*, 533; *Edinburgh Courant*, Mar. 12, 1849.

15. Ibid., 543; JAMIE, *John Hope*, 336–7.

16. CHAMBERS, *Social Science Tracts*, V. 2.

17. BLAIKIE, *Autobiography*, ch. x.

18. Ibid., *Soc. Science Assocn.* (1860), 783–4; BLAIKIE, *Better Days*, 183–4.

19. *Witness*, Feb. 19, 1853; FOULIS, op. cit.
20. *Report of Commn. of Working Classes* (1860); *Soc. Science Assocn.* (1860), 783–4.
21. SMITH, *Memoir of Begg*, II, 309–10; BEGG, *Happy Homes*, 16; *Soc. Science Assocn.* (1860), 785; *Royal Commn. on Friendly Societies*, 2nd Report (1872), 171–3.
22. *Royal Commn. on Housing* (1884–5), 2nd Report, 37–8; GEDDIE, *Water of Leith*, 140.
23. BEGG, *Happy Homes*, 19–20, 107; CHAMBERS, *Social Science Tracts*, V, 9–15; SCRATCHLEY, *Benefit Building Societies*, X–XI; *Witness*, Oct. 30, 1861.
24. *Report of Commn. of Working Classes* (1860); cf. *Courant*, Sept. 18, 1858; *Edinburgh Evening News*, Mar. 31, 1934.
25. *Tait's Magazine*, Nov. 1860, 594–9.
26. BEGG, *Happy Homes*, 25–8; H. G. REID, *Housing the People* (1895), passim.
27. BEGG, op. cit., 76–105; *Reports of Edinburgh Co-op. Building Co.*, passim.
28. BEGG, op. cit., REID, op. cit.; *Soc. Science Assocn.* (1863), 499–500; *Edinburgh Courant*, Nov. 30, 1861.
29. *Witness*, Oct. 26, 1861; *Courant*, Oct. 24, 1861; *Scotsman*, Oct. 25, 1861.
30. *Reports, Co-op. Building Co.*, passim; cf. BEGG, op. cit., 25–50.
31. *Social Science Assocn.* (1863), 625–30, 750–1, 765.
32. JOHNSTON, *History of Working Classes*, 376–7; *Edin. Directory*, 1863–4; *Edinburgh Courant*, Oct. 6, 1861, Jan. 14, 1865.
33. *Reports*, ut sup.; B. JONES, *Co-operative Production*, II, 540–5; REID, op. cit.; BALLINGALL, *Edinburgh Past and Present* (1877), ch. v.
34. *Scotsman*, Jan. 12, 1892; *Royal Commn. on Housing* (1884–5), 2nd Report, 35–7.
35. *Comm. on Sc. Housing*, 267.
36. SMITH, *Memoir of Begg*, ch. xlviii; cf. "Housing Policy in Europe" (International Labour Office, 1930), 147.
37. *Courant*, Dec. 27, 28, 31, 1861.
38. *Edinburgh*, 1329–1929, 34.
39. REID, op. cit.; *Soc. Science Assocn.* (1874), 914.
40. MCKAY, *History of Kilmarnock* (2nd edn.), 195; HALL, *Galashiels*, 528.
41. NIMMO, *Stirlingshire*, I, 270.
42. MACLEOD, *Dumbarton, Recent Events*, 49–55.
43. *Sc. Housing Commn.*, 49, 266–7.
44. MITCHELL, *Dalkeith*, 100–2, 227.
45. SMILLIE, *Life*, 143; *Sc. Housing Commn.*, 151–2; *New Statistical Account*, VI, 760–61; *Scottish Land Report*, 411–2.
46. *Sc. Housing Commn.*, 124–5, 145.

47. Sc. Housing Commn., 151–2.
48. Commn. on Employment of Children (1842), 1st Report, Evidence, 314.
49. MACLEOD, Clyde District, 129.
50. Comm. on Trade Unions, 4th Report (1867), 80–8.
51. Ibid., Final Report (1868–9), Appx. LXII, and pp. 342–46; CHAMBERS, Soc. Science Tracts, I, 22.
52. Sc. Housing Commn, 267; cf. W. MAXWELL, St. Cuthbert's Co-op. Assn., 196, 275.
53. CHAMBERS, Improved Dwelling Houses, 10; Soc. Science Assocn. (1860), 783; WYLIE, Disruption Worthies, 256.
54. Edinburgh Courant, Nov. 25, 28, 1861; Witness, Nov. 27, 1861; BEGG, Happy Homes, 24.
55. W. ANDERSON, Poor of Edinburgh (1867), passim.
56. GILBERT, Edinburgh in 19th Century, 142; Edinburgh, 1329–1929, 33–4; CHAMBERS, Memoir, 102; Edinburgh Evening News Jubilee.
57. Royal Comm. on Housing (1884–5), 2nd Report, 38–42.
58. THOMSON, History of Dundee, 156; PATON and MILLAR, Dundee, 94; GROOME, Ordnance Gazetteer, I, 423.
59. Royal Commn. on Housing, 2nd Report, 68.
60. Ibid., 74; RUSSELL, Leith, 454; IRONS, Leith, II, 335–7.
61. J. B. RUSSELL, Public Health Administration, ch. i, Royal Commn. on Housing, 2nd Report, 44; Municipal Glasgow (1914), 48–51; MACKINNON, Social History, 253–4; JEANS, Western Worthies, 155–7.
62. North British Daily Mail, Nov. 7, 1866; Hundred Glasgow Men, 37–9; Lord Provosts of Glasgow, 238.
63. Glasgow Herald, June 25, 28, 30, 1870; cf. Hundred Glasgow Men, 40–2; Soc. Science Assocn. (1874), 594–609.
64. GILLESPIE, Glasgow, 13.
65. CHISHOLM, Municipal Enterprises (MCLEAN, Industries of Glasgow, 248).
66. RUSSELL, op. cit., ch. iii, esp. 57.
67. Glasgow, Past and Present, XXVI–XXX; NICOL, Statistics of Glasgow (1881–5), 2, 5, 49.
68. NICOL, Statistics of Glasgow (1891), 129–34; RUSSELL, ut sup.; MACKINNON, op. cit., 254–5; BELL and PATON, Glasgow, 218–32 ; CHISHOLM, op. cit., 248–54.
69. Encyclopaedia Britannica, 11th edn., XIII, 818.
70. Royal Commn. on Housing, 2nd Report, Appx. C., 135.
71. D. MACLEOD, Non-Churchgoing and Housing of Poor (1888).
72. MAVOR, My Windows, I, 154; BELL and PATON, op. cit., 230.
73. MAVOR, op. cit., I, 156–8; BELL and PATON, ut sup.; GEMMELL, Societies of Glasgow, 76–7.
74. CHAMBERS, Soc. Science Tracts (1861), No. 6; Glasgow Herald, Feb. 23, 1870; JEANS, Western Worthies, 184–90.

75. *Scotsman,* April 12, 1890; BELL and PATON, op. cit., 230–31; MAVOR, op. cit., I, 162.

SCOTLAND AT THE END OF THE NINETEENTH CENTURY

1. M. ATKINSON, *Local Government in Scotland,* Pt. I, ch. iv.
2. *Census of Scotland,* 1891, Vol. II, Pt. II, xii–xiv.
3. Ibid., 15; cf. GROOME, *Ordnance Gazetteer* (1885), III, *Survey,* 80–2; MCLEAN, *Industries of Glasgow,* 140.
4. Ibid., 5, 6, 9.
5. Ibid., XVI.
6. MURPHY, *Captains of Industry,* ch. v; J. R. NAPIER, *David Elder,* 3–14; ABERCONWAY, *Basic Industries,* ch. xvi.
7. *Life of Sir A. Yarrow,* 192–7.
8. THOMSON, *History of Scottish People,* VI, 599; cf. MCLEAN, op. cit., 98.
9. MACKINNON, *Social History,* 112–3.
10. *Glasgow Herald,* Nov. 14, 1927; *Scottish Notes and Queries,* VI, 67; GROOME, *Ordnance Gazetteer,* II, 376; MACINTOSH, *Galston,* 32–3; Ibid., *Ayrshire Nights,* 396.
11. "James Young" (*Scottish Educational Journal,* June 19, 1932).
12. J. S. JEANS, *Iron Trade,* 55–6; Ibid., *History of Steel,* 87, 104; BESSEMER, *Autobiography,* 263–72, 289–95; *Dictionary of National Biography,* XXXIX, 430–2.
13. MURPHY, *Captains of Industry,* 257–63.
14. MACKINNON, op. cit., 134–43.
15. THOMSON, *Scotland's Work,* 669; LINDSAY, *History of Shipping,* IV., 178–84, 260–2, 287–90, 439–43.
16. MCLEAN, op. cit., 283–8.
17. MACKINNON, op. cit., 151; cf. THOMSON, *History of Scottish People,* VI, 60–1.
18. KERR, *Banking in Scotland,* 288–9.
19. Ibid., 270–71; ANDERSON, *Commercial Bank,* 65–73.
20. Ibid., 341.
21. H. W. MACROSTY, *Trust Movement,* 230, 241; cf. sup., Pt. II, ch. i.
22. THOMSON, *History of Scottish People,* VI, 592–624.
23. HUME BROWN, *History of Scotland,* III, 360–1; COCKBURN, *Journal* II, 219–22; FLEMING, *Church in Scotland,* 152; *Life of G. Hope,* 251; C. COWAN, *Reminiscences,* 259.
24. KING, *Feudalism in Scotland,* 196–210.
25. THOMSON, ut sup.; MACKINNON, op. cit., 60–2; *Life of G. Hope,* 253–9.
26. DAY, *Public Administration,* 182–3, 190–4; BEATON, *Highlands,* 74–7; M. M. LEIGH, *Crofting Problem,* VII.

27. DAY, op. cit., 4–7, 373–400.
28. W. MAXWELL, *History of Co-operation in Scotland*, passim; J. LUCAS, *Co-operation in Scotland*, esp. 31–33, 46–54, 55–8; B. JONES, *Co-operative Production*, passim.
29. J. B. RUSSELL, *Public Health Administration*, passim; A. K. CHALMERS, *Century of Public Health; Edinburgh*, 1829–1929, 11–34.
30. J. S. CLARKE, *An Epic of Municipalization* (1928).
31. A. MORGAN, *Scottish Education*, 138–40; Ibid., *Scottish University Studies*, 80–2.
32. "Mechanics' Institutes in Scotland" (*Journal of Adult Education*, VI, 3 (1933), 292–309).
33. W. STEWART, *Keir Hardie*, esp., 35–45, 72–4; D. LOWE, *Souvenirs of Scottish Labour*, esp. 1–5, 18–23, 81–7.
34. Cf. J. R. FLEMING, *Church in Scotland* (1843–74), esp. 149–55, 238–40; ibid., *Church in Scotland* (1874–1929), passim; H. F. HENDERSON, *Religion in Scotland*, ch. v; J. W. HARPER, *Social Ideal and Dr. Chalmers;* CARSWELL, *Brother Scots*, Preface.

BIBLIOGRAPHY

I. GENERAL HISTORIES

P. HUME BROWN, *History of Scotland*, Vol. III, Cambridge, 1911.

R. L. MACKIE, *Short History of Scotland*, Oxford, 1931 (ch. 29).

C. W. THOMSON, *Scotland's Work and Worth*, Edinburgh, 1910 (Vol. 2).

G. M. THOMSON, *A Short History of Scotland*, London, 1930 (ch. 24).

REV. TH. THOMSON, *A History of the Scottish People*, cont. by CH. ANNANDALE, Glasgow, 1893, Vol. 6.

R. S. RAIT and G. S. PRYDE, *Scotland*, Benn, 1934.

J. R. FLEMING, *The Church in Scotland*, 1843–74, Edinburgh, 1927.

D. BREMNER, *Industries of Scotland*, Edinburgh, 1869.

T. JOHNSTON, *History of Working Classes in Scotland*, Glasgow, 1920 (ch. 9–14).

J. MACKINNON, *Social and Industrial History of Scotland from the Union*, London, 1921, Pt. II.

H. HAMILTON, *Industrial Revolution in Scotland*, Oxford, 1932.

I. F. GRANT, *Economic History of Scotland*, 1934, London (Pt. IV).

E. S. HALDANE, *The Scotland of our Fathers*, London, 1933.

II. UNPUBLISHED MATERIAL

MSS. Records of Edinburgh Town Council, 1833–93, passim.

MSS. Minutes of Edinburgh Trades Council, 1859–76; 1881–9.

MSS. Minutes Society of Carpenters, Edinburgh, 1836–7.

Reports of Edinburgh Co-operative Building Co., 1862–1920.

An Economic History of Shipbuilding and Marine Engineering. Thesis for Ph.D., by W. S. CORMACK, B.SC., Glasgow, 1931.

III. REPORTS

Factories Inquiry Commission, 1st and 2nd Reports, 1833, XXI.

Returns Relating to Factories: Effect of Educational Provisions of the Factory Act, 1839, XIII.

Reports from Committees on Handloom Weavers, 1834, 1835.

Reports from Assistant Handloom Weavers Commissioners, 1839, XIII.

Report of Handloom Weavers Commission, 1841, X.

Report of Select Committee on Trade Unions, 1838.

Local Reports on the Sanitary Condition of the Labouring Population of Scotland (Poor Law Commission), 1842.

Report of H.M. Commission into Poor Laws of Scotland, 1844, XX.

Report of Select Committee on Payment of Wages, 1842, V.

Reports of Children's Employment Commission, First, 1842, XV; Second, 1843, XV.

Reports of Children's Employment Commission, 2nd Report, 1864, XXII; 4th Report, 1865, XX.

Report from Select Committee on Master and Servant, 1865, VIII.

Reports of Commission on Master and Servant Act, 1st Report, 1874; 2nd Report, 1875.

Reports of Commissioners on Trade Unions, 1st Report, 1867, XVIII; 4th, 1867, XXXII; 7th, 8th, and 9th, 1867–8, XXXIX; Final, 1868–9, XXXI.

Report of State of Education in Glasgow (Scottish Education Commission), 1866.

Report of Commission on Coal, 1871, XVIII.

Report of Commission on Truck, 1st Report, 1871, XXIII.

Owners of Lands and Heritages, 1872–3 (Scotland), 1874, LXXII.

Royal Commission on Mining Royalties, 1st Report, 1890, XXXVI; 2nd Report, 1891, XLI.

Royal Commission on Friendly Societies, 2nd Report, 1872, XIII; *Report of Asst. Commrs. for Scotland*, 1874.

Royal Commission on Depression of Trade and Industry, Reports, 1886, XXIII.

Royal Commission on Labour, 1st Report, 1892, XXXIV; 2nd Report, 1892, XXXVI; 3rd Report, 1893–4, XXXIV; 4th Report, 1893–4, XXXIX.

Royal Commission on Housing of the Working Classes, 2nd Report, 1884–5, XXXI.

Royal Commission on Housing of Industrial Population of Scotland, 1912–17.

Census of Scotland, 1891, 1892, XLVII.

Comparative Account of Population of Great Britain, 1801–31, 1831, XVIII.

PROF. R. COWAN, *Vital Statistics of Glasgow* (British Assocn., 1840).

A. WATT, *Vital Statistics of Glasgow*, 1843–4.

J. STRANG, *Vital Statistics of Glasgow*, 1855, 1861.

W. W. WATSON, *Vital Statistics of Glasgow*, 1863–80.

J. NICOL, *Vital Statistics of Glasgow*, 1881–5 (1885), 1885–91 (1891).

Reports of Proceedings of British Association for Advancement of Science, 1840, 1855, 1856, 1867.

Reports of Transactions of National Association for the Promotion of Social Science, 1860, 1863, 1874, 1877, 1880.

Report on Condition of Poorer Classes in Edinburgh, 1868.

Report of Committee of Working Classes of Edinburgh on Dwellings, 1860.

Scottish Land: the Report of the Scottish Land Enquiry Committee, 1914.

IV. LOCAL HISTORIES

EDINBURGH:

J. ANDERSON, *History of Edinburgh*, Edinburgh, 1856.

W. BALLINGALL (Ed.), *Edinburgh Past and Present*, Edinburgh, 1877.

W. M. GILBERT (Ed.), *Edinburgh in the Nineteenth Century*, Edinburgh, 1901.

J. GRANT, *Old and New Edinburgh*, London, 1880.

Edinburgh, 1329–1929 (600th Anniversary), Edinburgh, 1929.

J. C. IRONS, *Leith and its Antiquities*, 2v., Edinburgh, 1897.

J. RUSSELL, *The Story of Leith*, Edinburgh, 1922.

W. BAIRD, *Duddingston and Portobello*, Edinburgh, 1898.

A. HERON, *Merchant Company of Edinburgh*, Edinburgh, 1903.

W. STEVEN, *George Heriot's Hospital*, 1845, 3rd edn. by F. W. Bedford, Edinburgh, 1874.

GLASGOW:

J. D. BURN, *Commercial Enterprise and Social Progress*, London, 1858, chs. 5–9.

G. EYRE TODD, *Story of Glasgow*, revised edn., Glasgow, 1920.

R. GILLESPIE, *Glasgow and the Clyde*, Glasgow, 1876.

J. F. S. GORDON (Ed.), *Glasghu Facies*, 2v., Glasgow, 1873.

J. KNIGHT, *Glasgow and Strathclyde*, Edinburgh, 1931.

A. MCCALLUM, *Pollokshaws*, Paisley, 1925.

H. MACDONALD, *Rambles Round Glasgow* (1854), Ed. G. H. Morrison, Glasgow, 1910.

W. J. MILLAR, *The Clyde*, Glasgow, 1888.

"J. H. MUIR," *Glasgow in 1901*, Glasgow, 1901.

J. ORD, *Barony of Gorbals*, Paisley, 1919.

J. PAGAN, *Sketches of History of Glasgow*, Glasgow, 1847.

Ed., *Glasgow Past and Present*, Glasgow, 1884.

A. WALLACE, *History of Glasgow*, 1882.

OTHER TOWNS:

W. CADENHEAD, *New Book of Bon Accord*, Aberdeen, 1866.

W. ROBBIE, *Aberdeen, its Traditions and History*, Aberdeen, 1893.

VICTORIA E. CLARK, *Port of Aberdeen*, Aberdeen, 1921.

J. KNOX, *Airdrie* (Centenary Sketch), 1921.

J. M. MCBAIN, *Arbroath Past and Present*, Arbroath, 1887.

G. HAY, *History of Arbroath*, Arbroath, 1876.

P. C. CARRAGHER, *Arbroath the Royal Burgh*, Saltcoats, 1909.

T. J. SALMON, *Borrowstounness and District*, Edinburgh, 1913.

D. D. BLACK, *History of Brechin*, Brechin, 1839.

A. MILLER, *Rise and Progress of Coatbridge*, Glasgow, 1864.

A. MITCHELL, *Political and Social Movements in Dalkeith*, 1882.

D. MACLEOD, *Castle and Town of Dumbarton*, Dumbarton, 1877.
Dumbarton: its Recent Men and Events, Dumbarton, 1898.

J. THOMSON, *History of Dundee* (1847), Ed. J. Maclaren, 1874.
Memorial Volume, British Assocn. Meeting at Dundee, 1867, Dundee, 1868.

A. W. PATON and A. H. MILLAR (Ed.), *Handbook to Dundee and District* (British Assocn., 1912), Dundee, 1912.

REV. P. CHALMERS, *Historical and Statistical Account of Dunfermline*, Edinburgh, Vol. I, 1844; Vol. II, 1859.

R. GIBSON, *An Old Berwickshire Town* (Greenlaw), Edinburgh, 1905.

R. MURRAY SMITH, *History of Greenock*, 1921.

R. HALL, *History of Galashiels*, Galashiels, 1898.

R. WILSON, *History of Hawick* (1825), new edn., 1837.

A. MCKAY, *History of Kilmarnock*, 2nd edn., 1858; 3rd, edn., 1864.

T. WATSON, *Kirkintilloch*, Glasgow, 1894.

D. MITCHELL, *History of Montrose*, 1866.

J. PARKHILL, *History of Paisley*, Paisley, 1857.

R. BROWN, *History of Paisley*, 2v., 1886, Paisley.

REV. W. M. METCALFE, *History of Paisley*, Paisley, 1909.

W. F. MACARTHUR, *History of Port Glasgow*, Glasgow, 1932.

COUNTIES, PARISHES, ETC.:

A. SMITH, *New History of Aberdeenshire*, 2v., Edinburgh, 1875.

J. PATERSON, *History of Counties of Ayr and Wigton*, 5v., Edinburgh, 1863–66.

W. ROBERTSON, *Ayrshire*, 2v., Ayr, 1908.

JOHN IRVING, *History of Dumbartonshire*, 3v., 1917–24.

J. M. LEIGHTON, *Fife Illustrated*, 3v., Glasgow, 1840.

A. H. MILLAR, *Fife Pictorial and Historical*, 2v., Cupar-Fife, 1895.

J. WILKIE, *History of Fife*, Edinburgh, 1924.

A. MCCALLUM, *Midlothian*, Cambridge, 1912.

G. C. PRINGLE, *Peebles and Selkirkshires*, Cambridge, 1914.

F. MORT, *Renfrewshire*, Cambridge, 1912.

T. CRAIG BROWN, *History of Selkirkshire*, 2v., Edinburgh, 1886.

W. NIMMO, *History of Stirlingshire*, revd. edn. by R. Gillespie, 2v., 1880.

J. CAMERON, *Parish of Campsie*, Kirkintilloch, 1892.

REV. W. ROSS, *Busby and Its Neighbourhood*, Glasgow, 1883.

W. GIBSON, *Reminiscences of Dollar and Tillicoultry*, Edinburgh, 1883.

J. MACARTHUR, *New Monkland Parish*, Glasgow, 1890.

J. MACINTOSH, *Galston and Loudoun Parishes*, Newmilns, 1890.

D. PRIDE, *Parish of Neilston*, Paisley, 1910.

W. C. LEARMONTH, *History of West Calder*, West Calder, 1885.

P. MCNEILL, *Tranent and Its Surroundings*, Edinburgh, 1884.

G. HENDERSON and J. J. WADDELL, *By Bothwell Banks*, Glasgow, 1904.

H. M. CADELL, *Story of the Forth*, Glasgow, 1913 (ch. 9–14).

D. POLLOCK (Ed.), *Dictionary of the Forth*, Edinburgh [1891].

D. BEVERIDGE, *Between the Ochils and the Forth*, Edinburgh, 1888.

J. MYLES, *Rambles in Forfarshire*, Dundee, 1850.

R. GILLESPIE, *Round about Falkirk*, 2nd edn., Glasgow, 1879.

D. MACLEOD, *Dumbarton, Vale of Leven, Loch Lomond*, Dumbarton, 1884.

Historic Families, Notable People and Memorabilia of the Lennox, Dumbarton, 1891.

The Clyde District of Dumbartonshire, Dumbarton, 1886.

D. POLLOCK (Ed.), *Dictionary of the Clyde*, Edinburgh, revised edn., 1891.

V. PARTICULAR INDUSTRIES

BANKING AND FINANCE:

J. L. ANDERSON, *Commercial Bank of Scotland*, Edinburgh, 1910.

W. BAIRD, *The One Pound Note, 1885*, revd. edn., Edinburgh, 1901.

C. W. BOASE, *A Century of Banking in Dundee*, Edinburgh, 1864; 2nd edn. 1867.

J. S. FLEMING, *Scottish Banking*, 3rd edn., Edinburgh, 1877.

W. GRAHAM, *The One Pound Note in Scotland*, Edinburgh, 1886.

A. W. KERR, *History of Banking in Scotland*, 1884; revised edn. by F. H. Allan, Edinburgh, 1926.

N. MUNRO, *Royal Bank of Scotland*, Edinburgh, 1928.

SIR R. S. RAIT, *Union Bank of Scotland*, Glasgow, 1930.

R. SOMERS, *The Scotch Banks and System of Issue*, Edinburgh, 1873.

W. WALLACE (Ed.), *City of Glasgow Bank Trial*, Glasgow, 1908.

FENN'S *Compendium of Funds, Companies*, etc., 10th edn., London, 1869.

J. REID, *Manual of Scottish Stocks and British Funds*, 4th edn., Edinburgh, 1842.

A. SCRATCHLEY, *Industrial Investment and Emigration: Benefit Building Societies*, etc., 1847; 2nd edn., London, 1851.

G. GLASGOW, *Scottish Investment Trust Companies*, London, 1932.

J. FRANCIS, *Annals and Anecdotes of Life Assurance*, London, 1853.

W. FRASER, *Principles and Defects of Present Associations for Life Assurance* (1831), 2nd ed., Edinburgh, 1840.

D. M. EVANS, *Commercial Crisis, 1857–58*, London, 1859.

Facts, Failures and Frauds, London, 1859.

H. MILLER, *Words of Warning to the People of Scotland on Peel's Currency Scheme*, Edinburgh, 1844.

HEAVY INDUSTRY:

D. MILNE, *Memoir on Mid and East Lothian Coalfields*, Edinburgh, 1839.

A. S. CUNNINGHAM, *Mining in Mid and East Lothian*, Edinburgh, 1926.
Mining in the Kingdom of Fife, 2nd edn., Dunfermline, 1913.

R. L. GALLOWAY, *Annals of Coal Mining*, 2nd series, London, 1904.

T. S. ASHTON and J. SYKES, *The Coal Industry of the Eighteenth Century*, Manchester, 1929.

J. U. NEF, *Rise of British Coal Industry*, 2v., London, 1932.

J. S. JEANS, *The Iron Trade of Great Britain*, London, 1906.
Trial of J. B. Neilson v. Household Coal and Iron Co., Edinburgh, 1842.

R. HARVEY, *Early Days of Engineering in Glasgow*, Glasgow, 1919.
Dennys Dumbarton, Souvenir, 1908.
Two Centuries of Shipbuilding by the Scotts at Greenock, 2nd revised edn., London, 1920.
Development of Shipbuilding on the Upper Reaches of the Clyde, Barclay, Curle and Co., Glasgow, 1911.

TEXTILES:

A. URE, *Philosophy of Manufacture*, 1835.

Ibid., *Cotton Manufacture of Great Britain*, 2v., London, 1836.

A. J. WARDEN, *History of Linen Trade*, London, 1864; 2nd edn., 1867.

R. BROWN, *Flax, Its Culture and Preparation*, Revised edn., Glasgow, 1851.

M. BLAIR, *The Paisley Shawl*, Paisley, 1904.
The Paisley Thread, Paisley, 1907.

TRANSPORT:

Book of the Anchor Line, London, 1932.

W. M. ACWORTH, *Railways of Scotland*, London, 1890.

J. FRANCIS, *History of English Railways*, 2v., London, 1851.

H. G. LEWIN, *British Railway System to 1844*, London, 1914.
Early British Railways, 1801–44, London, 1926.

W. MCILWRAITH, *Glasgow and South Western Railway*, Glasgow, 1880.

H. SCRIVENOR, *Railways of United Kingdom*, London, 1849 (pp. 559–691).

C. E. R. SHERRINGDON. *A Hundred Years of Inland Transport*, London, 1934.

E. A. PRATT, *Scottish Canals and Waterways*, London, 1922.

J. L. CRAWFORD, *Forth and Clyde Canal*, Glasgow, 1891.

J. MAVOR, *Scottish Railway Strike*, Edinburgh, 1891.

W. S. LINDSAY, *History of Merchant Shipping*, Vol. 4, London, 1874.

B. LUBBOCK, *The China Clippers*, 3rd edn., Glasgow, 1916.
The Colonial Clippers, Glasgow, 1921.

L. C. CORNFORD, *The Sea Carriers*, Aberdeen, 1925.

OVERSEAS TRADE:

J. RANKIN, *A History of Our Firm*, Liverpool, 1908.
W. A. CARROTHERS, *Emigration from British Isles*, London, 1929.
J. M. GIBBON, *Scots in Canada*, London, 1911.
PROF. H. DRUMMOND, *Tropical Africa*, London, 1888.
M. FOTHERINGHAM, *Adventures in Nyasaland*, London, 1891.
SIR F. LUGARD, *Rise of East African Empire*, 2v., Edinburgh, 1893.
REV. N. MACLEAN, *Africa in Transformation*, London, 1913.
F. L. M. MOIR, *After Livingstone*, London, n.d.

GENERAL AND MISCELLANEOUS:

Notices of some of the Principal Manufactures of the West of Scotland
   (Leading Industries of Glasgow and the Clyde Valley. British
   Assocn.), Glasgow, 1876.
A. MCLEAN (Ed.), *Local Industries of Glasgow and the West of Scotland*
   (British Assocn.), Glasgow, 1901.
BARON DUPIN, *Commercial Power of Great Britain*, 2v., London, 1825;
   Vol. 2, 122–259.
W. S. MURPHY, *Captains of Industry*, Glasgow, 1901.
LORD ABERCONWAY, *Basic Industries of Great Britain*, London, 1927,
   chs. xiv–xvi.
A Century of Paper Making, Robt. Craig & Sons.
J. O. MITCHELL, *Two Old Glasgow Firms: Wm. Connal & Co.; the
   Crums of Thornliebank*, Glasgow, 1894.
J. O. MITCHELL, *Old Glasgow Essays*, Glasgow, 1905.
G. STEWART, *Curiosities of Glasgow Citizenship*, Glasgow, 1881.

VI. BIOGRAPHY AND MEMOIRS

The Dictionary of National Biography.
F. BOASE, *Modern English Biography*, 6v., 1892–1921.
T. H. WARD, *Men of the Reign*, London, 1885.
J. IRVING, *The Book of Eminent Scotsmen*, Paisley, 1881.
M. F. CONOLLY, *Eminent Men of Fife*, Edinburgh, 1866.
REV. J. A. WYLIE, *Disruption Worthies*, 2v., Edinburgh, 1881.
W. NORRIE, *Dundee Celebrities of Nineteenth Century*, Dundee, 1873.
A. H. MILLAR, *Eminent Burgesses of Dundee*, Dundee, 1887.
Biographical Sketches of Lord Provosts of Glasgow, Glasgow, 1883,
   2nd edn., 1902.
Memoirs and Portraits of One Hundred Glasgow Men, 2v., Glasgow,
   1886.
S. SMILES, *Industrial Biography*, London, 1863, ch. viii, ix, xv.
G. EYRE TODD, *Who's Who in Glasgow*, Glasgow, 1909.
E. GASKELL, *Lanarkshire Leaders*, n.d.

Chambers' Biographical Dictionary of Eminent Scotsmen, new edn., by T. THOMSON, Edinburgh, 1875.

W. T. PIKE (Ed.), *Contemporary Biographies: Edinburgh and the Lothians*, Edinburgh, 1904.

W. ANDERSON, *The Scottish Nation*, 3v., Edinburgh, 1859–63.

Memoirs of Life of Sir Andrew Agnew of Lochnaw, by REV. T. MCCRIE, Edinburgh, 1850.

By JAS. BRIDGES, Edinburgh, 1849.

A. AIRD, *Reminiscences of Editors*, etc., 1830–90, Glasgow, 1890.

Glimpses of Old Glasgow, Glasgow, 1894.

SIR A. ALISON, *My Life and Writings* (Ed.), Lady Alison, 2v., Edinburgh, 1883.

Arthur Anderson, A Founder of the P. and O. Co, by JOHN NICOLSON, Paisley, 1914.

ISABELLA H. ANDERSON, *An Inverness Lawyer and His Sons*, Aberdeen, 1900.

Sir William Arrol: A Memoir, by SIR R. PURVIS, Edinburgh, 1913.

W. E. Aytoun, Memoir by SIR T. MARTIN, Edinburgh, 1887.

The Bairds of Gartsherrie, by A. MACGEORGE, Glasgow, 1872.

Rev. Dr. Begg, Memoirs of, by REV. PROF. T. SMITH, 2v., Edinburgh, 1885.

Thomas Binnie, Memoir of, by T. BINNIE, junr., Glasgow, 1882.

Adam Black, Memoir ed. by A. NICHOLSON, Edinburgh, 1885.

Rev. Prof. W. Garden Blaikie, Autobiography: Recollections of a Busy Life. Ed. by REV. N. L. WALKER, London, 1901.

A. L. Bruce, In Memoriam, Edinburgh, 1894.

Rev. Dr. Robert Buchanan, Life of, by REV. N. L. WALKER, Edinburgh, 1877.

Robert Buchanan, Life of, by HARRIET JAY, London, 1903.

Sir George Burns, his Times and Friends, by E. HODDER, London, 1890.

WM. CHAMBERS, *Memoir of Robert Chambers*, Edinburgh, 1872.

Story of a Long and Busy Life, Edinburgh, 1882.

LORD COCKBURN, *Journal*, 1831–54, 2v., Edinburgh, 1874.

C. A. COOPER, *An Editor's Retrospect*, London, 1896.

C. COWAN, *Reminiscences*, Edinburgh, 1878.

D. CROAL, *Early Recollections of a Journalist*, Edinburgh, 1898.

Wm. Denny, Shipbuilder, Dumbarton, Life of, by REV. A. B. BRUCE, London, 1888.

Professor Henry Drummond, Life of, by REV. G. A. SMITH, London, 1899.

Thomas, 10th Earl of Dundonald, Autobiography of a Seaman, ed. by 12TH EARL, London, 1890.

David Elder, Memoir of, by J. R. NAPIER, Glasgow, 1866, reprinted, 1891.

John Elder, Memoir of, by PROF. W. J. M. RANKINE, Edinburgh, 1871.

Alexander Ewing, Bishop of Argyll, Memoir of, by REV. A. J. ROSS, London, 1877.

Jas. Ewing of Strathleven, Memoir of, by REV. M. MACKAY, Glasgow, 1866.

John Park Fleming, by J. B. FLEMING, Glasgow, 1885.

PROF. A. GEIKIE, *Scottish Reminiscences*, Glasgow, 1904.

Wm. Honyman Gillespie of Torbanehill, Memorial of, by J. URQUHART, Edinburgh, 1926.

Rev. Thos. Guthrie, D.D., Autobiography and Memoir, by D. R. and C. J. GUTHRIE, 2v., London, 1873.

J. Keir Hardie, From Pit to Parliament: Early Life, by D. LOWE, London, 1923.

By W. STEWART, London, 1921.

Writings and Speeches, ed. E. HUGHES, Glasgow, n.d.

William Harley, by J. GALLOWAY, Ardrossan (1901).

J. HEDDERWICK, *Backward Glances*, Edinburgh, 1891.

J. HODGE, *Workman's Cottage to Windsor Castle*, London (1931).

George Hope of Fenton Barns, by C. HOPE, Edinburgh, 1881.

John Hope, by REV. D. JAMIE, Edinburgh, 1900.

A. TAYLOR INNES, *Chapters of Reminiscence*, London, 1913.

HENRIETTA KEDDIE, *Three Generations*, London, 1911.

Lord Kelvin, Life of, by PROF. S. P. THOMSON, 2v., London, 1910.

By H. N. CASSON, n.d.

Chas. Macintosh, Biographical Memoir, by GEO. MACINTOSH, Glasgow, 1847.

Duncan McLaren, Life of, by J. B. MACKIE, 2v., Edinburgh, 1888.

J. MAVOR, *My Windows on the Street of the World*, 2v., London, 1923.

DR. ROBT. MUNRO, *Autobiographic Sketch*, Glasgow, 1921.

David Napier, Engineer, Autobiographic Sketch, by J. D. D. NAPIER, Glasgow, 1912.

Robert Napier, Life of, by JAS. NAPIER, London, 1904.

J. B. Neilson, Life of, by T. B. MACKENZIE, Glasgow, 1928.

R. SMILLIE, *My Life for Labour*, London, 1924.

JOHN TAYLOR, *Autobiographical Sketch* (Poems, Edinburgh, 1876).

Peter Taylor, Autobiography of, Paisley, 1903.

Alex. Thomson of Banchory, Memoir of, by REV. PROF. G. SMEATON, Edinburgh, 1869.

W. THOM, *Rhymes and Recollections of a Handloom Weaver* (2nd edn., 1845); ed. with biographical sketch by W. SKINNER, Paisley, 1880.

George Troup, Life of, by REV. G. E. TROUP, Edinburgh, 1881.

Randolph G. E. Wemyss, by A. S. CUNNINGHAM, Edinburgh (1910).

Walter Wilson, Merchant, Glasgow, by A. WILSON, Glasgow, 1920.

?. J. BURN, *Autobiography of a Beggar Boy*, London, 1882.

?. J. MYLES, *Chapters in the Life of a Dundee Factory Boy*, Edinburgh, 1850.

D. CARSWELL, *Brother Scots*, London, 1927.

J. S. JEANS, *Western Worthies*, Glasgow, 1872.

VII. LABOUR ORGANIZATION

T. JOHNSTON, *History of Working Classes in Scotland* (see under I).

S. and B. WEBB, *History of Trade Unionism*, London, 1894.

R. W. POSTGATE, *The Builders' History*, London, n.d

J. MARSHALL, *Report of Trial of Cotton Spinners* (Glasgow, 1838).

A. SWINTON (Ed.), *Report of Trial of Cotton Spinners*, Edinburgh, 1838.

A. H. MILLAR (Ed.), *Black Kalendar of Scotland: Records of Notable Scottish Trials*, 1st series, Dundee, 1884, 98–132.

Proceedings of Third Co-operative Congress, London, 1832.

W. MAXWELL, *History of Co-operation in Scotland*, Glasgow, 1910.

B. JONES, *Co-operative Production*, 2v., Oxford, 1894.

J. A. FLANAGAN, *Wholesale Co-operation in Scotland*, Glasgow, 1920.

J. LUCAS, *Co-operation in Scotland*, Manchester, 1920.

W. MAXWELL, *St. Cuthbert's Co-operative Association*, Edinburgh, 1909.

P. J. DOLLAN, *Kinning Park Co-operative Society*, Glasgow, 1923.

Amalgamated Society of Engineers, Jubilee Souvenir, London, 1901.

Trade Union Congress Souvenir, Glasgow, 1919.

Glasgow Council of United Trades, Annual Report, 1860.

   Report of Trade Union Appeal Case (Macfarlane v. Couper and Sons), Glasgow, 1879.

Edinburgh United Trades Council, Reports, 1886–7 till 1892–3.

S. and B. WEBB, *Methods of Social Study*, London, 1932, ch. viii.

VIII. POLITICAL INSTITUTIONS

MABEL ATKINSON, *Local Government in Scotland*, Edinburgh, 1904.

D. O. DYKES, *Scottish Local Government*, Edinburgh, 1907.

J. P. DAY, *Public Administration in the Highlands and Islands*, London, 1918.

R. P. LAMOND, *Scottish Poor Law*, 1870; 2nd edn., Glasgow, 1892.

SIR G. NICHOLLS, *History of Scotch Poor Law*, London, 1856.

A. A. CORMACK, *Poor Relief in Scotland*, Aberdeen, 1923.

S. H. TURNER, *History of Local Taxation in Scotland*, Edinburgh, 1908.

J. B. RUSSELL, ed. by A. K. CHALMERS, *Public Health Administration in Glasgow*, Glasgow, 1905.

E. L. HUTCHINS and A. HARRISON, *History of Factory Legislation*, revised edn., London, 1911.

R. W. COOKE TAYLOR, *The Factory System and the Factory Acts*, revised edn., London, 1912.

IX. SOCIAL THEORIES AND SCHEMES

A. and J. BETHUNE, *Practical Economy*, Edinburgh, 1839.

REV. PROF. T. CHALMERS, *Christian and Economic Policy of a Nation*, Glasgow, 1839.

J. CRAWFORD, *Philosophy of Wealth*, Paisley, 1837; 2nd edn., London, 1846.

REV. P. BREWSTER, *Chartist and Military Sermons*, Paisley, 1843.

H. MILLER, *Essays, Political and Social* (from the "Witness"), ed. by P. BAYNE, Edinburgh, 1862.

PROF. W. P. ALISON, *Management of the Poor in Scotland*, Edinburgh, 1840.

REV. J. SMITH, *Grievances of the Working Classes*, Glasgow, 1846.

REV. R. BUCHANAN, D.D., *The Schoolmaster in the Wynds*, Glasgow, 1850.

GEO. BELL, M.D., *Day and Night in the Wynds of Edinburgh*, 1849.

WM. ANDERSON, *The Poor of Edinburgh and their Homes*, Edinburgh, 1867.

R. FOULIS, M.D., *Old Houses in Edinburgh*, Edinburgh, 1852.

REV. J. BEGG, D.D., *Happy Homes for Working Men*, London, 1866.

REV. W. G. BLAIKIE, D.D., *Better Days for Working People*, London, 1867.

REV. D. MACLEOD, D.D., *Non-Churchgoing and the Housing of the Poor*, Edinburgh, 1888.

SIR H. GILZEAN REID, *Housing of the People*, Paisley, n.d.

R. CAMPBELL, *Provident and Industrial Institutions*, Manchester, n.d.

REV. R. WARDLAW, *Benevolent Associations for the Relief of the Poor*, Glasgow, 1818.

G. BURNS, *Principles and Management of Friendly Societies in Scotland*, Glasgow, 1821.

A. J. BEATON, *Social and Economic Condition of Highlands since 1800*, Stirling, 1905.

M. M. LEIGH, *The Crofting Problem* (Dept. of Agriculture for Scotland), Edinburgh, 1929.

D. MACLEOD, *Gloomy Memories of the Highlands* (1842); revised edn., Edinburgh, 1892.

A. MACKENZIE, *The Highland Clearances* (1883), revised edn, Stirling, 1914.

REV. J. GLASSE, D.D., *Pauperism in Scotland*, Glasgow, 1910.

REV. J. W. HARPER, D.D., *The Social Ideal and Dr. Chalmers' Contribution*, Edinburgh, 1910.

H. HUNTER (Ed.), *Problems of Poverty*, Edinburgh, 1912.

GRACE C. WOOD, *Dr. Chalmers and the Poor Law*, Edinburgh, 1911.

X. ENCYCLOPAEDIAS AND WORKS OF REFERENCE

Encyclopædia Britannica, 11th edition.
The "New" Statistical Account of Scotland, 15v., 1845.
S. LEWIS (Ed.), *Topographical Dictionary of Scotland*, 2v., London, 1846.
F. H. GROOME (Ed.), *Ordnance Gazetteer of Scotland*, 3v., Edinburgh, 1886.
J. R. MCCULLOCH, *Statistical Account of British Empire*, 1837.
J. H. DAWSON, *Abridged Statistical History of Scotland*, Edinburgh, 1853.
  Abridged Statistical History of Scottish Counties, 1862.
Oliver and Boyd's Edinburgh Almanac.
Who's Who.
Who Was Who (1897–1916, 1916–28).
T. WILKIE (Ed.), *The Representation of Scotland* (Parliamentary), Paisley, 1895.
Edinburgh and Glasgow Directories.

XI. PERIODICALS

Herald to Trades Advocate, Glasgow, 1831–2.
(Loyal) Reformers Gazette, Glasgow, 1831–6.
Scottish Reformers Gazette, Glasgow, 1837–55.
Chartist Circular, Glasgow, 1839–41.
Tait's Edinburgh Magazine, 1832–60.
North British Review, 1844–71.
Scots Magazine, 1888–1900, New series, 1931–
Scottish Liberal, 1890.
Scottish Farm Servant, 1926–30.
Scottish Notes and Queries, 1891–
Glasgow Courier (1840–60), passim.
Glasgow Argus (1833–47), passim.
Glasgow Sentinel, 1870–7.
North British Daily Mail (1859–79), passim.
Scottish Guardian (1837–57), passim.
Witness (Edinburgh), (1840–61), passim.
Edinburgh (Evening) Courant (1829–86), passim.
Edinburgh Advertiser (1830–47), passim.
Scottish News (Glasgow and Edinburgh), 1887.
Edinburgh Evening Post (1838, 1840).
Scotsman, Edinburgh, 1830–   , passim.
Glasgow Herald, 1830–   , passim.

Scottish Educational Journal, 1923–   , passim.
Scottish Historical Review, 1903–28.
Scottish Bankers' Magazine, 1909–   , passim.
Scottish Banking Magazine (afterwards, *North British Economist*),
    1879–90, passim.

INDEX

GEORGE ALLEN & UNWIN LTD
LONDON: 40 MUSEUM STREET, W.C.1
LEIPZIG: (F. VOLCKMAR) HOSPITALSTR. 10
CAPE TOWN: 73 ST. GEORGE'S STREET
TORONTO: 91 WELLINGTON STREET, WEST
BOMBAY: 15 GRAHAM ROAD, BALLARD ESTATE
WELLINGTON, N.Z.: 8 KINGS CRESCENT, LOWER HUTT
SYDNEY, N.S.W.: AUSTRALIA HOUSE, WYNYARD SQUARE

For Product Safety Concerns and Information please contact our
EU representative GPSR@taylorandfrancis.com Taylor & Francis
Verlag GmbH, Kaufingerstraße 24, 80331 München, Germany